To my parents, who taught me by example

Nicholas Dunbar studied physics in the UK at Manchester and Cambridge and finally in the US at Harvard University, where he gained a Masters degree in earth and planetary sciences. During this period his interests ranged from quantum mechanics and black holes to evolution and the history of global climate change. His teachers included Stephen Hawking at Cambridge and Stephen Jay Gould at Harvard.

In 1990, Dunbar decided to leave academia. He spent the next few years working in feature films and television, in a wide range of capacities. In 1996, after launching the television production company Flicker Films, a chance encounter with some old Harvard friends set him on a new path of finance and science writing, focusing on the derivatives industry. In 1998 he joined *Risk* magazine as technical editor. He is 34 and lives in London.

Inventing Money

'I finished *Inventing Money* over the weekend and I want you to know how much I enjoyed it. It was a comprehensive (and, I must thank you, comprehensible) survey of the history of financial innovation. The second half of the book was more a detective story than anything else. Your writing style is lucid and your ability to connect a series of very complicated dots was masterful.
I've since ordered 4 copies of the book to give to colleagues and friends. Thanks for writing such a wonderful book.'

Harris M. Lirtzman, Director, Risk Management, New York City Retirement Systems

'It was absolutely riveting – I could not put it down. I plan to suggest it as reading material for our MBA and PhD students.'

Alan White, Professor of Finance, University of Toronto

'. . . a great book. Your insights are both thoughtful and I think accurate. You have certainly recorded history within our industry.'

Jeremy Isaacs, CEO, Lehman Brothers Europe

'. . . there are many valuable lessons to be learnt from this tale. Nicholas Dunbar strips away the shroud of mystery surrounding the drama, and unveils previously undisclosed information in captivating and accessible terms.'

Scottish Banker

'. . . as good an explanation as we'll get of how the fund leveraged its way into becoming a market-distorting singularity.'

Red Herring

'The story of how LTCM was set up, its trades, and its ultimate demise make a ripping yarn, and Nick Dunbar tells it well. . . . well researched . . . a detailed and accessible account of what happened at LTCM . . . essential reading for anyone involved in proprietary trading and the hedge fund industry.'

Applied Derivatives Trading

Inventing Money

The story of Long-Term Capital Management and the legends behind it

Nicholas Dunbar

JOHN WILEY & SONS, LTD

Chichester · New York · Weinheim · Brisbane · Singapore · Toronto

This edition published in 2001 by John Wiley & Sons Ltd
First published in 2000 by John Wiley & Sons Ltd,
Baffins Lane, Chichester,
West Sussex PO19 1UD, England

National   01243 779777
International (+44) 1243 779777
e-mail (for orders and customer service enquiries):
cs-books@wiley.co.uk
Visit our Home Page on http://www.wiley.co.uk
or http://www.wiley.com

Other Wiley Editorial Offices

John Wiley & Sons, Inc., 605 Third Avenue
New York, NY 10158-0012, USA

WILEY-VCH Verlag GmbH, Pappelallee 3,
D-69469 Weinheim, Germany

Jacaranda Wiley Ltd, 33 Park Road, Milton
Queensland 4064, Australia

John Wiley & Sons (Asia) Pte Ltd, 2 Clementi Loop #02-01,
Jin Xing Distripark, Singapore 129809

John Wiley & Sons (Canada) Ltd, 22 Worcester Road,
Rexdale, Ontario M9W 1LI, Canada

British Library Cataloguing in Publication Data
A catalogue record for this book is available from the British Library.

ISBN 0-471-49811-4

Typeset by MHL Typesetting Ltd, Coventry
Project managed by Macfarlane Production Services, Markyate, Herts
Printed and bound in Great Britain by Biddles Ltd, Guildford and King's Lynn
This book is printed on acid-free paper responsibly manufactured from sustainable
forestry, in which at least two trees are planted for each one used for paper production.

Contents

Preface to the paperback edition

It was June 2000 and the mandarins of academic finance had staged a homecoming of sorts. The venue was Paris's hallowed Sorbonne University, and they were gathered to celebrate the hundredth anniversary of a PhD thesis written by a mathematician named Louis Bachelier. Obscure during his lifetime, Bachelier's work linking the mathematics of dust particles to the behaviour of stock markets would eventually change the world.

For the worse or for the better? Most finance theorists would say the latter. But then, in the Sorbonne lecture theatre that morning, Yale University professor and Nobel economics laureate Paul Samuelson was asked a question. 'What implications does the collapse of Long-Term Capital Management have for finance theory?'

The venerable professor thought for a moment. 'When it failed', he began, referring to the now notorious hedge fund, 'I sat down and satisfied myself with an explanation of what happened. But wild horses wouldn't make me repeat that explanation here today.'

Why was Samuelson so reticent? Perhaps it was tact – after all, only a few feet away from him was sitting his former PhD student and ex-LTCM principal, Robert C. Merton. Or perhaps it was because this uber-finance theorist didn't want to bring a sour note to Bachelier's anniversary.

When I completed the first edition of this book in October 1999, everyone that had anything to do with LTCM was very reticent indeed. None of the principals or employees of the fund would talk, nor would the Oversight Committee that was then in charge of its positions.

Any public comment that did leak out from LTCM supremo John Meriwether and his principals had the feel of bravado. There was the *New York Times* interview with Michael Lewis, and the tour of university economics departments by the fund's most junior partner David Modest, essentially defending LTCM's trading and risk management philosophy, and blaming the collapse on unforeseeable outside events.

A year on, all this has changed. Meriwether and his number two Eric

Rosenfeld have donned sackcloth and ashes, apologising profusely in print for LTCM's misdeeds. Yet in absolute terms they are still wealthy men, and more to the point they are managing a new $400 million hedge fund. *Plus ça change* ...

It says a lot for today's amnesiac, telescoped financial world that such a comeback is possible. It's also a testament to Meriwether's political skills in avoiding the stigma of outright bankruptcy. Sackcloth and ashes are more comfortable than tar and feathers. But the real lesson lies elsewhere.

LTCM was the expression of an idea that went too far. Hatched in academia by Samuelson, Merton, together with fellow LTCM partner Myron Scholes and a few others, the idea escaped from the labs and seemed to become an unassailable force of progress on Wall Street and beyond.

After LTCM, we should be much more ambivalent. Physics gave us the beauty of quantum mechanics, and the horror of nuclear weapons. Finance theory is the same. Combined with the greed of LTCM's principals, investors and counterparties, it became deadly. Like the Bomb, we can't put the genie back in the magic lamp. We have to control it, and can even harness it, just so long as by 'managing' risks we don't simply hide them beneath a flimsy intellectual crust.

As it turned out, the turmoil of late 1998 was contained. Markets rebounded quickly, ensuring that only the central players in the story felt any pain. That shouldn't make us complacent. According to Goldman Sachs Asset Management, during the crisis, the assets held by the UK's top 50 pension funds fell to 40% below the level needed to match their liabilities. However, no-one really noticed because the crisis didn't last long enough for these market valuations to filter through the system. Next time we might not be so lucky.

This paperback edition largely resembles the first in structure. I have added a few explanations here and there. Some of my interpretations of events have since been contested by former members of LTCM, but significantly, other players have championed them. Where appropriate, I have added clarifications.

The most significant change is the final chapter. This has been completely rewritten and expanded, incorporating an interview in *Risk* with the Oversight Committee who explain how LTCM's explosive portfolio was dismantled piece by piece. Their's was an important achievement, and deserves wider recognition.

Nicholas Dunbar
London
September 2000

Acknowledgements

I would like to thank Carole Jahme for her crucial support during the writing of this book.

I want to thank David Wilson and everyone at Wiley for making this happen in the first place.

I want to thank Peter Field, Mark Kemp and everyone at Risk Publications for backing me during this project.

I would like to thank the following people who have either generously given their time to discuss some of the issues covered in this book or have provided essential research material. There are others who remain anonymous at their request, and I apologise for any omissions.

Peter Bakstansky, Jamil Baz, Milton Bellis, Eric Briys, Hugo Calcagnini, Jonathan Chenevix-Trench, Neil Chriss, Craig Coats Jr, John Cox, Matthew Crabbe, Emanual Derman, Michele Faissola, William Falloon, Ramy Goldstein, Jay Higgins, Jeremy Isaacs, Philippe Jorion, Michael Kamal, Jean-Michel Lasry, TJ Lim, Bob Litzenberger, Saman Majd, Michael Maras, Merton Miller, Andrew Morton, Warren Mosler, Sean Notley, Bernard Oppetit, Ernest Patrikis, André Perold, Girish Reddy, Stephen Ross, Mark Rubinstein, Anthony Santomero, Til Schuermann, William Sharpe, Warren Spector, Nassim Taleb, Bill Winters

Introduction

The reader can hardly conceive my astonishment to behold an island in the air, inhabited by men, who were able (as it should seem) to raise or sink, or put it into a progressive motion, as they pleased.
Jonathan Swift, *Gulliver's Travels*

In September 1998, a country disappeared off the face of the planet. Like Swift's Flying Island of Laputa, its learned inhabitants had once gazed down on ordinary mortals with impunity. Like Atlantis sinking under the sea in ancient times, its plunge to earth caused devastating tidal waves.

Yet, none of this involved real oceans or landmasses. No-one died or was physically injured in the catastrophe. The country — if we may call it that — was a vast human construction, and in its own way was a true modern wonder of the world.

It was made out of money — not real cash or gold, but invisible billion-dollar financial contracts — and at its heart was a mysterious entity called Long-Term Capital Management, or LTCM. In the tangible, physical world, LTCM looked insignificant. It boasted three offices in London, Tokyo and Greenwich, Connecticut, and employed about 200 people.

But in the virtual world of money, LTCM was awe-inspiring. It was the pinnacle of a 30-year-long revolution in finance, which had done for trading and investment what the Apollo space programme had done for lunar exploration. Starting from nowhere, a few visionaries had constructed a great financial infrastructure, which allowed traders to fling trillions of dollars between continents in the blink of an eye.

With catch-phrases such as 'risk management' and 'financial engineering', these visionaries were cherished for bringing the discipline of science to what had once been a form of guesswork. Foremost among the visionaries were Robert C. Merton and Myron Scholes, who would win Nobel Prizes for their theory of option pricing.

Under the leadership of Wall Street's most aggressive warrior king, a trader called John Meriwether, Merton, Scholes and several others helped to found LTCM in 1993. Joined by one of the world's foremost banking regulators, US Federal Reserve vice-chairman David Mullins, LTCM styled itself as a sort of freelance police force of the markets, scouring the globe to remove 'inefficiencies' from the system. It also generated billions of dollars in seemingly risk-free profits.

As a precocious 18-year-old, Merton had written his first published paper about the mysterious magnetic effect that kept Swift's Laputa suspended in mid-air. Years later, Merton had created his own flying island in LTCM. For it was Merton's and Scholes's theories which said that equity – the base that anchors every normal company in the real world – was no longer necessary in the brave new world of scientific finance.

But in the summer of 1998, Merton and Scholes's theories suddenly stopped working, and LTCM crashed towards earth with terrifying speed. The King of Laputa could destroy enemies merely by letting his island fall on them. Now the world's 14 biggest investment banks faced a similar fate as this trillion-dollar flying island of money fell from the sky. These 14 banks saved themselves from the impact by providing a three-and-a-half billion-dollar cushion to support LTCM while it was dismantled.

So traumatic was this experience, that half of the world's financial markets seized up in fear. US Federal Reserve Chairman Alan Greenspan, arguably the world's most powerful man, was forced to take emergency action and cut interest rates to get them working again. It was as if a country had collapsed, but no-one could see which one.[1]

As for the 16 partners who had once gazed down like the King of Laputa at the mortals beneath them, they could only sit and watch as dozens of bankers crawled over LTCM's giant money machines, like earthlings inspecting a crashed alien spacecraft.

I had lunched with Merton and Scholes at the height of their success in April 1998. Now, *après le deluge*, I met one of the deposed LTCM kings in June 1999, at a glitzy hotel bar by Manhattan's Columbus Circle. He sat next to me at the bar, nursing a cranberry and grapefruit spritzer.

---

1. A real country, namely Russia, had gone bankrupt, but its direct impact on the US economy was minimal.

At first sight, this LTCM partner was a completely unremarkable, soft-spoken former academic. There were a few incongruities, such as a familiarity with the names of the richest people in America that you wouldn't expect from the average economics professor. For the most part, he talked in abstract terms, as if LTCM was a distant galaxy.

But his eyes gave him away. They were the eyes of the Ancient Mariner; they had witnessed scenes of indescribable violence and suffering. Not real bloodshed, but rather the sight of some beautiful, intricate construction being torn to pieces in front of its impotent creators.

How can you tell such a story? There are two temptations. One is to go for a natural metaphor. This is the 'perfect storm' theory, and is most popular with LTCM's partners, including the man in the bar.

According to this view, what happened during the late summer of 1998 was like a 100-year hurricane in the Atlantic. It was a freak event, beyond human control, and the world's most advanced trading vehicle – a storm-proof flying island called LTCM – was its victim.

But this picture is inaccurate. Although science has helped traders and investors, market crises are not hurricanes; they are created by human behaviour. LTCM was not like a ship tossed on the waves. It was more like an attempt to control the weather that went wrong.

This takes us to the second view, the 'human folly' theory. LTCM took flight because the world's biggest investment banks supported it. These custodians of the global financial system invested in LTCM, traded with it and lent it vast sums of money. By imitating LTCM, and building their own flying islands, these investment banks then made things even worse.

While LTCM's own partners were reckless or misguided, the real reason LTCM became so big and dangerous was because the people running the investment banks were greedy and ignored the risks. This view puts LTCM in the tradition of many historical boom and bust cycles, such as the South Sea Bubble of 1720.

The truth is a mixture of the two. And that is the subject of this book.

Fischer Black.

Robert Merton, standing in front of the Boston skyline on the Charles River.

Photograph: Popperfoto Reuters.

Myron Scholes.

Photograph: James McGoon/Sygma.

John Meriwether.

David Mullins.

I

The Theory of Speculation

'I can calculate the motions of heavenly bodies,
but not the madness of people'
Isaac Newton, after losing £20,000 in the stock market.

A man was crossing a bridge over the Charles River from Boston to the Massachusetts Institute of Technology (MIT) in Cambridge. It was October 1968 and there was plenty going on to distract Fischer Black. Richard Nixon was on his way to winning the presidential election, and the country was bitterly divided over the Vietnam War, where almost a million US troops were in action. Earlier that year, Martin Luther King had been assassinated, a bitter blow to those living in Boston's black ghetto of Roxbury. All over the world that year, riot shields confronted student banners.

But Black had other things on his mind. A tall, quiet man with slicked-back hair and chunky spectacles, he wore a dark suit, in contrast to the long hair and afghan coats of the students leaving their classes. Black didn't notice the students; he was deep in thought as he entered the MIT economics faculty. He was there at the invitation of a young Canadian academic, Myron Scholes, who had recently joined the faculty from Chicago.

Aged 30, Black was earning a living at Boston consulting firm Arthur D. Little, trying to advise mutual funds on their stock market investments. But Black's heart wasn't in his work. Instead, he was seeking Scholes's help in pricing an obscure type of financial contract called an option. Black didn't yet know about the brainy young student in the economics department, Robert C. Merton, who was interested in the same problem.

A talkative 27-year-old, Scholes showed his visitor into his office, and brought him a cup of coffee. He couldn't possibly know that the work he and Black were about to embark on would one day result in him and Merton shaking hands with the King of Sweden and accepting a Nobel Prize. He would have been insulted by the suggestion that shortly afterwards, their

1

activities at a hedge fund called LTCM (Long-Term Capital Management) would paralyse the global financial system.

The two papers on the subject that the trio eventually published nearly five years later don't look too inspiring at first sight. Black and Scholes's opus was called 'On the pricing of options and other corporate liabilities' while Merton's paper rejoiced in the title of 'The rational theory of option pricing'. Turn a few pages, and mathematical equations start dancing before one's eyes.

Yet, although the ideas of Black, Scholes and Merton didn't have much immediate impact in 1973, they eventually would change the world, along with the lives of their authors. Options would become vitally important to finance, but there was more to it than that. Black, Scholes and Merton had invented what came to be known as financial engineering.

Just as the engineering of digital bits would eventually lead to the Internet, the mathematically driven engineering of stocks, bonds and other securities would create the modern trillion-dollar financial system. Unlike the Internet, or the space shuttle, or any other engineering achievement, this one is largely invisible. Only when a disaster strikes, as would happen to Merton and Scholes and their colleagues at LTCM in 1998, do people notice.

Playing in the movie theatres in Autumn 1968 was the film by Stanley Kubrick, *2001: A Space Odyssey*. The film opens with a stunning sequence where a prehistoric hominid hurls a bone spinning into the air, which becomes transformed into an orbiting space station. The story of finance is no different. When combined with mathematics and technology, the ancient urge to make money is amplified into a force of awesome power.

Addressing Congress after the LTCM débâcle, what did Federal Reserve Board chairman Alan Greenspan mean when he spoke of 'mathematical models of human behaviour'? We can be sure of one thing. Markets arrived long before mathematics did. In fact, they go back to the distant origins of human behaviour, millions of years ago on the sweltering African savannah. Before we discover what Black, Scholes and Merton actually did, it's worth taking a brief excursion back in time to find out more.

The origin of trading

In chimpanzee communities, individuals exchange gifts (such as fruit or sexual favours) within a group to cement alliances, and punish those who attempt to cheat on such mutually beneficial relationships. Anthropologists believe that early humans started trading in much the same way. The word they use to describe this behaviour is 'reciprocity' and our personal relationships work on this basis.

Helped by the gift of language, humans took trading far beyond the level of immediate family groups. Like chimps, humans have a xenophobic streak. Nevertheless, realising the advantage of specialising in the production of certain commodities, tribes that had once interacted purely to kill and enslave each other began exchanging goods through barter.

The ability to specialise gradually increased everyone's wealth, encouraged innovation, and the life of a hunter-gatherer slowly gave way to civilisation – which brought advantages and disadvantages. Tribes that weren't interested in trading were either annihilated or forced to retreat to remote parts of the world where civilisations weren't viable. As agricultural economies replaced nomadic ones, one-to-one trading gave way to markets.

In a barter economy, cementing friendship is still a necessary part of exchanging goods. After all, if you needed to sell something, first you must look around for a partner who can offer you something worth while in return. Every barter trade is a unique, human event. It depends intimately on time and place, as well as the personalities and histories of those who took part. To make a living purely through barter, you need a network of friends and acquaintances whose needs you understand.

All this changed when people started using money, which was first developed in the agricultural states of the ancient Middle East. Money establishes the meaning of a 'fair' price. If a complex, tortuous negotiation could be summarised by a simple cash value, then it could be compared with other deals at different times and places. The value of this information was quickly realised by governments, who could use it to collect taxes, and pay their armies and bureaucrats. For this reason, the use of money was associated with an increase in state power.

That wasn't completely a bad thing. With state power came the rule of law. In the old barter economy, the only way to punish fraud or cheating was to seek out the cheat in person, and claim damages. If the cheat had returned to the safety of his village, this might be impossible. Once legal codes came into existence, plaintiffs could appeal to state authority to enforce agreements.

In time, confidence in the law increased so much that legal agreements such as bills of receipt or share certificates became readily exchangeable for cash. We would now call these bits of paper a form of risk management. In particular, shares were an important invention. Up to the seventeenth century, if you wanted to invest in a company, you had to join its owners in a partnership. If the company went bankrupt, you would be liable for its debts. But shares had something called 'limited liability', which protected investors from creditors. This very primitive form of financial engineering encouraged people to invest, and allowed economies to grow.

In a sense, the development of money and financial contracts was a democratic event. The knowledge of a fair price was hard to keep secret. Even in countries where prices are imposed by governments, such as communist states, 'real' prices soon emerge in the black market. Events with widespread economic impact, such as crop failures, are rapidly communicated to an entire population in the form of price changes, and can also lead quickly to political change.

The effect of money and law was to separate trading from friendship. The rule of law means that one no longer needs to build up a relationship of trust in order to trade. The priority becomes no longer to make a deal with the best person, but to obtain the best price. And the more impersonal things are, the better, in the sense that the best-price transaction is economically beneficial to everybody. Adam Smith was the first to comment on this:

> It is not from the benevolence of the butcher, the brewer, or the baker, that we expect our dinner, but from their regard to their own interest . . . This division of labour . . . is not originally the effect of any human wisdom, which foresees and intends that general opulence to which it gives occasion. It is the necessary, though very slow and gradual, consequence of a certain propensity in human nature which has in view no such extensive utility; the propensity to truck, barter, and exchange one thing for another.

The theory of markets starts with Smith, the Scottish Enlightenment philosopher who first argued that greed was good. In *The Wealth of Nations*, published in the year of the American revolution, Smith paints a picture of ruddy-cheeked butchers, bakers and brewers who each put their own interests first, and yet create wealth collectively.

Back in 1776, this was a radical idea. Before the industrial revolution, markets were seen as a low-grade human activity, which often fell under the Devil's influence. Greed was evil – it was a deadly sin – and its appearance in economic affairs should be curbed by monarchs and religious institutions that answered to God. And where was the evidence that contracts like shares actually helped anybody?

In 1720, when Smith was only three-years old, this hostile view of free markets had been confirmed by the scandal of the South Sea Bubble. Founded by a Tory minister in 1711, the South Sea Company was intended to profit from trade with the Spanish colonies, but instead, used shareholders' money to pay off the national debt. To stoke public interest, the directors of the South Sea Company sold additional stock, which investors could use as security to borrow money to buy yet more stock, and even issued a press release to promote their efforts.

This pyramid investment scheme gathered momentum, and by early 1720 it had spawned dozens of imitators. On 1 January 1720, South Sea shares sold for £128. By 24 June, they reached £1050. However, the market crashed in September, and by December, the share price was back at £128. Thousands of investors were ruined. Banks that had lent money against the value of the stock went bankrupt.

Even Isaac Newton, basking in the glory of having discovered gravitation, lost £20,000 in the scheme – a fortune in today's money. In the scandal's wake, chastened legislators passed a law forbidding new issues of stock without royal authority. Then, 55 years on, Smith was saying that all that control should be thrown out, leaving an 'invisible hand' to create human happiness.

To argue his case, Smith listed examples in which high taxes – a key economic tool of autocratic governments – had led to popular unrest. The American revolution was to provide a textbook example of Smith's argument. Unsurprisingly, the newly created United States took Smith's philosophy to its heart. And the bottom line was that the desire to make money was a natural law that should be allowed to run its course.

Smith's invisible hand has the air of science about it. Aren't Newton's laws of gravity an invisible hand guiding the planets? Notwithstanding Newton's sheepish comment at the head of the chapter, isn't it possible to write down a law of self-interest, that maximises wealth? Unfortunately, even if Smith had had the vision, the mathematical apparatus required even to attempt this wasn't yet available. Economic laws, if they indeed exist, must be approximate ones, and need statistics.

Of dogs and molecules

Ultimately, mathematics would find its way into finance, but statistics had to come first. Therefore, the road from Adam Smith to Black, Scholes and

Merton takes us on a detour away from the markets and into the laboratories and lecture halls of Victorian science who first exploited statistics. For the biologists and the physicists of the nineteenth century were modern in the sense that, where their predecessors thought about observations, they thought about data.

Up to the end of the eighteenth century, biology largely consisted of either dissection (of plants, humans and animals) and taxonomy, or classification. Observation meant going to the tropics, finding new species to be classified, and taking a few samples home for the collection. The Victorian naturalists changed all that. Obsessive cataloguers and note-takers, they made the bold step of seeing plants, animals and people as populations rather than individuals.

Consider 100 dogs, picked at random. Although they might range widely in size and appearance, an eighteenth-century naturalist would have focused on what these dogs had in common, in terms of internal anatomy, as well as their taxonomic relation to other species such as wolves.

A nineteenth-century biologist would have made lists: weights, heights, lifespans, size of litter and so on. The next step would be to take this list, say for heights, and take the average, namely, add up all the heights measured and divide by the total number of dogs (in this case, 100). However, this average or mean height might not correspond to any particular dog in the sample. There is no such thing as an 'average dog', only a number representing a given collection of dogs.

But there is a further step which is crucial to this book. Although the average is useful, what about the variation in size and appearance? Our Victorian naturalist can do more with his data. He takes the average, subtracts it from each height on his list and squares the results. He then calculates the average of this new list, and finally takes the square root to give a number called the standard deviation.

The standard deviation tells us how spread out the data are. For example, if our dog sample consisted of 100 Labradors of the same age, the standard deviation of the height would be small. If it contained every breed from Chihuahuas to Great Danes, the standard deviation would be large. Like the mean, the standard deviation is clearly not intrinsic to any particular dog, but is a property of the group.

Such observations of variation in animals were seized upon by Charles Darwin in the *Origin of Species* as important evidence for evolution. By arguing that the mean and standard deviation were intrinsic qualities of every species, Darwin made two radical suggestions. Firstly, that these qualities were passed from parent to offspring by inheritance (the science of genetics would later explain how). Secondly, that a variation in some quality (such as beak size in Galapagos finches) could, over long periods of time, and if geographical conditions encouraged it, lead to completely new species through natural selection.

The Victorian hunger for data led to another, more subtle discovery. Recall our imaginary dog study. Suppose the naturalist constructs a chart with height plotted on the horizontal axis, and the number of times a particular range of heights was observed plotted on the vertical axis. Such charts, called distributions, tend to have a peak around the mean value.

As more and more data was used to produce distributions, a peculiar property was noticed. Whatever the actual data involved – whether it measured animals, humans or plants – the distribution took on a characteristic humped shape. In recognition of its importance, the curve has a special name: the Normal distribution. Called the Bell curve in the US because of its shape, the curve is also known as the Gaussian distribution. This last name derives from the German mathematician C.F. Gauss who observed the same distribution of errors in cartographers' distance measurements.

The Normal distribution is symmetrical about the mean, and the standard deviation measures the width of the central hump. Beyond this hump, on either side, the curve then flattens out and soon becomes close to zero.

But the most striking feature of the Normal distribution is its meaning; it is nature's evidence that something is completely random. We can see why this is so by trying to construct a Normal distribution from scratch. This construction starts out with the quintessential random event: a coin toss. Toss a coin a hundred times and note down the number of heads. This gives you one data point. Do it again and again and again. Eventually, if you have not run out of patience, you plot the distribution of heads, and it will look very much like the Normal distribution.[1]

For mathematicians, the Normal distribution is very pure, and hence, a prized object. Aside from a vertical distance scale, its shape can be captured by only two numbers – the mean and standard deviation. If a real-life data distribution fails to reflect the Normal distribution as the amount of data increase, statisticians are trained to smell a rat, and look for something non-random in the data.

The Normal distribution has another, very reassuring property. Recall our naturalist who measures the heights of 100 dogs. There may be some

---

1. Although this is clearly the sort of task that computers were born for, the Normal distribution was first discovered in this way by the mathematician Abraham De Moivre in 1733.

specific reason why the distribution of heights differs from Normal. For example, in the area of study, large dogs might run away before being measured. In other areas there may be different problems. But if the naturalist repeats the experiment at many locations, the distribution of the means will eventually look like the Normal distribution. Statisticians call this the 'Central Limit Theorem', and it seems to be saying that pure randomness always wins out in the end. The Normal distribution plays an important role in the LTCM story, as we shall see.

While randomness would play an important, but subtle role under-pinning Darwin's theory of evolution, it became a central driving force in nineteenth-century physics. The idea that matter was made of atoms and molecules had been around since ancient Greece but for the first time, the idea could be tested. The goal was to explain the macroscopic properties of matter, such as heat flow and gas pressure, in terms of atomic behaviour.

With the tools of statistics at their disposal, theorists like James Clerk Maxwell in the 1860s were able to make intellectual leaps. Because no-one had ever seen a molecule (nor would they for another 100 years) Maxwell had to come up with a model. In the eighteenth century, the physicist Daniel Bernoulli had proposed that a gas inside a container consisted of countless tiny molecules, constantly bouncing off the walls and each other. Maxwell realised that this motion had to be random.

Maxwell started out by assuming that the gas was in equilibrium which means that on average, it wasn't gaining or losing energy to its surroundings. If the gas were in equilibrium, said Maxwell, the molecules' speeds in a given direction would have the Normal distribution, because of their randomness.

Clearly, the mean would have to be zero, because the molecules couldn't be moving anywhere on average in a closed container. The standard deviation was proportional to the temperature, and also the pressure exerted by the gas on the container walls. Without observing a single molecule, Maxwell had used statistics to explain the properties of gases.

Despite the elegance and power of Maxwell's 'kinetic' theory, many felt tricked by his statistical sleight of hand. These sceptics claimed that molecules were just imaginary constructs used by Maxwell, and his successor Boltzmann, to give the answers they wanted. The supporters of Maxwell's theory or the atomists, as they were known, needed to find some direct evidence. This came, in part, from a botanist called Robert Brown.

In 1828, Brown published a paper entitled 'A Brief Account of Microscopical Observations Made in the Months of June, July and August

1827, on the Particles Contained in the Pollen of Plants'. Brown reported that when he peered down a microscope at pollen grains in water, he observed the grains in incessant, random motion. At first, Brown thought the grains might be bacteria, but soon proved that this was not the case. Brown went on to note the same jiggling of dust particles from a wide range of sources, ranging from London soot to a pulverised fragment of the Sphinx.

By the 1860s, atomists began suggesting that Brownian motion, as it came to be known, was the result of the grains being randomly buffeted by invisible water molecules. The jiggling increased with temperature – the standard deviation of the molecules' speed, remember – supporting this theory.

However, anti-atomists poured scorn on the idea, correctly pointing out that individual molecules were far too small to move a pollen grain on their own. The effect had to be statistical in nature. But how? What held the atomists back was the lack of a mathematical framework to express their idea.

The invisible man

In the last years of the nineteenth century, Frenchman Henri Poincaré was renowned as one of the world's leading mathematicians. Taking a deep interest in physics, Poincaré did groundbreaking work in optics, classical mechanics and relativity. But when he gave the opening address to a packed hall in Paris at the International Congress of Physics in 1900, he talked about Brownian motion:

> Brown first thought that Brownian motion was a vital phenomenon, but soon he saw that inanimate bodies dance with no less ardour than the others; then he turned the matter over to the physicists ... We see under our eyes now motion transformed into heat by friction, now heat changed inversely into motion.

Across town, in the Sorbonne university, Poincaré's student, Louis Bachelier, was completing his doctoral dissertation. When he had suggested that Brownian motion would make a good thesis topic for Bachelier, Poincaré was handing him one of the plum problems of the day, and must have had high hopes for his young student. Bachelier in turn would have counted himself lucky to be part of the inner circle of Paris's star professor.

Here's what Bachelier did. The problem is how to reconcile two levels of randomness: the motion of a dust particle, which we can see, and the motion of trillions of molecules, which we can't see. Clearly, the scales of size are very different – because the particle is so much bigger than the molecules, a lot of molecules have to gang up together in order to move the particle. It is like the battle between Gulliver and the Lilliputians in Swift's *Gulliver's Travels*.

The time-scales of particles and molecules are different as well. The Lilliputians do a lot of running around and arguing, but on average they manage to co-operate enough to move Gulliver. Likewise, molecules do a lot of scurrying around in between every move made by the dust particle. This fact allowed Bachelier to make his crucial step.

Imagine Robert Brown, peering down his microscope, making notes. As the particle moves this way and that, Brown notes whether it moved left or right, and the distance it covered. He then plots this information on a chart, showing distance on the horizontal axis, and the number of times that particular distance was observed on the vertical axis. As with the naturalist observing dogs, we have another example of a distribution.

At first sight, the shape of this distribution should depend on what the molecules are doing at a given time – it should be different every time we do the experiment. But the difference in time-scales comes to the rescue. A move by the dust particle that Brown is capable of seeing in his microscope must be the sum of millions of tiny pushes given to it by molecules. These tiny pushes themselves each form a distribution, but when we add them together, the Central Limit Theorem means the visible movement of the dust particle always follows a Normal distribution.

In Swiftian terms, in the time it takes for Gulliver to move from one direction to the other, the Lilliputians have forgotten what they were doing, and act completely randomly. The only remnant of the molecules' behaviour, like a Cheshire Cat's grin, is in the standard deviation which describes how spread out the dust particles' distribution is.

You might think that over time, a particle would stay in the spot where it started out. After all, the Normal distribution tells us that a given movement to the left is as likely as the same move to the right – in other words, it is symmetrical. But once the particle makes a large, rare move in one direction, its next move is likely to be small, because the Normal distribution is peaked around zero. This means that the particle slowly drifts away from its starting point, making what is known as a random walk.

Because of the drift,[2] if you start out by clustering all the particles together,

---

2. Technical note: 'Drift' is used here in a non-mathematical sense. Strictly speaking, it refers to a non-random, increasing displacement over time. For a pure Normal distribution, the (mathematical)

they will spread out over time. We see this happening every day: cigarette smoke spreads out and disappears in a room, while a drop of ink spreads out in a glass of water. These are examples of what are called diffusion processes.

For a particle moving at constant speed, in the absence of molecules, the distance travelled is proportional to the time taken. When the molecules force the particle to take a random walk, it turns out that the average distance the particle travels is proportional to the square root of the time it takes. If you can measure both these quantities, then you can unlock the properties of the molecules captured in the standard deviation. The paper that first showed how to do all this helped make its author famous, and clinched victory for the atomists. In a testament to its popularity, the paper is still in the top ten list of all physics citations from before 1912.

However, that paper was not written by Louis Bachelier. It was written by Albert Einstein in 1905. And while Bachelier did indeed discover the mathematics of Brownian motion in his 1900 thesis, the motion of dust particles was not mentioned once. The paper was about the Paris stock market.

Reading through the 70-page thesis, entitled 'The Theory of Speculation', Poincaré must have suspected a practical joke. He didn't make the connection with Brownian motion, and from contemporary accounts, Bachelier seems to have been strangely unassertive. It doesn't pay to be too original in the presence of a star professor, and by doing so, Bachelier killed his career stone dead. For the rest of his life, disowned by his mentor, Bachelier struggled to find teaching work.

What had Bachelier done? 120 years after Adam Smith, and 180 years after Isaac Newton gave up on trying to understand the 'madness of people', Bachelier struck out into the unknown. Instead of a dust particle, Bachelier thought of a stock price as being buffeted up and down, not by molecules but by the invisible moods of thousands of investors and traders. Here was Alan Greenspan's 'model of human behaviour', written down for the first time.

Bachelier's reasoning is no different from that used to model the jiggling of dust particles. A large company (such as a component of the Dow Jones Industrial Average) has millions of shares in circulation. With thousands of speculators buying and selling the shares in the course of a day, each trade gives a tiny 'push' to the share price.

When we add the 'pushes' together, by using that statistician's party trick, the Central Limit Theorem, the changes in price follow a Normal

---

drift is zero, and the average displacement of the particle is zero. However, the random walk causes the *mean square* displacement to increase at a constant rate, proportional to the standard deviation.

distribution. Like Lilliputians, the speculators' constant to-ing and fro-ing means that by the time they have made a difference, they can't remember why. All one needs to know about the speculators' behaviour gets wrapped up in the standard deviation.

We'll come back to Bachelier's vision many times in this book, so it is worth putting it in context. What started hundreds of thousands of years ago as individuals exchanging goods on the African savannah had turned into an emerging global economy by 1900, with a dozen national stock and commodity markets in operation around the world.

The fear and greed in the market had disturbed Isaac Newton in 1720, and Adam Smith was forced to defend the system as being good for humanity. Since then, Karl Marx had argued that markets served the needs only of capitalists exploiting the workers. Now Bachelier was telling the world that the human drama in the market could be reduced to a science related to the mathematics of tossing coins. Discarded as a curiosity, his work would remain forgotten for over fifty years.

What Bachelier didn't have was an ideology. Capitalism had plenty of supporters in 1900, but finance and the markets were still seen as an appendage. Over that ensuing 50-year period, Russia and China would violently reject the system. Even in the United States, Adam Smith's spiritual heartland, markets were blamed for causing the Great Depression in the 1930s.

The change in climate would come during the early years of the Cold War. An intellectual revolution set in motion at the University of Chicago would bring mathematics into the markets, and eventually turn finance into science. Set loose in the US economy, this new science would flourish, and eventually help win the Cold War. We will join this revolution through the eyes of a Canadian youth – Myron Scholes.

The gurus of finance

Timmins, Ontario is about as close to the edge of the world as you can get. Located near Hudson Bay in the low-lying north-east of the Canadian province, the town owes its existence to the substantial gold deposits nearby. The average winter temperature of minus 15 °C quoted by the local chamber of commerce leaves out a vicious wind-chill factor. Only a few hundred miles further north, the surrounding pine forests give way to tundra that stretches half-way to the North Pole.

Myron Scholes was born in Timmins on 1 July 1941. His father, Jesse, was a dentist, and had moved there several years earlier to take advantage of the local economy during the Depression. There was certainly no shortage of gold for fillings in Timmins.

Scholes's mother, Anne, was a strong character. With the help of her uncle, she opened a department store in Timmins, and expanded the business into a chain of similar outlets. When her uncle died suddenly of a heart attack in 1950, his surviving family wrested control of the business away from Anne, with the help of crafty local lawyers. As Scholes later laconically put it, this was his 'first exposure to agency and contracting problems'.

Furious at the betrayal, Anne made the family move 500 miles south to the town of Hamilton where her brother ran a publishing and promotion business. Jesse Scholes had to abandon his dentistry practice and retrain as an orthodontist. Resigned to being a housewife, Anne now focused on her son.

Short-sighted and unco-ordinated, Scholes may have lacked ability in ice hockey or other Canadian sporting traditions. However, he was studious, had a head for figures and most importantly, got on with people. At high school he became treasurer of countless school clubs, making himself too useful to be bullied.

Meanwhile, Anne Scholes plotted out for him the business career in which she had failed herself. The plan was that Myron would join his uncle's publishing business after university. Feeling a close bond to his mother, Scholes dutifully worked for his uncle during school holidays, and even tried gambling, not to enjoy himself, but 'to understand probabilities and risks'. When her son reached fifteen, Anne opened a brokerage account for him, so he could learn about the stock market.

Then tragedy struck the family a second time. Diagnosed with terminal cancer, Mrs Scholes would never see the results of her investment. She died three days after Scholes's sixteenth birthday. The bereavement nearly floored Scholes. Shortly after the funeral, he developed scars on the corneas of both eyes, making him virtually blind.

For Scholes, reading a newspaper – let alone a textbook – was now a slow, painful experience. Years later, he managed to see the ailment in a positive light: 'I learned to think abstractly and conceptualise the solution to problems.' Leaving Hamilton was now out of the question, so Scholes enrolled at the local college, McMaster University, after which he would join the family business.

Living at home and commuting to class, Scholes worked hard. Jesse took over Anne's role in funding his brokerage account. Mapped out by his dead mother, Scholes's life now seemed on autopilot. However, half-blind as he was on the outside, Scholes was changing on the inside. 'Out of necessity, I became a good listener', he commented later.

Studying economics, Scholes listened especially carefully to a Professor McIver, who had got an economics PhD from the University of Chicago. According to McIver, Chicago was the place to be. Here were professors such as Milton Friedman and George Stigler, a new wave of free-marketeers who were revolutionising the subject. Here too, was a chance to escape from Canadian provincial life and live in a vast metropolis. Scholes was hooked, and when Chicago offered him a graduate school place in economics, he decided that his uncle's business could wait a little longer.

So what had been happening in Chicago? For the economists who arrived there in the 1940s and 1950s, their defining experience had been the trauma of the Great Depression. In particular, the Wall Street crash of October 1929 had shaken up everyone's ideas about investment. Until then, investing in stocks was like shopping. You would browse through the supermarket until you found a few select brands – or stocks – that you liked. Then you would stick with them for years, earning dividends while your investment grew in value.

1929 blew this cosy theory out of the water. Favourite brands of stock collapsed like dominoes along with the entire market. The companies that didn't go out of business completely, took years to regain their pre-1929 price and pay dividends again. Clearly stocks were risky. In an echo of the South Sea Bubble, laws were passed during the 1930s forbidding them as investments.

What happened next mirrored the changes in biology between the eighteenth and nineteenth centuries. Rather than trying to dissect individual companies, to see if they were 'good' or 'bad' investments, the new generation of self-styled financial economists started looking at pure data.

To see how radical this approach was, imagine investing in a modern company, Microsoft. The traditional approach would be to investigate Microsoft's products (for anyone using a personal computer, it's hard not to). Then you read its annual and quarterly earnings reports, to see how much money it is making, and how much it pays to shareholders. You might also read some interviews with Microsoft's CEO, Bill Gates, to see what his strategy was. At the end of all this, you make a decision whether or not to buy Microsoft shares.

The new generation would put all that carefully gathered information in the garbage can. Instead, they would sharpen their pencils, and focus on one thing: Microsoft's daily share price. They would gather a year's worth of prices and look at them using statistics. A single price – perhaps from the end of the year – no longer means anything. The new generation would define 'Microsoft' as a collection of share prices, measured one after the other, just as the nineteenth-century naturalist defined the species of dogs as a population of individuals.

With a share price – measured in dollars, pounds or whatever – the financial economists weren't quite ready to go to work. They needed a way to compare different stocks. For example, if the price of Microsoft rises by $5, that means something different from IBM rising by the same amount. If one of these companies pays out a dividend, that means something different again. To get round this problem, the early financial economists used the concept of returns – the percentage increase in the value of an investment after a day, a month and so on. Dividends were included as part of the return.

Like the heights of dogs in our earlier example, daily returns can be averaged, and that says something meaningful. The fact that Microsoft had an annual return of 114 per cent in 1998, while for Netscape the figure was 149 per cent, clearly tells us that Netscape was a better investment. Perhaps it's enough to stop there, sell Microsoft and buy Netscape. Many investors do just that.

However, it is the standard deviation – the Cheshire Cat grin of Bachelier's speculators – that we have forgotten about. Known as volatility in finance, the standard deviation of price returns tells us how the returns are spread out around the average. And that tells us something about risk. For example, Netscape has a higher volatility than Microsoft, suggesting that it is a riskier investment.

It was in Chicago, in 1952, that a graduate student named Harry Markowitz first brought this idea into finance. A tetchy and unsocial man, Markowitz made few friends among the Chicago economics faculty, and was nearly denied his PhD by a hostile thesis committee. But Markowitz's idea would change finance.

In order to say something useful about investment, Markowitz considered a portfolio, or group, of stocks. It's straightforward to calculate the average return and volatility of each individual stock. But what about the whole portfolio? To deal with this Markowitz looked at a statistical measure, the correlation, of how much each stock moved in line with the others.

Correlation takes us into new territory. Rather than being a property of a single collection of data, it provides a link between two separate distributions. As we shall see later in the LTCM story, it is one of the most subtle and treacherous tools in statistics. But it worked a miracle for Markowitz.

To see how, imagine a portfolio with two risky stocks: an ice cream company and an umbrella company. Ice cream sells when the weather is sunny, and umbrellas sell when it is rainy. The first company does well when the other does badly, and vice-versa. In the language of statistics, we say that their returns have negative correlation.

Now think about the total value of the portfolio. Day by day, this value is the sum of the two stocks. The volatility of each stock tells us how much its return fluctuates around the mean. However, when ice cream moves up, umbrellas move down — at least on average. Because of this, the portfolio value hardly fluctuates at all, or in other words, its volatility is low.

Low volatility means low risk. By not putting all our eggs in one basket, we have made a safer investment. As Markowitz would put it, the risk has been diversified away. Fifty years on, this idea seems like no more than common sense. Back in 1952, it seemed revolutionary.[3]

In his thesis, Markowitz suggested that his correlation trick could be used to build portfolios. All one needed to do, he said, was maximise the total return, at the same time as minimising the volatility, or risk. Markowitz dubbed a collection of stocks having this property as an 'efficient portfolio'.

It was this insight that earned Markowitz a Nobel prize years later. Back in the 1950s, however, there was a problem: how to handle the data needed to come up with useful results. First of all, one might calculate the annual return and volatility for a single stock. In one year, there are 252 trading days, which means 252 individual numbers – daily returns – needed to obtain the result.

Now consider a portfolio consisting of the Dow Jones Industrial Average, which contains 30 stocks. We now calculate using our 252 daily returns, and repeat this 30 times. That means handling 7560 numbers. For 30 stocks, there are a total of 420 correlations we need to calculate. To do this, a total of 106,000 numbers must be obtained and added together.

Today, desktop computers can do this in less than a second. In the 1950s and 1960s, the primitive machines available would require hours or even days. This bottleneck had two consequences. Firstly, it made technology a force in finance, and second, it made the younger generation who knew how to get the most out of these early computers especially valuable.

---

3.   A British civil servant, A.D. Roy discovered the idea independently, but never exploited his work, and ended up in obscurity.

In the summer of 1963, completing his first year at the University of Chicago, Myron Scholes made one of the smartest decisions of his life. Despite having no experience, he pressured the dean of the economics department into giving him a summer job programming the department's computers.

Scholes later recalled what happened next: 'During my first few days on the job, several professors asked for computer-programming assistance on their research projects. I was able to fend them off by arguing that the senior programmers would soon be on scene to assist them. They never did show up. By the third day, I could no longer fend off the aggressive professors.'

Scholes quickly taught himself programming, and suddenly had professors who previously ignored him now treating him like gold dust. There was no question now of returning to his uncle's business in Ontario. In fact, two of the department's top guns asked him to stay for a PhD. One of them was Merton Miller – we will see more of him later. The other was Eugene Fama, who was just completing his own thesis.

Fama was one of a select group of financial economists who picked up the ball from Markowitz and ran with it. Clever as it was, Markowitz's efficient portfolio raised more questions than it answered.

For a start, there was the calculation problem. One of Markowitz's students, William Sharpe, made that problem a lot easier by showing that one could focus on a stock's correlation with an index (such as the Dow Jones Industrial Average) rather than with each other individual stock in a portfolio. With this information, Sharpe could then ask if a particular stock was under- or over-valued. Sharpe's technique became known as the Capital Asset Pricing Model (CAPM).

But what about the real world? On Wall Street in the 1950s and 1960s, no-one could care less about financial economics. The majority of fund managers and investment advisers (then and now) took the traditional approach to picking stocks. They researched companies before recommending buying or selling, often claiming that they had superior information to their rivals. For this service, they charged high fees.

The new generation of economists was infuriated by this cosy arrangement. How could the fund managers justify their claims? In a recent cartoon series, *King of the Hill*, a character claims that 'all Americans are above average'. The fund managers' universal claims that they could beat the market were equally absurd.

Suppose you are a smart fund manager, trying to beat the market. At lunch you overhear a conversation that suggests a certain pharmaceutical company stock is underpriced. For example, the company may be getting government approval for a new drug. You call your broker and buy some of the stock.

However, the broker knows you are smart. He decides that you must be buying for a reason, and buys some stock too. Gossip starts spreading from brokers to analysts, some of whom are as smart as you, and guess why you are buying. Suddenly everyone else is buying too, enough to move the stock up in price. The stock is no longer underpriced. The next moment, someone else hears a negative rumour about the company – perhaps the drug has side effects. They realise the stock is overpriced and sell, the gossip spreads, and pretty soon the stock falls to a new fair value.

Here we have Bachelier all over again. The 'smart people' – the fund managers – end up appearing no smarter than the molecules buffeting a dust particle. Like the dust particle undergoing Brownian motion, the stock takes a random walk. All that's left of the fund managers is the standard deviation, or volatility.

In an influential 1965 paper entitled 'Random walks in stock market prices', Fama gave Bachelier the ideology he had lacked back in 1900. The existence of 'smart people' using information to buy and sell stocks meant that stock prices resulting from this trading didn't contain any secrets. Fama's vision – called the Efficient Market Hypothesis – was of a market where traders and investors devoured information like army ants stripping the jungle bare. Stock prices were like bones picked clean of their information.

In its strongest form, Fama's hypothesis asserted that no-one could beat the market. Even the smart people with information couldn't survive long before the gods of chance wiped them out. Scholes, whose PhD involved testing the efficient market hypothesis, was entranced with the logic of this argument.

But it was not Fama who brought Bachelier back into finance, but a contemporary of his on the East coast, Paul Samuelson at MIT. Not only did Samuelson shake fifty years of dust off Bachelier's work, but he smartened it up too. For example, Bachelier had the stock price taking a random walk. If the price was pushed down far enough it could go negative.

Samuelson realised that this was impossible, for legal reasons. Ever since shares were first invented in the seventeenth century, shareholders have had limited liability. That means the value of shares cannot fall below zero. Samuelson solved the problem by having stock returns take a random walk, rather than prices. In statistics language, this means that while returns follow

Brownian motion, stock prices are described by something called geometric Brownian motion, which is always positive.

No-one detested the active fund managers as much as Samuelson. He even wrote a paper urging them to figuratively 'drop dead', adding that 'few people will commit suicide without a push'. But how could that push be given? Efficient market theory was a negative statement – you couldn't beat the market – but Samuelson wanted a positive statement as well. What should an investor do?

Markowitz had supplied part of the answer with his efficient portfolio, and Sharpe had gone further with the CAPM. However, these models answered the question at only one particular time. Samuelson wanted a continuous time theory, that investors could use day by day, and so send the fund managers packing once and for all.

The answer lay in Bachelier's random walks, but Samuelson couldn't work out how to do it. An urbane, eclectic man, Samuelson had advised the Kennedy administration on economic policy, and was the sort of traditional economist John Maynard Keynes would have been comfortable with. What he needed was a mathematical gunslinger to take the problem off his hands. That man was Robert C. Merton.

The middle initial is a crucial one, because there are two Robert Mertons with distinguished academic careers – father and son. While the son would model human behaviour with mathematics, his father Robert King Merton covered a similar territory without ever using a single mathematical formula. He was a sociologist.

When Robert C. was born in July 1944, Robert K. was entering the most fruitful period of his career. At the Bureau for Social Research at New York's Columbia University, over the next few years he developed ideas that would enter the popular lexicon. One example was the 'focus group', a market research method which today's politicians have come to depend upon.

Robert K.'s most famous brainwave was the 'self-fulfilling prophecy', which he first defined in 1948, in an article in the *Antioch Review*. As a positive example, he said that by believing in a child's ability, the child was motivated to make that belief come true. Robert C. would spectacularly vindicate this hypothesis.

As a negative example, Robert K. discussed runs on banks, where the mere opinion that a bank is insolvent actually brings about insolvency when depositors all attempt to withdraw funds. How could Robert K. possibly know that fifty years later, during September 1998, that kind of self-fulfilling prophecy would haunt his son Robert C. during the LTCM crisis?

Back in the late 1940s, only the positive side of this deep thinking touched the young Merton. He experienced none of the misfortunes that dominated Scholes's early life. Living in the town of Hastings-on-Hudson, about ten miles north of Manhattan, Merton enjoyed a privileged life in the suburbs. While Robert K. commuted to his Columbia office every day, Robert C. stayed in Hastings with his two sisters, his mother, his grand-mother and about 25 pet cats.

Cosseted in this female household, Merton was allowed to pursue his own interests. At first it was baseball, and then cars that obsessed him. As he later wrote: 'On my bedroom wall, I put a large sheet of paper with 1800-plus numbers: one to be crossed out each day until I would be old enough for my driver's license. As I had known all the batting averages and pitching records of big league baseball players, so I came to know the horsepower and engine size of just about every automobile in the post-war era.'

The feeling of belonging to an elite was reinforced at the local high school, where many Columbia professors – some of them Nobel prizewinners – sent their children. Mathematics became Merton's favourite subject, not least because he found it easy enough to let him concentrate on cars. Hooked on the smell of motor oil, the teenage Merton spent every spare moment visiting stock car races and he later recalled the thrill when older car fanatics let him help with repairs: 'Handing tools to older, amateur buffs working on their cars was an outlet for my passion.'

When Merton occupied the family garage to rebuild a second-hand car as a hot-rod drag racer, his father must have wondered if his son would spend the rest of his life in greasy overalls. He needn't have worried. From under the layers of sump oil, a confident, good-looking youth was emerging. Merton's ability in maths easily won him a place at Columbia University, where he studied engineering. A week before his seventeenth birthday, some friends organised a blind date for him with June Rose, a pretty young TV soap opera star and a regular guest on Dick Clark's American Bandstand. Rose clearly saw her date's potential as a high flyer, and married him when he graduated from Columbia.

By now, Merton had lost interest in cars and machines. Soon after starting graduate school in applied mathematics at Caltech in Pasadena, California, he decided to switch to economics, seeing a better outlet for his talents. As he later recalled: 'I had a much better intuition and "feel" into economic matters than physical ones.'

Merton had toyed with the stock market since childhood, but now trading became a new obsession. Rising at dawn, he would visit a brokerage house to catch the New York Stock Exchange when trading opened at 6.30a.m., local time. There he would 'watch the tape' and do some trading before classes started.

One trade in particular was a harbinger of things to come. In late 1963, two US companies, Singer and Friden, announced a merger. Merton noticed that the share price of Singer was higher than Friden, despite the fact that if the merger was successful, the two stocks would become identical, and would have to have the same price.

Merton bought Friden, the cheap stock. He then sold Singer, the expensive stock, 'short' at the current price. All Merton had to do was wait for the merger to go through, and enjoy a virtually risk-free profit when the prices converged. As we will see, this is an example of an arbitrage trade.

Rejected as a PhD candidate by several economics departments, Merton was offered a place at MIT, where he was immediately steered in the direction of Paul Samuelson. For Samuelson, here was the mathematical gunslinger he had been waiting for.

The problem confronting Merton was to do calculations with stock prices, which seemed to follow a geometric Brownian motion – the kind of jagged, back-and-forth movement that Robert Brown had seen in pollen grains. In particular, if something depends on the stock price – in mathematical terms, if it is a function of the stock price – how does it change when the stock price changes?

The standard tool for dealing with rates of change is called the calculus, and was invented by our South Sea Bubble investor Isaac Newton back in the seventeenth century. At its heart, calculus depends on a simple trick. Functions can be drawn as curves on a graph – imagine the profile of a distant hill as a function of height. The function's rate of change is the slope of the curve.

Here's how the trick works. Suppose you zoom in on the curve with a telescope. From a distance, it undulates, but as you get close in, smaller and smaller segments of the curve fill your field of vision. Eventually, it starts looking like a straight line – for which the slope is a constant number.

If a curve is smooth, mathematics allows you to zoom in in this way. It's called 'taking a limit'. The paths taken by all sorts of objects ranging from cricket balls to planets follow smooth curves, allowing this trick to be used to great effect. But what about the jagged, jiggly Brownian curves followed by stock prices? To nineteenth-century mathematicians, these looked like nothing on earth.

In fact, there are plenty of things on earth that look like stock price curves. Snowflakes, coastlines, mountain ranges, all share the property of

Brownian curves to some degree; they are zoom-resistant. A small segment of the curve looks like a copy of the entire curve – jagged in every detail. Such curves are called fractals, and can't be reduced to straight lines.

At first sight, the situation seems hopeless. But the Normal distribution comes to the rescue. Recall how its mathematical purity appeared in the heart of Brownian motion, which conveniently hid the hurly-burly of Bachelier's speculators in the standard deviation. Because of this purity, the nastiness in the rate of change of a Brownian function reduces to a single extra bit dependent on volatility and time, which is added on to what you would expect from old-fashioned calculus.

This mathematical exorcism, called Ito's formula, was discovered in 1951 by Kiyoshi Ito.[4] Ito was a self-styled pure mathematician, which means he wasn't interested in applying his work to the real world. Indeed, when invited to a conference celebrating his contribution to economics many years later, Ito seemed bemused at all the fuss, and claimed not to remember deriving the formula in the first place.

What his formula does is allow you to do tricky calculations with Brownian motion. Here, it seemed was an answer to Newton's complaint. The madness of speculators had apparently been tamed once and for all.

For Merton, discovering Ito's formula was a Godsend. All the other economists working on continuous time problems in the late 1960s were waving sticks in the air. Merton now had an 'Ito machine gun'. Over the next few years, he would blow the big problems to smithereens, one by one.

Around the same time that Merton found Ito's formula, Myron Scholes arrived at MIT and started working with Fischer Black. The race to price options had begun.

4. Pronounced 'EE-toe'.

2

The Science of Fear and Greed

*If any one owe a debt for a loan, and a storm prostrates the grain, or the harvest fail,
or the grain does not grow for lack of water; in that year he need not give his creditor
any grain, he washes his debt-tablet in water and pays no rent for this year.*
Code of Hammurabi

In November 1968 Myron Scholes was seeing the world in a new light, literally. Before leaving Chicago, he had had new corneas grafted on his eyes, still scarred since his mother's death ten years earlier. When Fischer Black entered Scholes's MIT office that November, he noticed dozens of newspaper clippings on his desk.

They weren't news stories, but small classified advertisements taken from the financial section of the Sunday papers. The ads were for options, offered by companies with names like Ragnar & Co, and Thomas, Haab and Botts. With his new vision, Scholes was scanning the ads carefully, looking at the option prices.

Although the options allowed the purchaser the right to buy stock in well-known companies such as IBM or Eastman Kodak, the ads looked decidedly low-rent. A casual observer might mistake the wares on offer for discount furniture. So embarassingly obscure did options seem in the 1960s, that in his eventual paper, Merton referred apologetically to them as 'relatively unimportant contracts'.

But options are far from obscure. They certainly weren't in September 1998, when Merton and Scholes would watch helplessly as bad options trades on stock market indexes caused some of LTCM's billion dollar losses. The blow was especially bitter for the two men because it was they, together with Black 25 years earlier, who had made the breakthrough on how to price these 'unimportant contracts'.

There are two sides to options, which can be crudely labelled fear and greed. The fear aspect, more commonly known as risk, justifies their existence. The greed side, known as arbitrage, justifies their price. It was only after Black, Scholes and Merton completed the loop and showed how arbitrage could do this, that options broke out of their obscurity.

Options are examples of derivative contracts, so called because their existence is derived from something else that is already traded. In Scholes's newspaper ads, that something was stocks, but it can be anything capable of being bought and sold. Derivatives have a bad name outside finance, and have been blamed for causing a string of disasters over the years. At $4 billion, LTCM experienced the greatest derivatives loss in the history of finance.

Yet derivatives were invented to reduce risk, and they perform this job highly effectively today for millions of people. For anyone whose livelihood depends on a market price – stock prices, bond prices, oil prices and so on – derivatives have a useful role to play. We can trace derivatives, in particular options, back in time to the origins of markets. As soon as markets were invented, derivatives were invented too.

The risk managers of Babylon

In 1902, a team of French archaeologists uncovered an eight-foot high slab of black stone buried in the desert sand near Susa, Iraq. Carved on the stone in ancient Babylonian script was the world's first complete set of written laws – the famous Code of Hammurabi.

Hammurabi, who lived about 3800 years ago, was the king of Babylon and in his Code he claimed his authority from the Gods. The most common punishment for breaking the Code was death. According to legal scholars, the Code was largely a revision of common law existing at the time; in other words Hammurabi was effectively rubber-stamping the individual 'eye-for-an-eye' codes of personal retribution which were then in use.

But one of Hammurabi's laws, paragraph 48 (quoted at the head of this chapter), was different. It doesn't mention punishment, but only says that in the event of a crop disaster, those who owe debts need not pay any interest for one year. The Babylonians used clay tablets for writing on, and in Hammurabi's words, debtors could 'wash the debt tablet in water', or erase the loan contract, for the year of the crop failure.

At first sight, paragraph 48 resembles insurance. After all, it refers to debts being payable in grain, while the word 'rent' is used instead of 'interest', suggesting that a typical debtor would have been a farmer paying a mortgage on his property. In a year of crop failure, farmers suffer losses, and like a good politician Hammurabi is insuring them against being unable to pay their debts.

However, paragraph 48 is more subtle than that. Firstly, there is that issue of payment in grain, which suggests farmers were involved. But the Babylonian economy was founded on grain, and while loans were made in silver, it made sense to use grain to repay the debts because it was available everywhere.

And if there is one thing we can be sure about with grain, when the harvest fails, the price goes up because demand outstrips supply. In modern finance, we would say that debtors were 'exposed' to the grain price. This brings us to the second point. Insurance is about losses, which have to be proved before claims can be paid. Yet, paragraph 48 doesn't mention losses, and nor does it mention farmers, who after all might even benefit from inflated grain prices. So it can't be insurance.

Then what is paragraph 48 all about? When a crop failure happened, the debtors had the right to pay nothing that year. The lenders, on the other hand, had no choice in the matter: they had to do without the interest. In other words, the debtors had an option to call upon the lenders to cover their interest payments in the event of crop failure, which effectively put a cap on their grain price exposure.

Paragraph 48 is the earliest written example of an option contract, which is often mistakenly attributed to the Greek philosopher Thales, who lived 1200 years later. Hammurabi's option derives its value both from the existence of a loan – it's worthless without one – and also from crop failures which impact the price of grain. What's missing from paragraph 48 is how crop failure was defined in practice, and one wonders how often Hammurabi himself was asked to settle disputes between lenders and borrowers seeking to 'wash their tablets'.

What does Hammurabi's option tell us about risk? The risk of crop failure hasn't been removed, but only transferred, to lenders. Being wealthy, the lenders might be better suited to take on the risk. Then again, they might not want to, but disobeying Hammurabi tended to result in excruciating death.

However, Hammurabi doesn't say what the interest rate should be on loans. More recent archaeological research has shown that there was a thriving loan market in ancient Babylon where borrowers could search for the best rate, just as homebuyers do today.

Now imagine that we are lenders in the market of Babylon, and we have just heard that Hammurabi is to make us give an option to every borrower. If we are smart, we should increase the interest rate we charge to compensate us for the extra risk. That involves pricing the option – in other words, charging today for what we might have to pay tomorrow. While there is no historical evidence that Babylonian lenders ever actually did this, the problem is similar to that tackled by Black, Merton and Scholes 3800 years later.

The pit bulls of Chicago

There are three main branches to the derivatives family, and options belong to one branch. Another type, swaps, will make their appearance later on in this book. The third derivative, futures, is simpler to understand than the others and possibly for this reason, had established a tenacious foothold in American finance some hundred years before Black crossed the Charles River to work with Scholes.

Like Hammurabi's option, futures help manage risk. But their story shows how the flip side of derivatives – greed – enters the picture too.

The story begins 2000 miles west of MIT, in the Chicago futures exchanges. These freewheeling bastions of market forces had started out in the early nineteenth century, when the great prairies of the Midwest were first ploughed up and planted with corn.

By virtue of Chicago's position on the Great Lakes, its merchants would become the principal intermediaries between the Midwestern farmers and the hungry masses of the East coast. As the industry grew, buying and selling wheat became increasingly cumbersome. Attracting finance from the banks on the East coast was also difficult for the Chicago grain dealers. So they decided to protect their interests.

The group of businessmen who founded the Chicago Board of Trade (CBOT) in 1848 were the antithesis of Hammurabi. Out of sight of the Federal government in Washington DC, they incorporated themselves under local state law. Above all else, their intention was to govern themselves and avoid interference along the lines of paragraph 48.

The CBOT founders were themselves upholding a tradition. While not as old as Babylon, mercantile self-governance goes back to the Middle Ages, when agricultural fairs in southern France organised 'courts of the fair' to arbitrate in disputes between merchants. Then and now, the idea is the same: keeping the law of the land out of business.

By the time the American Civil War began in 1861, Chicago was fast becoming the biggest agricultural trading centre in the United States. Geography and industrial technology played a part – Chicago dealers pioneered the idea of grain elevators, giant structures which could rapidly transfer grain from train wagons to ships.

But the CBOT was equally important. With so many grain dealers gathered in one place, its quality definitions and delivery requirements rapidly became industry standards. The CBOT price became the best price, simply because it allowed the largest number of buyers and sellers to meet in one place. Its 'pit' system would become a popular spectacle, with hundreds of traders yelling prices above the din, and gesticulating their orders conveyed through a code of hand signals.

The Civil War proved all this beyond doubt. While popular imagination focuses on shaggy-bearded generals planning campaigns, and infantrymen clashing bloodily in Virginia pine forests, the war was arguably won elsewhere. The Union army was simply a highly-visible contact point in a war where the North slowly strangled the South to death.

Abraham Lincoln's Republican administration had no interest in taking over food production. But it needed to feed vast numbers of men and horses in the field – numbers which increased as more Southern territory was occupied. However, just like the value of stocks, the price of food is volatile. The vagaries of supply and demand could make it hard for the government to pay for the war. Indeed, gold prices became highly volatile too, because of concerns that the US government would have to sell its reserves to raise cash.

The risk became clear in 1862. Driven by the need of the Army Quartermasters Corps to provision its horses, the price of a bushel of oats rose from 16 cents to 43 cents, and increased to 67 cents by mid-1863. There had to be a way of reducing this risk, and when Federal Trade Commission officials began meeting CBOT members early in 1862, they learned of a new type of contract that might just make this possible. At first called 'to arrive' and then later 'futures' contracts, these deals allowed delivery of grain and other foodstuffs to be made at a future date – at a fixed price.

Futures allowed the army to finance its campaigns more efficiently. Suppose it is May and you are a general ordered to occupy the state of Arkansas by October. Your quartermaster goes to Chicago and enters into a CBOT futures contract promising delivery of oats for your horses in September at the May price. If the price subsequently doubles, you aren't affected. In modern terms, you have 'hedged' your exposure.

Now suppose you are a Midwestern farmer due to harvest a crop of oats for sale in September. Your worry is that prices could go down. By promising you a fixed price in May for your harvest in September, the futures contract hedges this risk.

What makes the contract so useful? Each side of the trade – buyer and seller – wants to avoid the risk of prices going against them. Of course, prices could go in their favour giving either side an unexpected windfall, but that is less important for them than avoiding risk. With its fixed future price, the contract excludes the windfall possibility, but it also excludes the risk.

With its new tool of futures, the CBOT functioned as a vital organ to the Northern military organism, sucking food from the prairies, and pumping it to the Union armies, while the blockaded Confederates slowly starved. No less significant than the ironclad gunboat or the rifle musket, futures were a weapon of war. After the Confederate surrender in May 1865, Generals Grant and Sherman both visited the CBOT trading floor to express their gratitude.

One trader who shook hands with the two generals that June must have felt an equal gratitude in return. His name was Benjamin Hutchinson and the growth of futures trading during the war had turned him from a near-bankrupt to a millionaire. He was the first of a new breed of trader made possible by futures contracts: the speculator.

Before futures, the amount of trading at the CBOT matched the quantity of wheat and other commodities that were available. After all, if a dealer sold wheat and then failed to deliver it, he would face the wrath of his peers, and could be expelled from the exchange. As a result, sellers of wheat tended to own grain elevators or at least have grain stored in one. When Hutchinson arrived in Chicago he had neither.

By selling wheat in six-months time, the futures speculator didn't have to own it in the present. All he needed to do was buy it for delivery when the time came. If the price fell in the meantime, he could make a handsome profit. On the other hand, the speculator might use futures to buy wheat in six months. He had no use for the stuff, but if prices had gone up, he could promptly sell it and also make a profit.

Hutchinson saw his first opportunity in 1863. Like oats, the price of wheat had skyrocketed since the previous year. Hutchinson sold as many futures contracts as he could get his hands on. When the Union army won the battle of Gettysburg that summer, the fear that had gripped the markets about the US government subsided, and the price of wheat plunged as a wave of confidence crossed the country. Hutchinson was suddenly a rich man.

Today, Hutchinson's 1863 coup would be called a directional trade. Believing that the price of wheat would go down, Hutchinson used futures to make a massive bet. Over the next thirty years, Hutchinson – or 'Old Hutch' as he was known – became a legendary figure in Chicago, and spawned many imitators. Paradoxically enough, the lesson of 1863 was that gamblers like Hutchinson and thrifty users of the market like the Army Quartermasters Corps needed each other.

Concerned about grain prices going up, the Corps had used futures to protect itself, and didn't mind foregoing a potential windfall if the price went down. However, the 'natural' sellers of grain, the farmers, might not be prepared to sell the Corps the futures it needed. In the jargon of finance, such a market in which trade doesn't flow smoothly is 'illiquid'.

Speculators like Hutchinson provided a service by stepping in and allowing the market to function, like oil lubricating an engine. In recognition of its lubricant properties, this service is called providing 'liquidity' to the market. The profit earned by speculators is the price the market pays for the service.[1]

So far, so good. But the speculators brought in other, less desirable qualities which foreshadowed LTCM. Firstly, they introduced something called leverage, which means controlling a large amount of assets while only having a small amount of capital to your name.

This was possible because futures didn't require any downpayments. In the 1860s, so long as you were a member of the exchange, you could buy a million dollars' worth of grain futures and only be charged a small brokers' fee. Speculators would enter into such trades, then borrow money to fulfil their obligations.

Worse still, the speculators wanted more. It is one thing to make a directional bet and win, but losing is costly, particularly if you have borrowed money to take positions. How could they make money without taking so much risk?

Their answer to this question was a technique that would bring them notoriety: the corner. Speculators would attempt 'corners' by taking such a large position that the market would have to move in their direction. By owning virtually all the wheat due to be delivered in say, September, the speculator could then dictate the price at which he sold it.

For those who had sold futures due in the same month and needed to buy to fulfil their obligations, the results could be devastating. It was also often humiliating, as defeated 'shorts' would be forced to plead in person for lenient terms from their victorious opponent.

---

1. Liquidity has a slightly different meaning in banking where it describes the ability to turn assets into cash.

As corners became a regular occurrence, the Civil War goodwill towards the futures markets evaporated. After a notorious corner in which Hutchinson doubled the price of wheat over a single month in September 1888, Chicago newspapers began to blame suicides on being the victim of a corner.

Aggressive speculation increased volatility too. The farmers and consumers who were the reason the market existed in the first place started suffering from the wild swings in prices, and for the first time politicians took notice.

There was only one way for sellers of futures to fight back against a corner. By buying up grain at the outset of the futures contract, before the price gets forced up, you can deliver without being squeezed by speculators. For this reason, speculators were secretive about corners, and most people didn't find out until it was too late.

The mood was captured brilliantly by the novelist Frank Norris, who in his time was dubbed the 'American Zola'. Published posthumously in 1902, Norris's bestselling novel *The Pit* tells the story of Curtis Jadwin, a speculator who unsuccessfully attempts to corner the wheat pit, driving himself and his beautiful wife Laura into a metaphorical 'pit' of madness.

Jadwin is based on a real-life speculator, Joseph Leiter, who had attempted a notorious corner in 1898. Leiter failed when his would-be victim Philip Armour, who had sold futures, shipped in millions of bushels of wheat to Chicago using a privately-chartered fleet of boats on the Great Lakes. Norris described how futures speculators transfixed the popular imagination:

> In the Democratic press [Jadwin] was assailed as little better than a thief, vituperated as an oppressor of the people, who ground the faces of the poor, and battened in the luxury wrung from the toiling millions. The Republican papers spoke solemnly of a new era of prosperity upon which the country was entering . . .

In the meantime, another type of contract had made an appearance. Called 'privileges' these contracts resembled futures except for one key difference. While the seller of a grain future has to deliver regardless of whether the price has gone up or down, privileges permitted the seller to refuse the delivery if the price had gone up – in other words, if he faced a loss. Because of the 'privilege' of not delivering, the seller paid a premium up front. It's not hard to recognise privileges as options under another name.

But the national mood was changing. An emerging global power with millions of mouths to feed, and with an increasingly sophisticated electorate,

America could no longer leave its food supply in the hands of a few businessmen and financiers. So, by the First World War, regulators were paying close attention to Chicago futures markets. As speculators like Hutchinson openly boasted that they were betting on prices, lawmakers and their supporters began accusing the CBOT of being a glorified gambling den. Futures and options contracts should be banned, they said.

The traders' only line of defence was that futures ultimately resulted in a physical grain delivery, even if they changed hands dozens of times beforehand. To emphasise their case, the CBOT decided to sacrifice privileges, which were considered even more suspect because delivery wasn't always necessary. Reluctantly buying the argument, Congress banned all options on commodities in 1934, while permitting futures to remain.

However, this wasn't enough for the government. In the Great Depression, the writing was on the wall for futures speculators like Hutchinson and Leiter. After setting up a commission to monitor the futures markets, Congress made corners illegal under the Commodity Exchange Act in 1936. From now on, all large futures positions would have to be reported. Never again, in the United States at least, would a single speculator be allowed to control trading on an exchange.

Under the harsh light of government regulation, options became a furtive species of contract. The only type of options that were still legal after 1934 were options on stocks. A market in stock options crept along for the next thirty years, traded by a network of humble dealers in New York. Treated like lepers on the exchanges, the dealers would negotiate individual 'over-the-counter' contracts with their customers.

Many of these dealers couldn't even afford offices of their own, and conducted business from a restaurant near Wall Street. According to Herbert Filer, a leading option dealer at the time: 'There were telephone booths and a ticker in the restaurant, and the telephone booths were our offices. All the dealers walked around with a pocketful of nickels, ready to use a phone to call a customer and make a trade.'

Two types of options were traded in the restaurant. Call options allowed customers to buy or 'call' a stock at a fixed 'exercise price' in the future. Put options let them sell or 'put' a stock back to the seller at a fixed price. The option buyer paid a premium to the seller who was known as the 'writer' of the option.

What happened when the contract matured – usually a few months later – depended on the stock price at maturity. For a call option, if the stock price was higher than the exercise price, the option could be exercised by the buyer as a cheap way to buy the stock – which he could sell for an instant profit.

Otherwise, the option expired, now just a worthless piece of paper, and the profit was earned by the writer who kept the premium. It was these options that were being advertised in Myron Scholes's newspaper clippings.

The formula that changed the world

Before crossing the Charles River to join Scholes, Black had become interested in the same problem from another angle. Having joined Arthur D. Little in 1964 after training as an applied mathematician, Black had learned finance from his boss Jack Treynor. Today, Treynor is remembered as the man who discovered the CAPM independently of Bill Sharpe, but didn't bother publishing it.

Black inherited a number of traits from his mentor. Like Treynor, Black was reluctant to publish his work, not least because he wanted to be sure it was completely correct. Like Treynor, he was unimpressed by academia, and Black's opinion became even stronger after several years employment as a professor at the University of Chicago and MIT.

Black had an impact on everyone he encountered. According to Steve Ross, whom we will meet in Chapter 4: 'Black was the strangest man I ever met. He wouldn't respond to anything you said in conversation, but wrote it down instead. There'd be these long, embarrassing moments of silence while he wrote.'

Emanuel Derman, who worked with Black many years later at Goldman Sachs, says: 'If you said something he found useful, he'd write it down with his fine-pointed mechanical pencil on a fresh sheet of his ruled white pad, and then insert it into a newly labeled manila folder, which eventually went into one of his file drawers.'

While Scholes pondered over-the-counter options, Black was focusing on warrants, which are options issued by companies on their own stock. Black thought that the CAPM might provide an answer to the problem.

Recall what the CAPM is all about: if you start out with the historical returns of a stock and its correlation with an index, when you turn the handle, the model spits out a value for that stock. An option depends on the value of a stock — that bit was obvious. Black wanted to re-jig the machinery of the CAPM so it could do the same trick for options that it did for stocks.

Underlying the CAPM was the idea of equilibrium. A key concept in post-war economics, equilibrium is a sort of mathematical statement of

Adam Smith's original idea – that there is a stable, ideal world that holds when rational, self-interested players all agree on a price.

For investors in a CAPM world, this means that stock returns are there to compensate them for taking risks. As Black later put it: 'The notion of equilibrium in the market for risky assets had great beauty for me. It implies that riskier securities must have higher expected returns, or investors will not hold them.'

Put simply, this means that any fund manager offering a return higher than the stock market index is selling a riskier investment – and investors should be prepared to take the consequences. The fact that year after year, investors ignore risk in the hope of a fast buck is a source of grief to believers in the CAPM equilibrium, and was a driving force behind the invention of index tracking funds in the 1970s.

The balance between risk and return that the CAPM says exists during equilibrium can be written down as a mathematical equation. Black played around with the CAPM until he found an equation for options, which stated that the return on an option should be related to its volatility in a similar manner to the returns on stocks.

Because the option price had to depend on the stock price, the equation was complicated, and Black spent many days unsuccessfully trying to solve it. However, he noticed something strange. According to the CAPM, the value of a stock depends both on its additional return over the index, and the volatility. For example, if General Motors shares happened to have twice the return of the Dow, but half the volatility, a CAPM believer would tell you they were a bargain.

Yet according to Black's equation, the option's value depended on the volatility, but somehow didn't involve the stock return at all. What was going on? Suppose you have two stocks with the same volatility. One doubled in value last year – its return was 100 per cent – while the other halved, having a return of minus 50 per cent. A call option only pays out when the stock price goes up, so one might think that the tendency of that stock to go up or down in the past should affect the price of the option. But the equation said that options on each stock were worth the same.

As Black crossed the bridge to MIT, ignoring the girls in miniskirts, ignoring the Jimi Hendrix music blasting out of dormitory windows, this puzzle was driving him crazy. It was Scholes who gave him the nudge he needed. Rather than try and solve this difficult option equation directly, why not put himself in the position of a humble option investor, who had read the newspaper ads, suggested Scholes. Such an investor would want to look into the future, at the precise moment that the option expired, and ask the question: how much would it be worth on average?

Black picked up his notepad and got to work. The problem was straightforward. You could take the distribution of the stock price return day by day over the lifetime of the option and multiply this by the option payout. But that wasn't much use to anybody. Recall the lenders in ancient Babylon – they needed to know what Hammurabi's option was worth at the time they made a loan, not after a crop failure raised the price of grain at a later date.

Although the stock would follow an unpredictable random walk during the life of the option – volatility summed that up – on average, its value should increase along the way, at a rate given by the stock price return. What Black and Scholes thought of doing was to use this return and work backwards from the expected option value at maturity to the present. This would give today's price of the option. However, Black already knew that the option price didn't depend on the return. So it was back to the drawing board.

Then, in early 1969, Black and Scholes had the brainwave that would change their lives. Because the return wouldn't make any difference to the option price, why not pretend that during the option's life, the stock grew in value as if it was a risk-free loan. They worked back in time from the option maturity using the risk-free interest rate, which is the rate paid on government debt, and more importantly, is known in advance. Miraculously, the result fit Black's equation perfectly, and the celebrated Black–Scholes option pricing formula came into being.

Now Black and Scholes had a formula, but it seemed more like a result of tinkering than anything else. In particular it seemed to depend on the CAPM being true. People had done empirical research that supported CAPM, but there was no grand theoretical reason for it to be any more than another model of the real world. Black and Scholes wanted to know why their formula worked.

Replicating reality

The final breakthrough came later that year, from an unexpected direction. A stone's throw away from Scholes's office, in the economics department, Merton had just completed his PhD thesis with Paul Samuelson, whom we met in Chapter 1 as an early disciple of efficient market theory. Merton was studying how investors should best decide to save or consume when stock prices fluctuate randomly. It was to solve this problem that Merton had started using Ito's formula.

So impressed was Samuelson with his protégé, that he promptly nominated Merton to become a junior fellow in the economics department at nearby Harvard. However, the Harvard dons took one look at the mathematical somersaults in Merton's thesis and rejected him outright. It felt like *déjà vu* for Merton as economists at other universities refused to let him into the fold, and again MIT came to the rescue when the Sloan School of Management offered him a job. On the day of Merton's interview, Scholes met his new colleague, and soon showed what he and Black had been up to.

With his 'Ito machine gun' Merton was a man to be reckoned with. When he started writing *The Pit* seventy years earlier, Frank Norris had said 'I'm full of red pepper and ginger and am ready to stand up on my hind legs and yell *big*.' Merton was in a similar mood. He seized upon Black and Scholes's problem and made it his own.

For a start, Merton realised that Ito's formula could be used to derive Black's original equation, but he kept that to himself, and would publish his alternative derivation separately. But there was one observation he couldn't help but reveal.

The CAPM assumption wasn't necessary. The answer to the mystery lay in the risk-free lending rate that Black and Scholes had pulled out of a magician's hat to get their formula. How could you pretend that an option wasn't risky to work out its price?

To understand what Merton did, we can use a very simplified example. Suppose you have a share that is worth $100 today, but that in one month's time will either go up to $110 or down to $90. Up or down is equally likely, as we would expect if stock price returns follow a random walk. In reality, of course, shares don't have to have one of two values, but the argument still works.

Suppose also that you have sold a pair of options to a friend each giving her the right to buy one such share at $100 in a month from now. What you have is a portfolio: 'long' a stock (meaning that you own it) and 'short' two options (meaning that you have sold them).

What can happen in a month? If the share has risen in price, your friend can come to you and buy two shares for $100 each. To honour the contract, you must buy the shares on the market at a price of $110, then hand them over. The result for you is a payout of $20, and although the single share you own is worth $10 more, you have lost a total of $10 on the total value of your portfolio.

If the share falls in price, the option that you sold is worthless, but your share is only worth $90, so again you have lost $10. In this idealised world, where trading is free and you can borrow money at zero interest, the premium you charge your friend for each option should be $5, to ensure that you break even.

Regardless of whether the stock goes up or down, the value of your portfolio in a month will be the same. By owning stock in the right proportion to options you have sold, you can immunise yourself against any movement in the markets. This is the miracle that stumped Black and Scholes: that risk can be conjured away.

The existence of this 'replicating portfolio' is the reason why the option price depends on volatility, but not the stock price return. Higher volatility leads to a higher option price because it is harder for the replicating portfolio to break even when the stock price changes rapidly. Here the word 'derivative' really lives up to its billing. Because the option is 'derived' from the stock, its performance can be imitated, using the stock itself.

Of course, in real life, shares don't just move up or down – they trace out jagged, fractal-looking charts over time. And in real life, you would have to change the proportions of stock in your portfolio daily to immunise yourself from the risk of selling an option. However, the idea is the same: the price of the option should be just enough to ensure that your replicating strategy breaks even.

But there is still a problem. Why should we believe in the break-even price? Could we tell if it was wrong? Merton's answer was 'yes'. The nature of his answer was dramatic, and would change finance forever. It would bring him and Scholes the glory of a Nobel Prize, and would set them both on the path to LTCM.

The reason is frighteningly simple. Suppose your friend, in the example above, paid a premium of $10 on each option – twice the replication value. You could sell her the options, then construct their mirror image using the underlying stock and cash.

As we saw above, it's enough to charge $5 per option for the replicating portfolio to break even. What's more, there is no risk involved in holding this portfolio. But here, we have an extra $5 per option on top of the break-even price. Earned without risk, this financial free lunch has a name: arbitrage. It is the greed side of the options coin.

By paying the wrong price for her options, your friend will provide you with a guaranteed profit, so long as you can replicate the options you sell her. She will either have to reduce the amount she pays you, or find another option seller who offers a better price. The effect of this will be to drive the option price downwards.

Now suppose that your friend wises up after this experience, and now convinces you that she need pay only $1 per option. This time, the replicating portfolio leaves you in the red, and with other buyers clamouring at your door, you must either raise your prices or get out of the options business.

Meanwhile, it is your friend's turn to make a risk-free profit, either by promptly selling the options at their fair value, or constructing their mirror image with stocks and making money on the replicating portfolio.

In other words, according to Merton, arbitrage 'enforces' the Black–Scholes option price. Using any other price is far too dangerous, because someone out there will make a risk-free profit at your expense.

The hunt for free money

No-arbitrage arguments run in the face of traditional economic thinking. After all, the most important thing should be supply and demand. Equilibrium implies balance between these two forces, and prices – whether options or sausages – should reflect that balance.

For many people, no-arbitrage isn't 'real economics', because the myriad forces that drive the economy are ignored in favour of a few traders looking for a free lunch. There is also something morally suspect about arbitrage. It doesn't seem like fair play. And yet, without the possibility of arbitrage there is no way of knowing if an option is fairly priced or not.

In 1970, arbitrage wasn't new. In the nineteenth century, financiers such as Jay Gould had noticed that the price of gold was different in London and New York. Buying gold in one city, shipping it to the other and selling there earned these financiers a risk-free profit.[2] But never had arbitrage been applied to such a sophisticated problem before.

Fischer Black, whose guiding light was the CAPM, would always remain suspicious of the no-arbitrage argument, even though it explained why his formula worked. Myron Scholes, on the other hand, was inspired. For he had seen it used before, by his mentor at Chicago, Merton Miller.

Back in the late 1950s, Miller and the Italian economist Franco

---

2. The cost of shipping and insurance reduces the profit on this transaction.

Modigliani had shown that the value of a company should be independent of
its mixture of equity and debt. If this were not so, investors could exploit the
difference in share price between two similar companies, buying one and
selling the other to earn a risk-free arbitrage profit. Eventually, Modigliani
and Miller would earn a Nobel prize for this discovery.

But early on, the Modigliani–Miller theorem, as it was called, had
attracted intense hostility from orthodox economists opposed to the no-
arbitrage argument. Nor did the theorem appear directly relevant, partly
because it contained unrealistic assumptions such as zero taxes, and also
because the arbitrage involved required simultaneous use of equity and debt
markets, which was difficult in the 1960s.

By 1970, the first drafts of Black and Scholes's, and Merton's papers
began to circulate among the academic community. Because it appeared
rooted in equilibrium theory, Black and Scholes attracted more attention.
Their supporters, in particular Miller and Fama, began to spread the
word.

When the first draft of their paper was brusquely rejected by three
academic journals in October 1970, Miller and Fama took over, suggesting
changes that made the paper more acceptable to mainstream economists,
finally steering it towards the Chicago-based *Journal of Political Economy*.
Although the journal's editors at first suspected that Black and Scholes's work
was a mathematical gimmick, some discrete lobbying by Miller persuaded
them to change their minds.

Meanwhile, in July 1970, Wells Fargo Bank sponsored a conference on
finance theory at MIT. Black and Scholes gave a talk on their work. Merton
was due to attend but overslept and missed the seminar. Then Harry
Markowitz stood up to speak.

Since his epochal work of the early 1950s, Markowitz had been
somewhat sidelined by the CAPM, which was easier to work with than
Markowitz's portfolio theory. Now working at US military think tank, the
RAND corporation, Markowitz devoted his time to finding ways of
speeding up the computer calculations needed for his theory.

Perhaps resenting the young Turks who taken the centre stage,
Markowitz decided to try his hand at pricing options. Rather than mess
around with novel ideas like replicating portfolios, Markowitz took a
down-to-earth approach. He used market prices for options, and attempted
to fit a line relating option prices to stock prices.

The problem for Markowitz was that he used a straight line. Because options allow buyers to walk away from their contract if stock prices go against them, the line must go up when the stock goes up, but stay flat if it goes down. In other words, the line is curved.

Black and Scholes watched Markowitz in silence, but finally another member of the audience piped up: 'Which formula did you use to straighten out that curve, Mr Markowitz?' Markowitz surveyed the lecture theatre for a moment, then haughtily replied: 'That's proprietary'.

This was the last straw. Everyone in the audience knew that Black and Scholes had an exact option pricing formula, and here was Markowitz trying to pull rank, claiming his work was too valuable to explain to mere mortals. The sound of laughter started to spread across the auditorium. Irritated, but not quite understanding what had just happened, Markowitz returned to the Rand Corporation. The new generation was taking over.

There was another reason that the no-arbitrage argument took a while to catch on. Who were these people enforcing the correct option price? Surely it couldn't be the New York put and call dealers. Fired up with their formula, Black, Scholes and Merton went back to the Sunday newspapers and scanned the option ads carefully.

Scholes would later recall making lists of the options on sale and comparing their prices with the predictions of his formula. The following Monday morning, he would phone up the New York dealers, offering to buy the options that were the most undervalued. However, these cheap options were always sold out and the dealers would try to sell Scholes something else instead. It was then that Scholes realised he was the victim of a 'bait and switch' sales technique.

Clearly, the put and call dealers had some kind of instinctive cunning that protected them from arbitrage. One reason for this was the tiny size of their business. To survive, they had to charge high prices for the options they sold.

The fly-by-night image of options and the dubious sales practices employed by the dealers, still kept most people out of the market. When one of Scholes's students later analysed prices from a put and call dealer in detail, he found that transaction fees would have wiped out any profits from mispriced options.

As would-be enforcers of arbitrage pricing, where else could Black, Scholes and Merton test their theory? Warrants were a better proposition. Although they are options to buy stock under another name, warrants are listed on stock exchanges, where the threat of regulators ensures that 'bait and switch' techniques aren't allowed.

The trio immediately started applying the option formula to warrants. Like all mathematical formulae, it works like a sausage machine: you put the meat in, turn the handle, and sausages come out. The Black–Scholes formula asked you to put several ingredients in. Most of these were already at hand: the initial stock price, the strike or exercise price, the maturity or lifetime of the option and the risk-free interest rate.

There was one more ingredient that needed a little cooking before the handle could be turned, however – the volatility, or standard deviation of the stock price return. Strictly speaking, this should be the volatility during the life of the option, but that wasn't known in advance. The next best thing was to use the volatility for a period of time just before the option contract was agreed. This is what Black, Scholes and Merton did.

By this time they were not alone. The US brokerage firm Donaldson, Lufkin and Jenrette (DLJ) dabbled in the options and warrant markets for its clients, and in early 1972 DLJ's head options trader, Leon Pomerance heard about some young MIT professors who had a theory of option pricing. He offered Scholes and Merton a part-time consulting job, pricing and hedging options for him. Earning modest academic salaries at the time, Scholes and Merton jumped at the chance. At the same time, Black went in the other direction, and accepted a professorship at the University of Chicago.

Meanwhile, the warrant market seemed ripe for the picking. Years later, Black recalled what happened: 'We estimated the volatility of the stock of each of a group of companies with warrants outstanding. We noticed that several warrants looked like very good buys. The best buy of all seemed to be National General new warrants.'

Black continued: 'Scholes, Merton and I jumped right in and bought a bunch of these warrants. For a while, it looked as if we had done just the right thing.' Then, in mid-1972, disaster struck. Another company called American Financial announced a take-over bid for National General, and the terms of the offer looked bad for warrant holders.

Black, Scholes and Merton's investment plunged in value, and the warrants expired, worthless. Disheartened, the trio went back to the drawing board. What had they done wrong? In fact, there was little they could have done to anticipate the take-over. Only the insiders who traded the warrants on the New York stock exchange had known it was a possibility, and this made the National General warrants look like bargains.

Black commented: 'The market knew something that our formula didn't know. Although our trading didn't turn out very well, this event helped validate our formula. The market was out of line for a very good reason.'

Although warrants had more liquidity than over-the-counter options, both markets were sideshows compared to the huge stock market, at the time reaching all-time highs. How could options ever break out of the ghetto? In fact, just as Black, Scholes and Merton were completing their papers, plans were being hatched that would bring options into the modern era. Who was behind this initiative? The Chicago Board of Trade.

By the late 1960s, the CBOT had shed much of its raffish, piratical air. By now carefully regulated by Washington, the scandal-ridden days of Hutchinson and Leiter were long gone. The CBOT itself had reduced risks still further by adopting a system, called a clearing house, which made sure that no-one who defaulted on a futures contract could ever cause losses to other futures users. The business of futures trading had become respectable in Chicago.

However, things were not all good at the CBOT. For a start, there was a rival exchange, the Chicago Mercantile Exchange (CME), snapping at its heels with a new futures contract on live cattle. Worse still, its crowning glory, the wheat futures pit, was in the doldrums, the victim of government policies which had created huge food mountains and reduced the need for trading.

While a gold-plated statue of agricultural goddess Ceres stared across the Chicago skyline atop the CBOT's stunning art deco building, far below, exchange members sat on the pit steps reading newspapers. To protect the exchange's livelihood, a search began for new contracts to trade. Options on grain were illegal and hence out of the question. But what about options on stocks? Could these be traded on an exchange?

The problem was, while commodities were regulated by one authority, stocks – or 'securities' in legal parlance – were overseen by another Washington regulator, the Securities Exchange Commission, or SEC. The SEC is feared on Wall Street as America's toughest financial regulator, and often imprisons those who break its rules. And the SEC was known to take a dim view of futures markets, let alone options.

The CBOT didn't take any chances. After sketching out how pit trading of options might work, the CBOT members commissioned a study by Washington consulting firm Robert Nathan Associates. The objective was to demonstrate to the SEC that options could perform a service to society, and several eminent economists were enlisted to help, including Merton Miller.

So what were options good for? The borrowers of ancient Babylon who benefited from Hammurabi's paragraph 48 knew the answer to this question – they gained protection against the risk of crop failure.

Although he was not involved in the Nathan report, perhaps the best answer to the question had already been given in 1953, by another economist, Kenneth Arrow. It was he who gave intellectual weight to the fear argument we discussed at the beginning of this chapter.

Working at the height of the Cold War, at Stanford University, Arrow and a colleague, Gerald Debreu, had a vision of a world where everything was assigned a value on a market. In this utopia, every possible state of the world, past, present and future, from a stormy July evening in Patagonia to England winning the World Cup, had a financial payoff associated with it.

They called this utopia the 'complete market', and the hypothetical contracts that were so carefully tailored to the countless states of the world were called 'Arrow–Debreu securities'.

Arrow was motivated by idealism. Markets, in his view, were not there to make a few greedy people rich. They existed to increase freedom of choice for all people by allowing risks to be transferred and shared. For Arrow, risk created fear, and in 1953, with the nuclear arms race in full swing, fear was clearly a bad thing.

Arrow–Debreu securities were the means to reduce risk. If you worried about a certain risk, you could buy one as insurance. Once you had covered yourself against loss, you could take on some risk yourself, perhaps by selling an Arrow–Debreu security to someone else. If the market worked properly, everyone should benefit.

Old-fashioned insurance contracts were one approximation to Arrow's mythical contracts. But as we saw at the beginning of this chapter, insurance has grown up to cover specific types of loss, which have to be proven before payments are made. Moreover, the insurance industry specialises in covering a few types of risk; if yours fell outside these types, insurance would be prohibitively expensive.

That was fine if one was worried about a house fire or car theft, but in the early 1950s, one of the greatest fears was of the stock market crashing like it had done in 1929. There were no insurance contracts covering that. But options were ideal for this kind of risk. In particular a 'put' on the index would provide precisely the coverage needed. This argument resembles the reasoning behind Hammurabi's paragraph 48.

Such thinking, in a watered-down form, appeared in the Nathan Report. One analogy given was the decision to carry or not carry an umbrella when concerned about rain during a journey. The report's authors pointed out that having the option to postpone the journey was a great advantage, and the same argument applied to options on stocks.

The Chicago school of financial economists, and its MIT offshoot, was barely aware of Arrow's work in the late 1960s. Many years later, Merton would attempt to reinvent himself as Arrow's intellectual heir. Scholes, infused with Chicago school rigour, felt that the Nathan Report was unnecessary. The usefulness of options was irrelevant, Scholes argued. The point of the new exchange was to provide an existing service at a lower cost.

In other words, if people needed options they would always find a way to trade them in the cheapest way possible. Scholes's efficient market viewpoint is reminiscent of the apocryphal story about the Chicago professor who denies the existence of a $100 bill on the pavement because the market is too efficient to allow it.

Arrow's vision of the markets was the flipside of the Chicago school. While Arrow at Stanford would go on to give economic justifications for social welfare payments, the Chicago school would culminate in the neo-conservative Reagan era of the early 1980s, as we shall see.

The Nathan Report did the trick. Primed by the report, as well as the CBOT's careful lobbying, the SEC sent a cautious, but encouraging letter in October 1971. It said '. . . the proposed options exchange does not appear to be inconsistent with statutory requirements . . .' The backers of the project at the CBOT were delighted.

On 27 April 1973, the new options exchange – called the Chicago Board Options Exchange (CBOE) – opened for business in the former CBOT members' smoking lounge. On this first day, only 911 options were traded, but within two months positions equivalent to two million underlying shares had been taken on the exchange.

One of the CBOE board of directors was DLJ's Leon Pomerance, and with his encouragement, the options traders started using the Black–Scholes formula, which was finally published in May 1973. Merton's paper was published the same month. 3800 years after Hammurabi, options had come of age.

Yet the Black–Scholes–Merton theory contains the seeds of its own destruction. The seeds lie buried deep in the small print of the theory – in its underlying assumptions. The most important assumption is that the underlying market – such as stocks – functions properly. In the summer of 1998, this and other assumptions would break down.

The consequence of this breakdown was that arbitrage stopped working. As an edifice founded on arbitrage, LTCM would collapse as a result. But that still lies in the future. It is time to leave Black, Scholes and Merton enjoying the first flush of success, and meet the enigmatic character who pushed their ideas to the limit: John W. Meriwether.

3

Trading in Time

John Meriwether is a very talented bond trader
Richard Sandor

Who is John Meriwether? One of his former colleagues at Salomon Brothers describes him like this: 'I'm a huge fan of JM. He's a very smart guy, very savvy. He's a traders' trader. He inspires loyalty – he has charisma.'

This is a glowing accolade for someone implicated in the near meltdown of the global financial system. Hank Greenberg, chairman of the American International Group, a giant financial conglomerate, was more blunt. After Meriwether used a newspaper interview to accuse AIG traders of hastening LTCM's downfall, Greenberg said: 'John Meriwether is the author of his own misfortune.'

While it was Black, Scholes and Merton who showed how important arbitrage was as an idea; it was John Meriwether who turned the idea into a business. It was he who held up a mirror to the academics, and taught them how to turn equations into fabulous power and wealth. Then, as the founder of LTCM, he would eventually bring them to disaster.

Meriwether's world was the bond market, where traders buy and sell the value of time itself. More obscure than the stock market that was the backdrop to Black, Scholes and Merton's early work, the bond market is also much larger. It takes a certain way of thinking to understand bonds, but it's the key to understanding Meriwether. And once again, this way of thinking takes us back to the sun-baked ruins of the ancient Middle East.

Children of money

The notion that time equals money is as old as money. A dollar received today is worth more than a dollar tomorrow. A dollar paid back in thirty years is worth much less than today's dollar. This is called the time value of money, and in financial terms, it means charging interest for loans.

When people first started lending things to each other, it was as friends. You might lend a spear to a friend going hunting, or lend your time to help gather in the harvest. These loans didn't last long, and were repaid in kind.

What about a lending for longer periods of time? The most important possession people had was livestock, but animals have a unique property – they breed. If you borrow a herd of cattle for a year, you probably will end up with more than you started with. The number of calves represents the time value of cows.

In the first cities of the ancient Middle East, where money was invented, interest was devised according to the same principle. Indeed, the Sumerian word for interest was the same as the word for calves. This is also the case in Greek. Over time, money breeds money, and this principle was established as early as 5000 years ago. By the time of Hammurabi, 2000 years later, Babylonian children were even being set problems on calculating interest in school!

The time value of money contains one big assumption – that the money will be paid back. But despite the best intentions, many borrowers have trouble repaying their loans. From the lenders' perspective, this is called credit risk, and they traditionally have had some kind of legal claim on borrowers' assets to compensate them for taking this risk. In other words, as soon as loans were invented, bailiffs and repo men were invented too.

The threat of such sanctions was not enough for the Babylonian lenders. To ensure repayment, they demanded collateral, or something that could be readily turned into cash if the loan couldn't be repaid. Collateral will make its appearance in the LTCM story, as we will see. Borrowers in the ancient Middle East without something valuable to hand would have to pledge themselves as collateral, and if they couldn't repay the loan, they would become slaves.

Because of such possibilities, the relationship between lenders and borrowers has often been tense. With the threat of slavery hanging over his citizens, Hammurabi used paragraph 48 to make sure that lenders protected borrowers from the effects of crop failures. Other kings would periodically cancel all the debts of their subjects.

The bad reputation of debt became official 2000 years later, with the rise of Christianity. But it was not the threat of bailiffs that worried theologians. It was the time value of money. Since time was ordained by God, charging interest for the time value of money was a sin, known as usury. In Dante's

Inferno, usurers had to spend eternity sitting under a rain of fire with purses bulging with money hung round their necks.

However, the need for Renaissance princes to borrow money to fight their wars meant that lending gained in respectability. Usury ceased to be a sin, and although it has retained this status for Muslims, it is now reserved in the West to describe the exorbitant rates charged by loan sharks. As Shakespeare's 'pound of flesh' makes clear, the rights of lenders over individuals would always be controversial, but for borrowers with armies at their disposal, it wasn't an issue.

At this stage, a loan was still a contract between two parties. To some degree, it involved a personal relationship. However, there is the possibility of *selling* loans. The borrower stays the same, but now an investor pays the original lender for the time value of money locked inside the loan, and receives the loan contract in return. The contract holder is now, legally, the lender.

As states grew in size and scope, government appetite for borrowing grew. When shares became popular in the seventeenth century as a means of enabling widespread investment, clever financiers thought of applying the principle of selling loans to government borrowing. This is how the bond markets were born.

In many respects, bonds are identical to loans. They both involve a borrower – in this case a government – and a lender, who is compensated for the time value of the initial sum – called the principal – by being paid interest. The length of time involved is defined in advance.

Yet bonds are different. Loans are contracts between two parties, which sit in someone's drawer. Bonds are securities which can be freely bought and sold in the open market. Traditionally, they have come in the form of engraved certificates on which are printed four key pieces of information: the issuer (meaning the borrower), the face value of the bond, its maturity date and the interest – usually paid annually as a 'coupon'.

The name of the lender is not written on the bond. Instead of one lender, as with most loans, there is a multitude, called bondholders. Every bondholder is a lender, earning interest in recognition of the time value of money. That status is theirs no matter how briefly they own the bond. While loans often 'amortise' or return principal to the lenders during their lifetime, bonds tend to repay principal in one lump sum at maturity.

The impersonal nature of bonds adds another, crucial difference. The interest rate on a loan is the result of private negotiations between the borrower and lender. Once signed, the loan agreement can sit in a drawer, unaffected by conditions elsewhere.

Bonds, on the other hand, are sold publicly to hundreds of investors, who only hand over their cash if they think that the interest rate rewards them sufficiently. In the spirit of Adam Smith, the interest rate on a bond is essentially a price on the value of time set by the market. If the interest engraved on that certificate isn't high enough, they won't pay up, and the borrowers must either increase it or leave the market empty-handed.

The first bonds were issued by governments, shortly after the first banknotes started circulating. As governments started issuing bonds and banknotes, and stopped depending on lending relationships with a few select banks, they needed to manage the myriad pieces of paper floating around containing their name. Central banks were the answer.

The Bank of England is one example. Founded as a private bank under a Royal Charter in 1694, the Bank's prime role was – and still is – to raise money for the country by issuing bonds, called Gilts. This model was put into practice across the continent in the eighteenth century by the legendary Rothschild family, which founded central banks in Germany, France, Austria and Italy.

Another example is the United States. During the War of Independence against Britain, the thirteen rebel states issued bonds to pay for the war. With the war won, and the business of building a new country a priority, there was political pressure to renege on the bonds, or at least repay them selectively.

The first US secretary of the Treasury, Alexander Hamilton, made a momentous decision. Resisting the pressures around him, in particular the opposition of Thomas Jefferson, Hamilton called the debt the 'price of liberty' and insisted that it be repaid in full. Recalling the debate years later, Jefferson wrote: 'this measure produced the most bitter and angry contest ever known in Congress, before or since the Union of the States.'

The message was clear: the United States never defaults on its debt. Hamilton ensured that his new nation joined the select group of countries, led by Britain, whose bonds have always been repaid. If you buy a government bond in one of these countries, and hold it until maturity, you can be sure of getting all your money back, principal plus interest. When we talk of a risk-free return, this is what we mean.

With this money-raising tool at their disposal, the central bankers had a new dimension to play with – time. If a large bond was due to be repaid next year, all you needed to do was issue a new twenty-year bond, and use the new bondholders' money to pay the old bondholders. Not surprisingly, national debts tended to grow rather than shrink, as repayment was left to future generations. By 1981, the US owed more than a trillion dollars.

Exploiting their new dimension with some finesse, the central bankers went further. They issued bonds with a whole spectrum of maturities, ranging from a few months to over thirty years. In the US Treasury bond market, this spectrum has its own inner language. Bonds with maturities of a few months are called Bills. Those repayable in about five years are called Notes. Only those that cast their shadow further than ten years into the future are granted the distinction of being called Bonds.

By the early twentieth century, companies were issuing bonds too. Not backed by governments, companies occasionally go bankrupt. The corporate bonds issued must pay more than the risk-free, or government interest rate, to compensate investors for this default risk.

As the bond market grew, some governments began defaulting on their debt too. The elaborately engraved bond certificates issued by the pre-revolutionary Russian and Chinese governments are collectors items today. But aside from this ornamental value, they are now worth precisely zero, after the debt was repudiated by the communists.

Investment bankers such as the Baring family in London or John Pierpoint Morgan in New York developed a business issuing or 'underwriting' these bonds for their clients – often building on an existing lending relationship. It was then that the shadowy world of bond trading developed. While the names traded in this market mirrored those stocks traded under the full light of public gaze, bonds didn't get so much attention.

In the US, this exclusivity was reinforced in 1933. Alarmed by the failure of several banks under the ravages of the Great Depression, and picking up on the prevailing anti-capitalist mood, two senators, Carter Glass and Joseph Steagall, passed a law dividing the banking system in two. Henceforth, there would be commercial banks that were allowed to make loans and take deposits, and securities firms that could issue and trade shares and bonds.

If John Milton had written *Paradise Lost* about the US banking system instead of Adam and Eve, the Glass–Steagall Act would have been the bit where half the angels get thrown out of heaven. It was America's backlash against the scowling visage of John Pierpoint Morgan, who although long dead by the 1930s, still embodied the popular image of capitalism.

As for his legacy, JP Morgan & Co. itself – the bank that had helped finance the First World War – being excluded from the market in bonds and shares was a bitter blow. The part of JP Morgan & Co that had dealt in securities was cleaved off into a new firm called Morgan Stanley.

Ringfenced by the Glass–Steagall Act, the securities firms – including

Goldman Sachs, Merrill Lynch and Salomon Brothers – gained in mystique, and it was this quality that helped shape America's most talented bond trader, John Meriwether.

Man of mystery

Born in 1947, Meriwether grew up in the tight-knit Irish immigrant neighbourhood of Roseland on Chicago's South Side. As he would recall many years later, the Meriwethers were part of an extended family where everyone on the block was apparently related, and four cousins lived across the alley. The Catholic Church added to the sense of closeness and Meriwether is said to keep his rosary beads with him at all times.

This close atmosphere is a theme in Meriwether's life. At Salomon Brothers and then LTCM, Meriwether has always worked with a tight-knit circle of cohorts, who show fierce loyalty. Meriwether is also obsessed with privacy, even after LTCM's near collapse made him a public figure – and those who work with him are expected to uphold a code of silence.

Meriwether's lifelong sporting interests offer another clue to his personality: horse riding and golf. A far cry from team contact sports, both activities involve intense concentration and iron-willed control, whether over a living horse, or a set of golf clubs. Combine that with ambition and a capacity for hard work, and you have John Meriwether.

By the age of 12, he had found work as a caddy at Flossmoor Country Club, a golf course set in manicured Illinois pastureland about ten miles south of his home. A popular course, and a regular venue on the American Junior Golf Association competitive circuit, Flossmoor gave Meriwether an early head start in the game.

By the time he got to high school, Meriwether was a skilled player, and headed the school team. Glory came when he twice won the Chicago Suburban Catholic League Tournament for his school. But there was another side to Meriwether that ultimately meant more to him.

Inheriting a head for figures from his father, an accountant, Meriwether got the stock market bug early, and started investing his caddying money in shares. To this day, he has not revealed how successful his early trading attempts were; but at this stage it was only a hobby.

After high school, Meriwether won a scholarship to study at nearby Northwestern University, which ironically enough, had enjoyed funding in its early days from one of Chicago's most successful futures speculators, James

Patten. However, Meriwether was discouraged from leaping into finance by his mother. An administrator at Chicago's Board of Education, Mrs Meriwether wanted her son to remain part of the Roseland community.

A dutiful son, and disciplined too, Meriwether followed his mother's guidance, and after graduation, he started work as a teacher in the Chicago public school system. But the rows of little faces watching him in front of the blackboard soon became a torment. Besides, he would never be able to afford membership of Flossmoor Country Club on his teachers' salary, let alone do any horse riding.

Then Meriwether heard the same siren's call that also changed Myron Scholes's life. In 1971, he quit his teaching career and enrolled as an MBA student at the University of Chicago business school. It was there that he saw the light, and realised what he wanted to be.

By this time, Meriwether was a wiry five-foot nine, and wore his brown hair in the boyish style that would remain his trademark. The dark and intense Irish youth from the South Side could not have been more different from his classmate Jon Corzine. A six-foot two soft-spoken blond giant who had grown up on a farm miles out on the Illinois cornfields, Corzine would one day end up at Goldman Sachs, staring at Meriwether across the table during September 1998. At the University of Chicago, they were on nodding terms.

As a believer in the market, Meriwether couldn't have arrived at a better time. There was George Schultz, the head of the economics faculty who would later become Ronald Reagan's secretary of state. There were the rising macroeconomists such as Friedman and Stigler. There was Eugene Fama, the apostle of efficient market theory. Fischer Black had recently joined as well, having just published his paper with Myron Scholes.

Meriwether has never publicly discussed his days at Chicago. But possibly the greatest influence on Meriwether was Merton Miller. Based in the business school itself rather than the economics faculty, Miller was already famous for the Modigliani–Miller theorem, which we discussed in Chapter 2. For his part, Miller claims to have no memory of Meriwether whatsoever.

One more professor should be mentioned, however. This was Richard Sandor, then a visiting scholar from Berkeley in California, who would be a key stepping stone in Meriwether's career, although the two men did not get to know each other until later.

Why was Miller so influential? Because he introduced Meriwether to the motivating principle of his career – arbitrage. The idea that markets contained free money there for the picking transfixed Meriwether. How could people be so blind, or plain stupid, to just leave it there?

Sitting in class, listening to Miller talk about how arbitrageurs enforced the 'law of one price', Meriwether wondered how it could be done in practice. For while Miller invoked these mysterious characters who kept the markets in line, on the other side of the fence, in the next class, there was Fama saying that the markets were too efficient for anything other than a fleeting moment of additional profit. The tyranny of the index was absolute. Fama's empirical research seemed to show that there indeed were no free lunches in the stock market.

Meriwether pondered the question some more, and made up his mind. After graduating with his MBA degree in 1973, coincidentally the same year that Black, Scholes and Merton published their famous papers, Meriwether went to Wall Street and joined Salomon Brothers as a government bond trader in 1974.

The bond brotherhood

Outside of the cloistered excitement of the University of Chicago, it didn't seem like a great time to be starting out on Wall Street. A vicious bear market was underway in stocks. Confidence was in short supply with the Watergate scandal unfolding in Washington, and the oil crisis in the Middle East.

At the time, bond trading was a backwater on Wall Street. While the underwriting business – the traditional investment banking activity of issuing bonds – was still lucrative for those securities firms allowed to do it, trading was the opposite. In those days, few bond investors were active in the market.

With their fixed interest coupons and maturity dates, bonds were considered to be safe, predictable investments, compared to stocks that jiggled around like dust particles. The parts of investment banks that dealt in them were – and still are – called 'fixed income' departments, in homage to this predictability. That is why most finance research up to the 1970s focused on the stock market.

However, this feeling of security was an illusion. The income earned on a bond is only fixed if certain things don't change. In 1974 things were changing very fast. To understand how we need to take a walk on the wild side, and get inside the dark mind of a bond trader. We need to imagine ourselves at Salomon with John Meriwether in 1974, learning how the business worked.

For a traditional bond investor, life is simple. You buy newly-minted bonds, either from the government or large companies, and you sit on them, earning interest as a return on your investment. At the end of the bonds' lifetime, the issuer pays you back the principal, which you are free to re-invest in new bonds.

For a bond trader, life is harder. To see how, consider a very simple kind of US government bond. This bond pays a single interest coupon at the end of its life, along with the principal. On the bond certificate is written the total amount due to be paid back – the face value – and the date.

To make things simple, we will imagine all these bonds have the face value of a dollar. So we might have a 'one-year dollar' and a 'ten-year dollar'. These bonds are sold at a discount to their face value, to reflect the time value of money locked up inside them. For example, if a newly-minted one-year dollar sells at 91 cents, that means it pays an interest rate of 10 per cent per year.

You are given a desk and a phone, and told to buy and sell these bits of paper every day. Now suppose the one-year dollar is issued on a Monday at its price of 91 cents. By Thursday, there is an international crisis, and investors all over the world decide to buy US government bonds – in particular the one-year dollar. Your phone rings constantly, and the one-years are so popular that the price rises to 95 cents.

Now you examine one of the bond certificates. It still says it will be worth a dollar eventually. But while on Monday, an investment would have given you 10 per cent interest after a year, on Thursday, you can only get 5 per cent if you were to buy the same bond and wait until maturity.

So if one-year dollars go up in price, the interest rate that they pay has to go down. If these bonds had gone down in price – say to 80 cents – then the interest rate would have risen to 25 per cent. Over the year of its life, the one-year dollar goes up and down in price, and the interest rate, called the yield to distinguish it from the initial rate that it paid, goes up and down too. While the stock market thinks in prices, bond traders think in yields.

Part of their mystique stems from this topsy-turvy view of the world. With their 'yield goggles' on, the traders see a peak in prices become a deep pit in yields. If prices plunge, yields soar into the stratosphere.

Something else that makes bond traders different is their view of time. In the stock market, a company issues millions of shares, and they float around the market for years, going up and down in price. Individual bonds – the actual bits of paper – may go up and down in price for a while too, but ultimately they expire, and are cashed in for their face value. Time passes them by.

To avoid getting confused by which bonds are young, middle-aged or about to expire, the traders think in 'bond time'. It's as if the special goggles do not only turn the world upside down, but they give tunnel vision too.

With their goggles on, bond traders have their eyes always fixed on a bond having a given number of years to live.

At the beginning, this bond could be a brand new five-year bond, but after a year this only has four years left and isn't any good. What the goggles do is pick out another bond with five years left to go – perhaps a six-year bond with a year of its life gone – and keep track of that one instead. While ordinary time unfolds around us, bond time stretches out before the trader, never getting any closer. The US Treasury makes things easier for the traders by regularly issuing new bonds as well.

When John Meriwether started at Salomon, bond traders would be assigned to work on specific maturities. Meriwether himself traded the long bond – the 30-year US Treasury bond (known simply as T-bonds). On Meriwether's right, a trader would be yelling into a phone, trading the ten-year bond, while on his left, it would be five-year notes that were being bought and sold. It would be the same across Wall Street, and for each maturity, the traders would buy and sell that particular bond from each other, independently of the others.

With their goggles on, traders watched the yield of the bond they traded go up and down – in the random fashion that Bachelier had identified sixty years before. When the traders took their goggles off – perhaps to speak to investors – the yield stopped moving, and became a 'fixed income investment' that paid a fixed rate of interest for five, ten or thirty years. That is why the interest rate on 30-year bonds is called a 'fixed rate'.

In contrast, very short term bonds, with maturities of three or six months, belong to the world of 'floating rates'. In this world which is known as the money market, investors and borrowers have to buy or sell new bonds every few months, and are forced to be aware of the changes in the time value of money.

During Meriwether's early years at Salomon, the head of bond research, Marty Liebowitz, was teaching the traders to think about their market in a new way. Rather than restrict themselves to a single maturity, they looked at all of them: six months, a year, five years and so on all the way up to thirty years or more.

For each maturity in their yield goggles' vision, they would track the yield. By drawing a line through all the yields, traders then came up with a curve in bond time, called the yield curve. The bit nearest to the present time is called the short end, while further out at the other extreme is the long end. Today, all bond traders think like this.

Like a wave passing through water, the yield curve moves forward through time. Because they are free from default risk, only government bonds are used to calculate the yield curve. Sitting on top of the curve, like foam on the wave, the yields of corporate bonds float above their government counterparts.

As yields change – due to bond price changes – the curve changes shape, watched avidly by the bond traders. In the world of fixed income, bond traders are expert surfers on the yield curve. If they judge its movements wrongly, they can get wiped out.

Rising and falling, twisting and flexing, the yield curve in some ways is as much a prey to sentiment as the stock market, as people buy and sell their bonds. But there is a big difference. The most important player in the bond market has traditionally been the government itself. For while King Canute never believed he could control the waves, the US and other governments have tried, to varying extent, to control the yield curve.

Governments attempt to control the yield curve for two main reasons. At any time, the curve tells you the basic cost of borrowing. If you have a mortgage or a business loan linked to a government lending rate, an upward flick of the curve can drive you into bankruptcy, unemployment and even homelessness. Borrowers tend to be voters, so governments have a good reason to stop the curve rising too high.

How can a central bank stop the curve from rising? At the short end, the yield curve turns into the overnight lending rate, at which the central bank supports other large banks in the same country. Being able to quickly lend banks money – and stop them getting into difficulties – has become an important additonal role for central banks in the last 100 years, and was the main reason that the US Federal Reserve System was founded in 1913.

If the yield curve goes up, the central bank can do two things. It can reduce the lending rate, and make the supply of money easier for other banks, or it can buy back government bonds. If the central bank buys enough of its own bonds – one-year dollars, for example – they will rise in price, and the yield will go down.

But life is never that easy. Making it easier to borrow at the short end, or paying cash to buy back huge amounts of bonds at the long end, has the same effect – you need to pump money into the economy. But where does the money come from? If you don't want to cut spending, the central bankers' alternative is to print more money instead. That means inflation.

Inflation is the other big reason for trying to influence the yield curve. However, at the end of the 1960s, the consensus among the economists who ran the central banks was that inflation wasn't a problem. Following the lead of the English economics guru J.M. Keynes, the central bankers believed that unemployment – the bane of the 1930s – was the real danger.

This remarkable consensus had been cemented during World War Two in 1944, when the about-to-be-victorious Western powers, under Keynes' guidance, organised the famous Bretton Woods conference in New Hampshire. It was a conscious attempt to dam the rivers of international money whose flows had worsened the effects of the Great Depression. The most important result of Bretton Woods was that foreign exchange rates between different countries were to be permanently fixed in relation to the US dollar. Each dollar, in turn, was backed by a fixed amount of gold.

Interest rates too stayed roughly constant. In the US, there was even a law that put a limit on how much interest savings and loan banks could pay on deposit accounts. Meanwhile, if yields rose in the bond market, the Federal Reserve was always standing by ready to flood the economy with money, to keep interest rates constant, and thus keep unemployment at bay. It was this kind of climate that made the bond market a backwater, because the volatility of interest rates – and hence bond prices – was so low.

Around 1970, this sensible, comforting system started blowing itself apart. I was only five-years old then, and I remember watching the news on TV. Palestinians had hijacked three airliners, and then after evacuating the passengers, blew them up, one by one in the desert. These explosions in the desert would be mirrored in the financial world, for which the 1970s would be a series of one shocking event after another.

Under Bretton Woods, central banks could alleviate international strains between different economies by buying and selling their gold reserves. By the early 1970s, these strains had become too much to bear, largely because the US government had printed too many dollars to fight the Vietnam War, pushing up inflation.

At the instigation of European governments, Bretton Woods was replaced by a system of floating currency rates. At the same time, the Organisation of Petroleum Exporting Countries (OPEC) was aggressively raising oil prices. By the time John Meriwether started trading US Treasury bonds at Salomon Brothers, annual inflation in the US was over 10 per cent.

The effect on bondholders – and lenders in general – was disastrous. Suppose you lent $100 at interest of 10 per cent for a year. When the year was up, you would get $110 back, but because of inflation, it would only be worth $100. Trying to stay in business, lenders raised their rates. To bring them down again – as economic orthodoxy said it should – the Fed could buy back its bonds, but this would make inflation worse. The end result was a severe recession.

Bond traders suffered too. There are two ways in which an investment bank bond trading department – or a 'desk' – makes money. The first is by doing trades for clients and charging a commission. By doing this, the traders pick up useful information about the market, which they can use in the second money making technique: proprietary trading.

In a broad sense, proprietary trading means trading for the investment bank's own account rather than for a customer. In practice, it can mean many different things, from temporarily taking positions in the market to help a client's deal go more smoothly, all the way to the kind of aggressive, sophisticated operation run by Meriwether at Salomon in the 1980s.

For bond dealers back in the mid-1970s, 'prop trading', as it is called in the industry, was mostly a part-time activity. At this stage, traders would lay bets on the shape of the yield curve. For the most part, this involved trying to second-guess what the US Government was going to do. You didn't need an office in Washington for that. The US Government already had an outpost on Wall Street. It is called the Federal Reserve Bank of New York.

Based in its fortress-like building at the southern tip of Manhattan, the New York Fed is entrusted with the job of buying and selling Treasury bonds in the open market. It also issues new Treasury bonds by auctioning them to the Wall Street dealers. These quarterly auctions work as a tap for the US government to quickly pour its debt into the market. For the hungry bond traders, the Fed auctions are like feeding time at the zoo, as they snap up the assortment of bills, notes and bonds for their clients.

By watching the bond auctions, and keeping track of the important economic indicators like unemployment or inflation, the prop traders thought of strategies. How did they make their bets? It was just like surfing. Some traders thought the entire curve would rise or fall. So they would watch a single point on the curve – the crest of the wave perhaps – and buy or sell a bond of that maturity.

A more discerning trader might predict that the curve was going to steepen, as if rearing up towards a beach. They'd need to follow two points for that, perhaps buying the near end and selling the long end. Yet another trader might guess that the curve would develop a hump in the middle. This strategy involved three different bond maturities.

Some traders made modest fortunes in this way. Others lost money, and were told to clear their desks. The bond market may have been more arcane than the stock market, requiring special 'yield goggles' and an ability to think in bond time. An ability to understand its special nature should give some advantages. Yet the problem was, as John Meriwether saw it, that by betting on prices going in a single direction, it was still too easy to be wrong.

With the unravelling of Bretton Woods, and the surge in inflation, a lot of the old tricks didn't work. Traditionally, when stocks went down, bond prices went up. In 1974, bonds plunged along with the Dow. Even the Fed, floundering about trying to control the yield curve, was harder to predict in its behaviour. Right, left and centre, bond traders were falling off their yield curve surfboards.

For Meriwether, there was another way of doing things. By betting on the curve, the Wall Street bond traders were trying to out-guess the market. But they were the market, and very often, they all thought in the same way. Their real advantage, as Meriwether saw it, was that they knew the prices, day-in and day-out, and how to turn them into a yield. If someone at another firm offered Meriwether a Treasury bond at a particular price, he could work out whether it was cheap or expensive relative to the total amount it would earn during its life.

One example would become a Meriwether favourite. Because the Fed makes its newly-minted bonds – called 'on-the-run' Treasuries – so readily available, they can be bought and sold quickly in the market. To the traders who make a living by buying and selling them, this availability makes them more valuable. As a result they tend to be very slightly more expensive than their seasoned, 'off-the-run' equivalents which get salted away by investors and traded less often.

Over the life of the bond, these discrepancies gradually disappear, as the new bond loses its shine. For instance, a ten year on-the-run Treasury bond and a nine-and-three-quarter year off-the-run bond with the same face value will by definition converge to the same value by the time they are paid back.

Because all the other bond traders wore the same 'yield goggles' as Meriwether, and would seize upon any opportunities for an easy profit, these discrepancies or mispricings were usually small, and didn't last for longer than a few weeks or perhaps months. You would need to buy $1 billion worth of mispriced bonds just to make a few hundred thousand. Even if you did that, your profit would be swamped by the ebb and flow of the yield curve.

The only way to escape this pitfall would be to buy or sell the mispriced bond, and at the same time take the exact opposite position on another bond sitting very close to it on the yield curve. For example, sell the on-the-run Treasury and buy an equal quantity of off-the-runs. By doing this, you could immunise yourself from the great wave of the yield curve.

Some Salomon traders, in particular two fellow bond traders Craig Coats Jr and Don Green, were already doing the on-the-run/off-the-run trade for a modest profit. But Meriwether wanted more. To make a reasonable profit from these tiny discrepancies, however, Meriwether would have to trade in billion dollar size chunks. Unfortunately, on Wall Street in the mid-1970s, that was difficult. Look again at the on/off-the-run Treasury trade. You might want to buy a huge amount of Treasuries in the auction, but the supply is not unlimited. As we will see in Chapter 5, the greediness of one Salomon trader in these auctions would, in 1991, nearly ruin Meriwether's career.

If instead, you tried to buy the bonds in the market, it was even tougher. Other dealers, who were in fierce competition with you, might not co-operate. Even if you spread your trading around dozens of firms to appear innocuous, the bid-ask spread – the dealing cost taken out of each trade – was more than 1 per cent of the bond's value in the 1970s (it is far less today). That was enough to wipe out your profits from the actual trade.

It was even more dangerous to sell a large quantity of bonds. If you didn't own them in the first place, you would have to borrow them first, again from rival firms, to make the sale. When your trade had run its course, you would then buy the bonds on the market – hopefully at a lower price – and repay the loan in kind. This procedure is called selling 'short'.

The danger would arise if a shortage of bonds occurred in the meantime. This might happen because other firms, unknown to you, had done the same trade, and were due to repay bonds at the same time as you. The resulting shortage of bonds was called a 'short squeeze', and could drive the price up to ridiculous levels, causing you to suffer heavy losses.

Apart from these formidable obstacles, there was an ingrained culture at Salomon opposed to Meriwether. According to this traditional view, government bond trading involved either second-guessing the Fed and the direction of the economy, or trading against rival firms in the market. The traditionalists at Salomon were represented by people like Coats. These men did 'day trading' in government bonds – constantly working the market eeking out a few cents in the dollar every day, making a good living in the process. For these old-fashioned traders, Meriwether's ideas on price discrepancies were little more than glorified accounting tricks.

Meriwether was not discouraged. If the market wasn't ready for his ideas, then the market would have to change. This was already happening in the foreign exchange markets, and the initiative had come not from Wall Street, but Meriwether's home town, Chicago.

With Bretton Woods on the scrap heap, foreign exchange rates were floating freely. Many investors in US Treasury bonds were taking advantage of this. They would sell their Treasuries for dollars, then exchange their dollars for something else like Swiss Francs. The idea was to escape the ravages of inflation by buying government bonds in a lower inflation country.

This flow of money out of the United States lowered the value of the dollar by 50 per cent over the space of a year. With their money worth less, importers suffered the effect of this currency swing, which was made worse by rising oil prices. But in Chicago, a new development offered hope. In 1972, the CME, the CBOT's cross-town rival, had set up a new trading floor called the International Monetary Market (IMM) to trade currency futures.

The Saturday night massacre

These futures would allow importers to pay close to today's exchange rate at a future date, functioning as a sort of poor man's Bretton Woods. Thus, if you got ten francs to the dollar today, you could protect yourself against the danger of only getting five francs in six-months time.

Not only importers seeking to hedge their currency risk used these new contracts. What Meriwether immediately noticed were the arbitrage opportunities. Before the IMM started, it had only been possible to arbitrage triangles in spot currency rates – an example discussed in Chapter 2. With the futures, one could close the loop in new ways.

One example actually determines the price of currency futures. Suppose the one-year interest rate was 10 per cent in the US and 5 per cent in Switzerland, and the exchange rate is two Swiss Francs to the dollar. You borrow two million Swiss Francs in Zurich, at 5 per cent, and immediately convert them into $1 million. Wiring the funds to Wall Street, you lend at 10 per cent. Most important of all, you enter a futures contract to convert your dollars back into Swiss Francs at today's rate in a year's time.

After a year, the loan is paid back to you, and you have a total of $1.1 million in New York. You now exercise the futures contract, and convert the dollars into 2.2 million Swiss Francs. Wiring the money to Zurich, you repay the two million Swiss Francs you borrowed, plus 100,000 in interest. The remaining 100,000 Swiss Francs, after trading commissions have been deducted, is your risk-free profit.

Taking the opposite side of the futures contract is the nervous US company treasurer, who hedges his next year's Swiss Franc earnings by entering a contract to convert them into dollars. Just as speculators like Hutchinson and the US Army Quartermasters Corps were on two sides of the CBOT wheat pit in the 1860s, hedgers and arbitrageurs become bedfellows in currency futures.

However, in reality, this arbitrage opportunity wouldn't last long, as other traders got wind of this opportunity to make free money and started exploiting it too. The consequences would be twofold. Firstly, the rush to sell dollars in a year's time would use up the supply of dollars available from hedgers like the corporate treasurer above. This imbalance in supply and demand would then weaken the dollar against the Swiss Franc.

Secondly, the eagerness of traders to borrow in Zurich and lend on Wall Street would affect the bond markets. Wearing 'yield goggles' it's easy to see how: borrowing means selling bonds, reducing their price, and driving up Swiss interest rates; lending means buying bonds, raising their price, and lowering US interest rates. The net effect would be to make the trade less profitable. The only way to continue making the same profit would be to pour even more money into the trade – thus hastening its demise.

Here we have the 'law of one price' all over again. The eagerness of currency traders to enforce this law contributed to the great sloshing about of international capital that followed the collapse of Bretton Woods, and so confused the traditional bond traders. After all, if you were used to scanning unemployment and house building statistics, the relevance of currency speculators wasn't immediately apparent.

At this stage, trading US government bonds for Salomon, Meriwether wasn't ready to borrow in Zurich and lend in New York. Even if he was, currency futures arbitrage was too obvious for him. It had too many players already. But if currency futures were so successful, bond futures should be more so, with there being both a need for hedging and an appetite for arbitrage. Meriwether had that appetite, but he lacked the tools to do it.

The answer to his prayers was Richard Sandor. They had crossed paths briefly, while Meriwether was doing his MBA at the University of Chicago. But now Sandor would have a crucial impact on Meriwether's career, by giving him the tools he needed to make his name on Wall Street.

A Brooklyn native, Sandor had been a business school professor at Berkeley in California during the 1960s. When he describes Berkeley at that time as an 'exciting place' he isn't referring to the student unrest on the campus, but the intellectual climate. Teaching his MBA students about futures, Sandor started thinking about new uses for the contracts. In particular, there were two places where he thought they might be useful: interest rates and insurance.

Sandor was not familiar with Kenneth Arrow's work at the time, but his ideas were in the same spirit as the complete market that we discussed in Chapter 2. Both insurance and interest rates represented a price: of an insurance policy and a loan respectively. However, because these couldn't be hedged with futures, in the same way as wheat, these prices were higher than Sandor felt they should be.

When he first tried to popularise the ideas of interest rate and insurance futures, Sandor had a rude awakening. First, a colleague went to London, to canvass the Lloyd's insurance market, but was cold-shouldered and had to give up. Sandor then toured Wall Street touting interest rate futures, but as he recalls: 'I got kicked out of most places in New York because people said that interest rates weren't volatile, so there was no need to hedge. You can imagine the look in peoples' eyes, a professor from Berkeley proposing to trade interest rates.'

Then came the oil crisis and inflation, and suddenly Sandor's ideas didn't seem so far-fetched. Meanwhile, the CBOT had heard of this wide-eyed futures prophet – and hired him on the spot, giving him the title 'chief economist'. Alarmed by the success of the IMM currency futures, which had given its arch-rival 30 per cent of the market, the exchange was desperate for new ideas after launching the CBOE.

The first contract that Sandor designed for his new employers – while temping as visiting scholar at the University of Chicago – was not the straightforward Treasury bond future that Meriwether would use later. In 1973, the bond markets were only starting to wake up. Instead, Sandor designed a futures contract that had a far more direct influence on ordinary peoples lives, because it allowed lenders to hedge the cost of mortgages.

The problem with mortgages was that as far as Wall Street was concerned, they were too tiny to bother with. With a typical corporate bond having a face value of several billion dollars, a $100,000 mortgage was loose change. As a result, despite the fact that the total amount of outstanding mortgages was bigger than the corporate bond market, mortgages in the US were mostly left to small savings and loan banks (S&Ls). The equivalent of building societies in the UK, the S&Ls were expected to finance their mortgages with the money received from savers.

Unfortunately, these S&Ls were often too conservative to bother lending to the kind of young family that really needed a mortgage, particularly if they hadn't accumulated enough savings. Urged on by a few financiers, the US government stepped in with a deft bit of financial engineering. It set up an agency called the Government National Mortgage

Association (GNMA), whose purpose was to buy mortgages from S&Ls, package them together, and sell them as bonds.

These bonds were called mortgage-backed securities (MBS), and because they paid more interest than Treasuries, they appealed to investors. Because they were big, bond traders sat up and took notice. 'Mortgage-backs', as they are called, contain secrets that Meriwether's circle at Salomon would one day exploit for a vast profit.

With the GNMA bonds – nicknamed 'Ginnie Maes' by traders – housing developers could organise mortgage financing from a bank before laying a single foundation.

When the houses were completed, they could be advertised to home-buyers as having mortgages attached – which would guarantee a quick sale. However, changes in interest rates could ruin such deals by wiping out either the bank's or the developer's profits. This process is called securitisation, and has grown into an industry that allows ordinary people to borrow money on favourable terms unprecedented in history.

This is where Sandor and the CBOT came in. The Ginnie Mae future, which started trading in October 1975, worked just like the wheat future, but involved delivery of bonds instead of bushels. Wall Street soon overcame its reluctance. In particular, a Salomon bond trader named Lew Ranieri became the biggest MBS trader on Wall Street, helped in part by Sandor's Ginnie Mae future.

The CME quickly hit back, however. A year later, it launched the first futures contracts on US govenment debt in the form of a future on six-month Treasury bills.

This move prompted Sandor to go for broke. As he would recall: 'You didn't have to be a genius to realise that the real prize was the long bond' – in other words the 30-year Treasury bond that served as a benchmark long-term interest rate for the US economy. However, notwithstanding the enthusiasm of a few traders like Meriwether, the government bond trading establishment was hostile.

According to Sandor: 'The less progressive amongst them didn't like price transparency. A lot of people thought that would take the profitability out of the cash market.' To ensure that the new contract wouldn't get boycotted by hidebound Wall Street bond desks, Sandor carefully included a sweetener in the future's delivery specification. Instead of a single Treasury bond, sellers of the future could pick from a range, and deliver whatever was cheapest.

Sandor explains the purpose of this tweak: 'Since there were a whole load of bonds that could be delivered, you created arbitrage opportunities in trying to find the cheapest to deliver. Therefore you got a huge amount of liquidity, because there wasn't a lot of price risk if you were doing that arbitrage, in a very narrow band. So it provided liquidity for long-term hedgers because of short-term arbitrage.'

For Sandor, the first day the T-bond future started trading, on 22 August 1977, is an indelible memory. The bond that the future corresponded to was due to be paid back in July 2007, so inevitably, it became known as the 'James' bond. In a few years, the new contract would become the most heavily traded future in the world.

Meriwether moved in quickly. Salomon Brothers already ran its own team of Chicago futures pit traders through a subsidiary called the Plaza Clearing Corporation. Meriwether became a vice-president of Plaza, and would shuttle back and forth between New York and Chicago, giving orders to each team of traders.

Meriwether's New York traders would buy and sell the physical Treasury bonds, either at the Fed auctions or on the open market. Meanwhile, his Chicago pit brokers would buy and sell the equivalent T-bond futures, in a mirror image of the New York trade. If New York went down, Chicago would go up and vice versa. Immunised against the great surges in interest rates that so obsessed the traditional yield curve surfers, Meriwether could calmly pick off small arbitrage profits without taking any risks at all.

But Meriwether was not the only one to see the value of the new futures contracts. Craig Coats and another trader, John Eckstine, were already doing the same thing with the CME's T-bill future, which they would sell while physically holding the T-bills.

Meriwether's response was to rethink his strategy. Rather than merely do these arbitrage trades on a part-time, opportunistic basis while being part of the government bond desk, why not set up a special unit devoted to doing these trades and nothing else? So after much cajoling and persuasion, Meriwether's superiors, Tom Strauss and John Gutfreund agreed in late 1977 to let him set up a specialised arbitrage desk. With his own mini-kingdom at Salomon, Meriwether would not only trade in larger sizes, but now had a springboard from which to conquer Wall Street.

As Meriwether increased the size of his trades, small profits became big profits. It was now that Meriwether's secretive style came into its own. For his big two-way bets to work, it was essential that no-one else was in on the game. As we found with the dollar-Swiss Franc currency futures example above, arbitrage opportunities are victims of their own success, as traders pile in to enforce the law of one price. With his own arbitrage group sworn to secrecy, Meriwether could keep everyone else in the dark.

Over the two years following the launch of Sandor's contract, Meriwether's bond arbitrage operation grew in size. Yet even at Salomon he remained in obscurity. His lifestyle was modest. At the time he still shared an apartment on New York's Upper East Side with two roommates, although he could by now afford to play golf and ride horses at suburban country clubs. Meriwether's golf skills, in particular, earned him a grudging respect. Coats recalls that Meriwether had a handicap of six and was the top player working at Salomon. But what Meriwether needed was some kind of coup, to put his name on the map. This came in October 1979. Ironically, it was not arbitrage, but hedging that did it.

While bond trading was growing fast as a business, the prestige at investment banks still lay with the bankers who put corporate bond issues together, rather than those who bought and sold them. This underwriting business had grown too, for the simple reason that issuing debt made good sense at a time of high inflation. With the stock market moribund and many investors (such as insurance companies) still forbidden from investing in it, the bond business was a seller's market.

However, investors were increasingly aware that inflation was deadly for bondholders. Corporate bond underwriters would often have to buy up their clients' new issues themselves, and sit on the bonds until buyers could be found. With different securities firms competing for the same business, it was important to offer this service. But it was also risky for the banks, since if interest rates went up, the value of the bonds on their books would fall, and they would have to sell at a loss.

This is where Meriwether came in. In September 1979, while the US was transfixed by the Iranian hostage crisis, IBM issued a large, $1 billion bond through Salomon. Holding the bond as inventory while looking for buyers, the Salomon corporate finance department realised it was essentially making a huge bet that interest rates would not rise. How could it hedge the risk? Gutfreund set up a meeting with the government bond traders.

Shorting Treasury bonds of the same maturity was one way. But as we saw earlier, shorting in such large sizes carried risks of its own. Meriwether proposed using T-bond futures as a cheap alternative. His idea was accepted and by Friday 5 October, the Plaza pit brokers had sold a large futures position for Salomon.

We will never know how much of what followed was due to foresight or pure luck. For it was that same weekend that saw the US government dump 40 years of Keynesian monetary policy in the garbage can. How did this happen?

Firstly, there had been an intellectual shift among economists. The old Keynesian idea of using money as a fire hose against unemployment had been discredited, largely because the market had learned how to predict what was coming. Developed by the economist Robert Lucas, this insight was known as 'rational expectations'.

Meanwhile in the two years leading up to that October, inflation had become a political hot potato. The two noisiest professors at the University of Chicago, Milton Friedman and George Schultz, had allied themselves with the neo-conservative right wing of American politics, and lobbied to have monetary policy changed. Congress listened.

While Congress rescinded the law keeping deposit account rates fixed, the beleagured President Carter tried to keep up by appointing a tough new chairman of the Federal Reserve: Paul Volcker. And it was on Saturday 6 October 1979 that Volcker came to a King Canute-like conclusion. He would stop trying to control that mighty wave known as the yield curve. From now on, interest rates could find their own level.

Volcker's decision would become known on Wall Street as the 'Saturday Night Massacre' because of what happened the following week. Interest rates went through the roof. Looking through the yield curve goggles, what happened to Treasury bond prices? On the Monday they fell by 11 per cent, and continued to fall by two percentage points a day for the rest of the week. The investment banks who were sitting on piles of government and corporate bonds lost millions.

But not Salomon, or at least the part handling the IBM bond. Because of Meriwether's bright idea to hedge with futures, the losses were negligible. Even though he would not claim direct credit for this idea, Meriwether's career took off after this point, and his power base at Salomon became virtually unassailable.

For the next few years, Meriwether would continue doing simple, futures-based arbitrage trades, the kind he could think up himself. But it was a spiralling increase in sophistication that was soon to hit the market which would make him famous.

4

The Garden of Forking Paths

We do not exist in the majority of these times; in some you exist and not I; in others I, and not you; in others, both of us . . . time forks perpetually towards innumerable futures. In one of them I am your enemy.
Jorge Luis Borges, 'The Garden of Forking Paths'

In 1973, it looked like the story was already over. Black, Scholes and Merton had published their papers, and the CBOE allowed people – in the US at least – to openly trade stock options for the first time. The shady 'over-the-counter' market that had preceded the CBOE would disappear for ever. The young professors could relax in the congenial obscurity of an academic career, having established a name for themselves. End of story.

For a few years it seemed like that. But in the 1980s, this cosy world would be turned upside down. Over-the-counter (OTC) options and other derivatives would make a spectacular comeback, growing into an industry worth trillions of dollars. As for the professors, they would become the gurus of Wall Street. LTCM was the final result of this revolution.

What made it happen? Two independent breakthroughs were involved. The first happened in academia, and brought a new generation of option theorists to prominence. The second happened in banking, and directly paved the way for the sudden rise of John Meriwether.

Breaking down the ivory tower

In the 1970s, financial instability had become a byword, starting with the collapse of Bretton Woods and ending with the Saturday Night Massacre. With the end of stability came volatility, that imprint of Bachelier's speculators. In Kenneth Arrow's complete market utopia, some contract would be out there, ready to protect you against these dangerous new times.

But despite the efforts of people like Richard Sandor, the market was woefully incomplete.

By pricing options, Black, Scholes and Merton had shown a way forward. But no-one could understand them. The mathematical wizardry needed to deploy Ito's formula may have put Merton on the road to fame, but it also worked as a high fence keeping all but the most dedicated outside. Options theory sat high above the markets in an ivory tower.

At the pinnacle was the Black–Scholes option formula itself. And that was the problem. Like a painstakingly-constructed chronometer, the formula was so elegant and perfect that it seemed like an end rather than a beginning. It was useful to the CBOE pit traders, but only as sort of oracle, that could crank out numbers when needed. This unthinking approach was enshrined by the computer company Texas Instruments which incorporated the formula into one of its pocket calculators.

Anyone who wanted to tinker with the formula, and adapt it to price options with slightly different properties, was soon out of their depth. For example, what about a so-called 'American option' which can be exercised at any time before its expiry date? The Black–Scholes formula gave an exact price for 'European options', the kind that can be exercised only on expiry, but even today there is no exact formula for American options. That slight, extra twist of flexibility was enough to completely jam up the formula's mechanism.

If the Black–Scholes formula was a delicate chronometer, what the financial industry needed was a disposable watch. Something that could be broken down into the most basic parts, that an idiot could understand, but that still did the job required and could be customised too. The solution would come from an unexpected source.

The man responsible for bringing options theory down to earth, and helping to spark off the biggest explosion of free market activity the world has ever seen, started out as a Marxist radical. As a young undergraduate studying physics at the California Institute of Technology in the 1960s, Stephen Ross was in a dilemma.

On the plus side, he was fortunate to be attending lectures given by a star of twentieth century physics: Richard Feynman. In Chapter 1, we saw how the development of statistics in the nineteenth century led to the triumphs of classical physics, explaining everyday things like gas pressure in terms of invisible molecules. In the twentieth century, physicists looked at these molecules more closely and found a world that seemed incomprehensible: the world of quantum mechanics.

For the classical physicists, it may have been convenient to assume that molecules moved around randomly, but it was only a convenience: they believed that molecules, if it were possible to actually see them, followed the predictable paths of Newtonian mechanics.

In reality, the paths of molecules, atoms and other tiny particles are unpredictable. The mere act of trying to pin one down, and fix its speed or position, has the effect of making its behaviour more uncertain. To those brought up on nineteenth-century certainties — such as Einstein — this was a shocking discovery.

For much of the 1920s and 1930s, physicists worked hard trying to rescue some of that cherished predictability. They tried working with a mathematical form called a wave function. However, there was no escaping the strange consequences of these equations, which said that particles could happily be in two or more places at once. Many concluded that the question of what a particle *really* did was not a question that could be answered. Physicists would have to make do with statistics as a description of reality.

Then in the 1940s, Feynman entered the scene. He was working on a problem called quantum electrodynamics, which sought to unify everything that was known about electricity, light and quantum mechanics in a single theory. Feynman's main problem was to explain the behaviour of electrons — the fundamental particles found in atoms.

Rather than stand back like everyone else when it came to the electron's behaviour, Feynman had a clever idea. He accepted that the quantum world was mad by everyday standards. The electron not only *could* be in two places at once; it *had* to be in two places at once, or even everywhere at once. Electrons travelling between two places took every possible route to get there.

Instead of a wave function that had to be carefully interpreted, Feynman found a mathematical way of adding up the effect of an electron taking every possible route. Although Feynman's technique — called a sum over paths — gave the same statistical predictions as other methods, it had the advantage of embracing quantum mechanics from the start.

One of Feynman's colleagues, Freeman Dyson, later recalled how strange the idea seemed at the time:

> Dick Feynman told me about his version of quantum mechanics. 'The electron does anything it likes' he said. 'It goes in any direction at any speed, forward or backward in time, however it likes, and then you add up the amplitudes and it gives you the wave function.' I said to him, 'You're crazy'. But he wasn't.

Twenty years later, Stephen Ross was dazzled by Feynman's brilliance. Sitting in the Caltech lecture theatre, he wanted to be a physicist too, but there was one big obstacle. Feynman may have solved the puzzle of quantum electrodynamics, and later won a Nobel Prize for his efforts. But he also helped develop the atomic bombs which the US Air Force used to devastate Hiroshima and Nagasaki in 1945. This was the negative side as far as Ross was concerned.

Nearly all of the leading quantum theorists were involved in developing atomic weapons, and the existence of these weapons is a sort of grim flipside to the beautiful theories of the quantum world. As an avowed Marxist, and fiercely opposed to the Vietnam War, the young Ross felt uneasy about this connection.

When his classmates in the Caltech physics department would cheerfully take summer jobs at the nearby Lawrence Livermore weapons laboratory, helping the US government build bigger hydrogen bombs, Ross looked for a way out. He found one by chance, while taking a compulsory economics class.

The subject of the class was game theory, a branch of economics invented in the 1940s to deal with situations involving negotiation or bluffing. One famous example was the Cuban Missile Crisis in 1962, where President Kennedy and his counterpart Nikita Kruschev each had to anticipate their opponent's moves. Game theory tries to find out if a single outcome exists that satisfies each side.

For the young Ross, here was a connection between the excitement of political activism and the beauty of mathematics. He was hooked, and after graduating from Caltech, went to Harvard where he received his PhD. It was at Harvard that Ross met Kenneth Arrow, and soon after that, in 1970, he encountered Fischer Black.

By this time, Ross had left his radical roots behind and would soon become a world-class finance theorist. But he was unimpressed with the traditional supply and demand arguments behind equilibrium theories like the CAPM. Instead, Ross saw in the 'law of one price' as enforced by arbitrage something that reminded him of physics. Arbitrage fascinated him more than anything.

Theoretical physicists have found over the years that by imposing very simple, but universal conditions upon nature – such as conservation of energy – different observations, from the scale of atoms up to galaxies, can be unified and explained. The principle that greed eliminates opportunities to make free money seemed to have a similar potential to unify much of finance.

Now a professor at the Wharton School in Pennsylvania, Ross studied the CAPM, and devised a rival, which he called the Arbitrage Pricing Theory (APT). According to APT, arbitrage, not supply and demand, decided the relation between risk and return. Ross describes his theory: 'Whatever the systematic risks in the market, arbitrage will force excess expected returns to be proportional to the exposure to those risks.'

A pivotal moment for Ross came around 1972. Visiting MIT for a conference, Ross was invited to join some finance professors for an evening of poker. And there, facing him across the baize tablecloth, was Robert C. Merton. Ross remembers Merton as an 'excellent player'.

Merton had already completed his option pricing paper but was sitting on it in order not to steal precedence from Black and Scholes, who were still waiting for publication themselves. Reading through Black, Scholes and Merton's work, Ross spotted the magic word 'arbitrage' again.

Working with a PhD student, John Cox – whom Ross describes as 'incredibly smart' – Ross decided to confront Merton head on and question the need for all those mathematical acrobatics. Rather than trying to do calculus with Brownian motion, which forced people to use Ito's formula, perhaps there was a simpler way.

Cox and Ross went back to basics. They imagined a cartoon version of the stock market. It contained only one stock. After a certain length of time – say a month – the stock would either go up or down by a fixed amount. Cox and Ross asked if it were possible to price options on this caricature stock.

We've seen this cartoon before, in Chapter 2. We used it to show how an option could be replicated using the underlying stock. But in that example we fudged the question of what the option price should be by pretending the stock was equally likely to go up or down. In reality, you can't make assumptions like that.

Yes you can, said Cox and Ross. It is the same reasoning that allowed Black and Scholes to get away with pretending that stocks behaved like risk-free government bonds. While for Black and Scholes it was a clever trick that got them to the right formula, for Cox and Ross it was a natural outcome of the most fundamental principle in option theory – the ability to replicate.

The CAPM was about balancing risk and return. More volatile stocks should compensate investors with a higher return. Cox and Ross turned this idea around. The important thing, they said, was not what stocks had done in the past, but what investors' opinion of them was. If investors were panicky and nervous, they would demand higher returns – above the risk-free rate – to compensate them.

According to Cox and Ross, the ability to replicate changed everything. Because of that, you could treat investors as if they didn't care about risk. In the jargon of finance, this is called being 'risk neutral' and it had allowed Black and Scholes to use their trick. In this imaginary world of indifferent investors, all stocks should earn a risk-free rate of return.

Cox and Ross took things further. In the real world, we should expect the price of an option to depend on the likelihood of the stock going up or down. This in turn depends on the unfathomable moods of thousands of investors, just like Bachelier had noticed back in 1900. However, if the opinions of investors didn't matter any more – and with replication they didn't – you could construct a fake, risk-neutral probability and use it to work out the option price.

The next bit was even better. Firstly, visualise Cox and Ross's up-and-down cartoon model as being like two branching trunks of a tree, laid sideways. The root of the tree is the present time. Then imagine that at regular time intervals – such as a day – each branch grows a pair of branches in turn, which sprout more branches, and so on into the future. If you make the time intervals small enough, a single path traced out along the tree, from root to tip, looks like the fractal, jagged curve of a stock price over time. Indeed it is.

Now suppose you want to price a stock option maturing in a month's time. Every single path – millions and millions of them – has a payoff associated with it. But instead of trying to do tricky Ito calculus with these forking paths, Cox and Ross showed that you could add them together to work out the option price. As long as you pretended that investors didn't care about risk, and used the fake probability, the result was the same as given by the Black–Scholes formula. Volatility was a measure of how spread out the branches of the tree were.

Ross was not that surprised. What he had done was re-discover Feynman's sum over paths version of quantum mechanics, and apply it to the stock market. In Ross's garden of forking paths, the price of a stock did almost everything it could possibly do, just like the electron in quantum electrodynamics.

Cox and Ross's work, published in 1976, gave a new philosophical depth to finance theory. But it was their next crucial paper that would galvanise the derivatives business. For this final step, they joined forces with another professor, Mark Rubinstein of Berkeley in California. An avid computer programmer, Rubinstein supplied the final piece of the jigsaw.

The problem was, how could this sum over paths on a stock price tree work in practice? Without an answer to this question, Cox and Ross's achievement would have remained an elegant curiosity. What Rubinstein did was look at the very last branches of the tree, leading up to the end of the option's life. Because the option payout was known in advance, it was possible to use the simple up-and-down model to work out the option's value just before this moment. One could then look at the branches before, and so on, all the way back to the root of the tree, where the branches converged to a single point.[1]

Using this technique, called backwards induction, Cox, Ross and Rubinstein discovered a way to calculate the value of any option they liked. It was also easy to understand, and economically rigorous. However, for realistic trees, with lots of branches, the calculation could be extremely laborious. But it was ideal for a computer. When the trio published their paper in 1979, the first PCs were just being invented.

Over the next ten years, the ability to calculate option prices on trees would vastly increase the number of derivatives that could be priced. Perhaps Ross hadn't lost sight of his radical past after all. For with his model he broke the stranglehold that Ito calculus had on the field. Indeed, he – together with Cox and Rubinstein – had broken into the ivory tower and brought option pricing to the people.

The swap shops

In 1979, the people, namely the bankers, weren't quite ready – yet. But they had already been bitten by a replication bug of their own. It was nothing to do with finance theory, but arose from fierce competition and the need to do things faster, cheaper and more discreetly. New derivatives would be invented to solve the problem, and they would in turn prepare the ground for an academic invasion of Wall Street.

The impetus came from those commercial banks that had been figuratively thrown out of investment banking heaven by the Glass–Steagall Act. In the US, the rivers of international capital that sprang up in the 1970s may have been frightening, but for those willing to jump in, there were rich pickings.

Away from the watchful eyes of the Fed, an offshore dollar lending market had taken root in London. These offshore 'Eurodollars' were at first

---

1. Rubinstein recalls that CAPM inventor Bill Sharpe discussed this idea at a conference several years earlier but never exploited it.

a despised currency, sold off by European governments in 1974 after the US government stopped promising to exchange them for gold. Today they are the currency of the global financial system.

But dollars were also the currency of the oil business, and suddenly a flood of oil money hit Europe. The Arab princes making fortunes from high oil prices wanted to invest their riches. With the stock market floundering, the action was in bonds. Setting up in the old-fashioned City of London – still populated by bowler hat-wearing 'stockjobbers' in the 1970s – a clique of bankers took this oil money and lent it out, either in bond issues called 'Eurobonds' or loans called 'Euroloans'.

Of course, rampant inflation lowered the value of these bonds and loans by the day. In the US it was this inflation that triggered a neo-conservative backlash and put the Chicago school into power. Margaret Thatcher would take the same approach in Britain. But inflation wasn't such a problem for the Arab princes who were making money faster than inflation could destroy it.

The US commercial banks smelt an opportunity. Opening or expanding their London offices, firms like JP Morgan, Bankers Trust, Citibank and others started issuing Eurobonds and loans. There was no Glass–Steagall Act in London or anywhere in Europe for that matter. As far as Europe was concerned, if it looked like an investment bank it was an investment bank.

Some of these US bankers noticed certain odd discrepancies between different lending markets. A German company, Volkswagen for example, might be able to borrow more cheaply in Deutschmarks, while a similar American company – maybe IBM – had an advantage when it borrowed in dollars.

This happens because lenders are less familiar with foreign companies and charge higher interest on their loans. As an extreme example, let's imagine that Volkswagen can borrow at 5 per cent in Frankfurt, but must pay a whopping 10 per cent in New York. The situation is reversed for IBM. Both companies want to borrow a billion dollars.

However, perhaps because each company planned to expand abroad, each wanted to access loans in a foreign currency. The bankers would bring the two companies together and propose a deal: first borrow in your home lending market, then swap the currency payments you didn't want to pay for ones that you did. So while IBM borrows $1 billion in New York at 5 per cent, Volkswagen borrows a billion euros in Frankfurt at the same rate (assume the deal happens today, with $1 = 1 euro).

Thus, Volkswagen would receive 5 per cent euro payments from the American company, which would cover the loan. It would make 5 per cent dollar payments in return. The effect would be to transform a euro loan into a dollar one, and vice versa for the American company. However, both companies have avoided the penal 10 per cent interest rate which they would have to pay on the market.

It was a win-win situation for everybody. The two companies borrowed in the currency of their choice, at below the market rate. The investment bank sat in the middle, taking a cut from the deal. When these deals were first done, the two companies would do the swap as a mutual loan – dollars for euros in our example.

However, for some companies, particularly American ones, accounting rules meant that these mutual loans would have to appear publicly on the company's annual balance sheet. This would wipe out any tax advantages that the company could gain from its separate home-currency loan.

The bankers' solution was to take the deal 'off balance sheet', where no-one could learn about it apart from the bank itself and a few lawyers who would draw up the contract. Prying eyes – whether belonging to share-holders, credit rating agencies, or especially the taxman – could be kept in the dark. Called a cross-currency swap, the deal was a brand new type of derivative contract.

Back on Wall Street, the securities firms that had the good side of Glass–Steagall – firms like Goldman Sachs, Morgan Stanley and Merrill Lynch – ignored these new-fangled swap transactions at first. Only one of them took notice: Salomon Brothers.

Spotting an opportunity for its client IBM, in 1981 Salomon structured a swap between IBM, which paid dollars, and the World Bank, which paid Swiss Francs. Perhaps hoping to wrong-foot its commercial bank rivals, Salomon leaked details of the swap to the financial press. The deal made headlines, and the swap market began to grow.

But an even more useful new derivative contract – the interest rate swap – was just being invented in the US. So popular would this contract become, that today it is simply known as a 'swap'. It would provide the raw material for some of LTCM's biggest bets.

In the US, the years of volatile, high interest rates that followed after Volcker's inflation-fighting Saturday Night Massacre would have devas-tating effects on many banks. The yield curve, placid in the 1970s, began to buckle and whip like an angry snake.

The banks that behaved in the traditional way, making loans at fixed rates, and paying interest on deposits at floating rates, went to the wall. Worst hit were the S&L banks, which had sold long-term mortgages at fixed rates of 6 per cent, but suddenly found themselves paying 12 per cent on their deposit accounts. In the 1970s, a total of 14 US banks went under. In the 1980s and 1990s, the list would be numbered in the thousands.

It was a process of natural selection. Those who could ride with the storm survived. These banks made it their business to reduce that deadly 6 per cent gap between their assets – the loans they had made – and their liabilities – the deposit accounts they had opened. The simplest way was to sell the assets in the hope of raising enough capital to make new loans at much higher rates of interest. The eagerness of S&Ls to do this played a large part in boosting the size of the market in mortgage-backed securities.

But selling assets had to be done at market prices. Because everyone was selling old fixed-rate mortgages off their balance-sheets, you could only make 70 or 80 cents on the dollar. It was a sign of desperation that many did so. Perhaps there was a smarter way of doing things using derivatives.

The T-bond futures contracts that had helped Meriwether hedge the IBM bond had certainly protected investment banks against short-term changes in bond yields. Another tool was created in 1982 when the CME, keen to hit back at its rival, launched Eurodollar futures. These contracts allowed people to hedge the floating interest rates paid on a three-month Eurodollar deposit. But neither of these contracts could deal with the killer 6 per cent mismatch.

What was needed was some way of turning a high floating rate payment into a low fixed rate one. The commercial bankers who had thought up currency swaps at the tail end of the 1970s invented the interest rate swap to solve this problem. It was the bankers' equivalent of turning water into wine.

Suppose you are a small retail bank stuck paying out floating rates – currently 12 per cent – on deposit accounts and receiving 6 per cent interest on fixed rate loans. JP Morgan comes to you with a proposal. For the remaining period of your loans, JP Morgan will pay you floating rate to cover your deposits. In return, you pay JP Morgan a fixed rate of interest, which although higher than the fixed rate you receive on the loans, is lower than today's floating rate. This gives you the breathing space you need.

But how can JP Morgan receive a low fixed rate without losing money? The reason lies in the fact that floating rates live up to their name. By looking carefully at the yield curve, JP Morgan's traders have noticed that the market expects floating rates to come down. This means that JP Morgan will end up paying less in the future – enough to compensate JP Morgan for receiving less today.

In practice, JP Morgan would find another company willing to take the other side of the trade. This might be, for example, a car manufacturer that already had fixed rate debt outstanding, but wanted to take a bet on floating rates coming down – without having to borrow any more money. A swap would allow it to transform its fixed payments into floating ones. All JP Morgan does is put the deal together and take a fee for its efforts.

At first, the bankers had to search high and low for two companies that wanted to trade at exactly the same time, for the deal to work out. Only a few deals were done every year, and each one was a cause for celebration. But news of these new contracts soon spread, and their popularity grew. Banks would sell a swap to one company, and then 'warehouse' the risk themselves until the other side of the deal could be found.

The advantages of swaps proved an irresistible combination. Firstly, they avoided the need for costly changes to the balance sheet, because only the interest payments changed hands rather than the underlying 'notional' amounts. Thus for a $1 billion swap, the actual sums involved are much smaller than $1 billion.

Then, there were the tax avoidance advantages of going off balance sheet. Finally, swaps were flexible – they could be done in any size, at any date, for any length of time. Swaps could be tailored to exactly the kind of problem you wanted to solve. Exchange-traded futures contracts, on the other hand, were only available at specific expiry dates.

This flexibility was possible because swaps were 'over-the-counter' derivatives, negotiated directly by a bank. It was like the 1960s OTC option market that happened in a Wall Street restaurant all over again, except that the sums involved now were hundreds of millions of dollars or more. Interest rate swaps would prove incredibly popular, overtaking currency swaps, and eventually becoming the most heavily traded derivatives in the world.

For the commercial banks, swaps were a clever way round the Glass–Steagall Act. According to Bill Winters – a leading dealer from JP Morgan – 'We had capital and we understood credit risk, but it was illegal for us to trade corporate bonds. Swaps were connected to the bond market we couldn't deal in, but it was as close as we could get to it, so we put our efforts into it.'

The early swap dealers were not finance theorists, and had not even studied under them. In the words of Bill Winters they were 'PPE types' from the Ivy League universities and Oxbridge in England. This background in politics, philosophy and economics (hence the acronym) gave them the right combination of market insight and cultural knowledge which went over well with their corporate clients.

An *eminence grise* among swaps dealers is Connie Voldstad, who built up the business from scratch at JP Morgan in the early 1980s. Voldstad's reputation came from his ability to warehouse large swap deals. To do this, he had to replicate the swap payments using the new futures contracts on the CBOT and CME. This was the first example of an important technique: using futures exchanges to hedge OTC derivatives.

Swaps weren't too sophisticated for the PPE types, because they could easily be broken down into a series of two-way payments. With a computer spreadsheet and a cheap PC, you could work out what a swap was worth. Options were a different story.

Digging for options

Some academics had already tried to bring options to Wall Street, but had focused on the stock market rather than interest rates. During the bearish stock market climate of the late 1970s, people certainly could have done with some help. For anyone investing in stocks, options were the ideal way, in the Kenneth Arrow tradition, to protect against that unpleasant downside.

However, when Merton and Scholes set up a venture in 1976 to manage a portfolio of CBOE stock options – to provide some potential upside – along with an interest-paying deposit account – to insure against the downside – they found few takers. After two years, the venture folded. No-one wanted 'unimportant contracts' when they could invest in the stock market itself.

But Mark Rubinstein, who had helped Cox and Ross make that final leap with their tree model, was not so easily discouraged. Joining forces with Hayne Leland, a fellow finance academic, Rubinstein targeted portfolio managers instead of ordinary investors. These managers already owned stocks, often in large quantities. What they needed were put options, that allowed them to sell their portfolios at a fixed price if the market plunged.

Unfortunately, the kind of options the portfolio managers would have found useful were not available. The CBOE contracts were mostly calls, rather than puts. They offered the right to buy a few specific stocks, and like all exchange-traded contracts, had only a small range of expiry dates.

Leland and Rubinstein's brainwave was to go back to the underlying theory of Black, Scholes and Merton. If you couldn't buy an option, why not replicate one, using the underlying stocks? Using his new baby, the tree model, Rubinstein wrote a computer program that calculated the necessary buy and sell instructions, one day at a time. They called it 'portfolio insurance'.

Guaranteeing to protect any portfolio from declining below a fixed level, Leland and Rubinstein set up a company called LOR. Based in Los Angeles, LOR was not itself a portfolio management company. Rather than hold assets, it dispensed buy and sell orders to its clients, which were churned out by Rubinstein's computer. LOR found a steady stream of business coming its way during the 1980s.

Although portfolio insurance was a success, it was still some distance from Wall Street proper. There were still no academics prowling the investment bank trading floors, and the financial theories of Black, Scholes and Merton were still obscure. That would change when the up-and-coming swap dealers started to trade options.

That there was a need for interest rate options was in no doubt. They started appearing around 1983. The simplest were options to buy or sell bonds. Then came 'caps', which were similar in spirit to Hammurabi's option of Chapter 2. Someone who had borrowed money at a floating rate could use a cap to stop the rate rising above a certain level. 'Floors' were an option that made sense for floating rate lenders, and would protect against falling rates. You might be considering an interest rate swap, but weren't quite sure. The solution was to buy an option on a swap, which was called a 'swaption'.

All these options needed to be priced, and most were beyond the scope of the Black–Scholes formula. But there was an even more fundamental problem. The options involved all sorts of interest rates – floating rates, fixed rates, swap rates, and bond yields all along that undulating curve. How were they all related?

The academics had been quietly thinking about this problem already. They called it the 'term structure of interest rates'. While John Meriwether was learning by the seat of his pants how to surf the yield curve as a bond trader, the academics, including Robert Merton, were trying to understand bond prices. Their goal was to do for bonds what Harry Markowitz and Bill Sharpe had done for stock prices.

At first sight, bonds and stocks are similar. They are both bought and sold daily in the marketplace. Supply and demand makes their prices go up and down in what we already know is a random walk. But as we saw in the last chapter, the analogy is flawed because bonds have a finite lifetime. The trick, as bond traders realised, was to strap on the yield curve goggles and focus on interest rates rather than bond prices.

The academics realised this in the early 1970s, and indeed, Fischer Black adapted the Black–Scholes model in 1976 to price options on bonds by making the yield earned on the bond follow Brownian motion – the principle that had made their model work in the first place. However, Black's model didn't say anything about the yield curve, which as we saw in Chapter 3, linked together bonds with different maturities.

The naïve approach would be to think of two different maturity bonds – say a five-year and a twenty-year Treasury – as being like different stocks – for example IBM and Microsoft. Each Treasury bond would have its own return and its own volatility – which would be used to price options on one bond independently of the other.

Being technology companies, we expect the fortunes of IBM and Microsoft to rise and fall together; in other words they should be correlated. We would expect the Treasury bonds to be correlated in a similar way. However, the correlation between IBM and Microsoft stock is purely a measure of historical statistical relationships. They are ultimately different companies with different management, and it would be dangerous to expect this correlation not to change in the future.

The Treasury bonds, on the other hand, are fixed-term debt obligations of the US government. They will both pay a known amount at a known time in the future. Any relative fluctuations in their values today should be more than just coincidence. Wall Street bond traders had an intuitive idea of this when they visualised the yield curve rising and falling like a wave. Unless it was unbelievably stormy, different points on the wave should move together in a predictable way.

One of the first term structure models with this property was devised in 1977 by Oldrich Vasicek. A mathematician who had fled Czechoslovakia after the Soviet invasion in 1968, Vasicek was working at the time for Wells Fargo Bank in San Francisco. Wells Fargo didn't trade bonds, but it was one of the few banks that had embraced the CAPM as part of its portfolio management operation.

Vasicek recalls how he started working on the model: 'The CAPM was an exciting development that had revolutionised my thinking, but I was bothered by the fact that it didn't address bonds.' Vasicek decided to go back to fundamentals. The Brownian motion of stocks, as we have seen, arises from the random back-and-forth pushing by thousands of invisible speculators. The naïve model of bonds says that each of a given maturity has its own, isolated corral of speculators independent of the others.

Vasicek argued that all the bond speculators were effectively in the same room, making decisions about the time value of money. A speculator who invested in a five-year bond and kept it for five years would compare herself to a nearby speculator who kept on buying three-month bonds for the same period. Who earned more from the time value of money?

It was these constant comparisons being made by the invisible speculators that linked three-month bond prices to five-year bond prices. To Vasicek's surprise, he found that the prices were enforced by arbitrage, rather than the supply and demand arguments of the CAPM. According to Vasicek's model, bond prices all along the yield curve were determined by what happened to the short-term interest rate.

Vasicek expressed his idea mathematically by taking the Brownian motion that worked so well for stocks and attaching it to the short end of the yield curve – in other words, the floating interest rate. Like a bluebottle attached to a piece of string, the short rate jiggled at random, and transmitted this movement to the rest of the yield curve.

The effect of Vasicek's paper, in his words, was like 'opening a Pandora's box'. Other term structure models soon followed. And moreover, for the first time these models allowed one to price interest rate options on any part of the yield curve while replicating them on another part. The mathematics was much more complicated than Black's model, and Ross's tree approach would become an essential part of using these models.

Rumours that there were models out there to price these new options started circulating among Wall Street fixed income dealers. If you couldn't solve that problem, there was the danger that another bank would. A race was quickly underway to find people who could understand yield curves and price options at the same time.

The idea was to take these 'quants' as they became known, and shut them in a back room full of computers behind the trading floor. Paid five times what they had earned in academia, these quants could spend the whole day working on the pricing models they knew and loved.

The dealers would periodically leave their noisy, testosterone-drenched trading floors and ask the quants to price something. Then, leaving the quants hunched silently in front of their computers, the dealers would return to the real world, get on the phone and make some real money.

Fischer Black would become perhaps the best known quant on Wall Street, long before Merton and Scholes. By 1984 he was fed up with academia, with its petty struggles for status and intellectual one-upmanship. Black would later quip that professors should be paid and hired for their teaching, and not for their research. When Goldman Sachs asked him to run its quantitative strategies department he jumped at the chance.

Black's quirkiness made him the consummate quant. Fast-talking Goldman traders would have to endure his famous two-minute silences while he thought about their questions. If that didn't kill the conversation, Black might then start programming his Casio calculator watch, or enter data into his personal organiser software, which obsessed him so much that he would phone the manufacturer with suggestions for improvements. And yet, Black's ultimate willingness to explain things in down-to-earth terms ended up making him a much-loved figure at Goldman.

Over at Salomon Brothers, John Meriwether had watched all these developments with interest. By 1983 he was head of the government bond division at Salomon and was becoming known as one of the most successful traders on Wall Street. Meriwether also set up arbitrage desks in London and Tokyo, to exploit the opportunities across different currencies. The bond markets had been good to him, although his arbitrage techniques were still shunned by most traders.

In particular, Salomon's head government bond trader, Craig Coats – said to be the model for the character of Sherman McCoy in Tom Wolfe's *Bonfire of the Vanities* – preferred a more macho, directional style of trading. For him, trading was like arm-wrestling with Paul Volcker every day. Junior traders would enter through a college graduate induction programme which stressed fraternity-style team building in the place of intellect.

Meriwether played along with the system, but was spending more and more time in the bond research department, where people actually understood the mysteries of the term structure. The department's boss, Marty Liebowitz, had been told by management to beef up his unit and start hiring. Although he was now looking out for finance professors, Liebowitz had traditionally plucked young Master's degree graduates from the Salomon induction programme and then trained them himself.

Two such graduates, Victor Haghani and Larry Hilibrand, had already impressed Meriwether with their ability to learn. But frustratingly, he had to share their skills with other traders at Salomon. Then in 1984, Meriwether had a meeting that would change his life, and would create LTCM inside the walls of Salomon Brothers.

Because neither man will discuss it today, let's imagine the meeting takes place over lunch in the oak-panelled dining room of Salomon Brothers' skyscraper headquarters. On one side of the table is John Meriwether, wearing a tailored suit and $500 silk tie. On the other side is a scruffy, long-haired academic from the Harvard Business School. His name is Eric

Rosenfeld. Rosenfeld had been Merton's star student at MIT, and was about to put into practice a whole new chapter of finance theory.

Rosenfeld had won his spurs in 1980 with a PhD entitled *Stochastic Processes of Common Stock Returns: An Empirical Examination*. It looked at the limitations of Black–Scholes–Merton theory, in particular, the assumption that volatility was constant. In the real world, it was noticed that volatility changed – although more slowly than the stock price itself. In his thesis, Rosenfeld compared two possible improvements to the theory: either keep Bachelier's random walk and let volatility change, or introduce occasional jumps and keep volatility fixed.

Early on during his PhD studies, Rosenfeld had befriended a young hippie called Mitch Kapor. A typical seventies drop-out, Kapor was deeply into transcendental meditation and had spent time in Switzerland trying to levitate. That didn't work out, and Kapor now wanted to get his life together. While working part-time as an orderly in a mental hospital, he had discovered personal computers, which had just been invented. Kapor bought one and taught himself how to program.

By this time, Rosenfeld was completing his thesis for Merton, and needed to do lengthy statistical analysis on years of stock market data. Unfortunately, MIT's mainframe computer was so heavily used by other graduate students that Rosenfeld couldn't get the time he needed to crunch through his data. However, Rosenfeld had recently bought an Apple II computer, and as a favour to his friend, Kapor wrote a program that solved the problem.

Rosenfeld was impressed by Kapor's program. Why not sell it? Working from home, Kapor and Rosenfeld began marketing the program, and sold it via mail order at $100 per copy. At Rosenfeld's suggestion, Kapor then took some MBA classes at the Sloan School before starting his own company to do the job properly.

The company was called Lotus in homage to Kapor's background in meditation, and its product, launched in 1982, was a spreadsheet called Lotus 1-2-3. It was based on the original program used by Rosenfeld. Catching the boom in personal computers with perfect timing, Lotus was a runaway success. Part of the success was due to Kapor's innovations such as a customer helpline – the first of its kind. When Kapor finally sold out his stake in 1984, he was worth $150 million.

Although Rosenfeld parted company with Kapor at an earlier stage, the experience of running a business made an impression. Turning down offers to do pure research at several other universities, Rosenfeld accepted a job teaching at the nearby Harvard Business School, where he could be closer to the 'real' world.

Becoming aware of the practical applications of finance theory, Rosenfeld started visiting Wall Street, and it was then that he met John Meriwether. By this time, Rosenfeld's stake in Lotus had already made him a millionaire. So it was with some confidence that he sat across the lunch table facing the most talented bond trader on Wall Street. Meriwether just listened.

Like his mentor Robert Merton, Rosenfeld was a deft user of Ito calculus which he showcased in his thesis, but since arriving at Harvard, he had started thinking about the US Treasury yield curve. Talking to Meriwether, Rosenfeld explained that the Treasury curve was the opposite of the sparse, incomplete equity option market that had forced Mark Rubinstein and Hayne Leland to invent portfolio insurance.

The Treasury curve, continued Rosenfeld, was over-complete. In its drive to borrow money, the US government had created such a rich universe of bonds, each with different coupons and maturities, that according to the new generation of term structure models, many of them could be replicated several times over. That meant that their prices ought to have a precise mathematical relationship, otherwise, in the words of Vasicek, 'profitable riskless arbitrage is possible'.

Yet the bond market – dominated by people like Craig Coats – didn't realise this. Absorbed by the daily flood of news and rumour, they flocked to buy certain maturities of bond, and shunned others. This distorted the market away from what the models said the curve should look like – and created opportunities for arbitrage profits. Of course, none of this analysis would interest a traditional bond trader, whose standard demand was 'I want to know what interest rates are going to do.'

Meriwether's stock response was 'I don't care, because I want to do arbitrage.' Indeed, he was already good at doing just that with on and off-the-run Treasuries as we saw in Chapter 3. There were also those Chicago futures contracts with their arbitrage potential, and recently the London International Financial Futures Exchange (LIFFE) had opened, giving even more opportunities.

But now, here was Rosenfeld sitting opposite him, explaining how a hypothetical arbitrage trader could systematically take the population of US bonds, solve that as a set of simultaneous equations, and come up with prices for bonds. When you looked at supply and demand, tax considerations, and all the things that might yield a reasonable amount of variation, added

Rosenfeld, the possible trades were endless. The same thing could also be done in other countries, where governments issued risk-free debt.

There was still the short-term rate to worry about: the buzzing blue-bottle that tugged the string in Vasicek's theory. But if you were careful enough to replicate and hedge away this randomness, perhaps using a Chicago futures contract, you could capture the predictable part of the yield curve that all the models claimed was there.

Meriwether wanted to grab this genius with both hands and push him onto the Salomon trading floor. But he restrained himself. 'What about options?' he asked Rosenfeld. Meriwether had in mind the growing market in OTC Treasury bond options and floating rate caps that was the talk of Wall Street. Rosenfeld responded that most options in the world went completely unnoticed.

What could Rosenfeld mean? 'You ought to talk to Bob Merton' came the reply. Rosenfeld then told Meriwether who Merton was. When we last saw Merton in Chapter 2, back in 1973, he was barely on the first rung of the academic ladder. Ten years later, Merton had moved on. By 1983 he could afford to rest on his laurels. He now had three children, and the job security of a tenured professorship at MIT.

After publishing his 1973 paper, and seeing the CBOE options market flourish, Merton had left the details of option pricing to others, like Cox and Ross. After the failure of his venture with Myron Scholes, he lost interest in the visible options market because he was becoming aware of a much larger, invisible one. Merton was hunting for hidden options.

Finance is full of hidden options. They lurk in the small print of share certificates and bond issues. Laws and financial regulations are full of them. Hammurabi's paragraph 48 contained an option, hidden until we saw how to find it in Chapter 2. The question Merton asked was, who owns these options and how much are they worth?

One classic example was analysed by Merton in 1974. Humble, old-fashioned equity, argued Merton, is actually an option. Why? In general, companies issue both equity and debt. Equity gives investors ownership in the company, and while debt holders have to forego this privilege, they do have the advantage of legal precedence if the company goes bankrupt.

Merton painted the life of a company as a sort of Manichean struggle between shareholders and debtholders. If the company goes bust, the debtholders are first in line at the bankruptcy court, ready to seize the company's assets, while shareholders usually get nothing. But at least they are protected from the debtholders – recall that the most important feature of equity is its limited liability nature. According to Merton, this is equivalent to saying that shareholders have an option not to pay the debtholders, even though they have a stake in the company. This option can be valuable.

There are many other such examples of such hidden options, and the art of finding them is known as contingent claims analysis. During the 1970s and 1980s, a cottage industry grew up around Merton at MIT dedicated to solving this puzzle. For instance, there was Greg Hawkins. Younger than Rosenfeld, Hawkins did a thesis for Merton on the value of options embedded in revolving credit agreements, a kind of renewable loan. Another student named Saman Majd was working on the hidden options that resulted from companies making investment decisions; for example, owning oil-drilling rights to a piece of land is equivalent to an option, because the decision to drill for oil will only pay off if oil prices are high enough to make it worthwhile.

Surely, suggested Rosenfeld, many of the new securities then appearing on Wall Street contained hidden options that hadn't been priced properly. And pricing options was like eating breakfast for Eric Rosenfeld. If the Ito calculus became too hair-raising even for him, there was always Steve Ross's garden of forking paths.

For Meriwether, this was virgin territory, but he saw the potential immediately. After the lunch was over, Meriwether went straight to his boss John Gutfreund, and got approval to make an unheard-of job offer.

Far more than money, Meriwether offered Rosenfeld power. He would not be entering Salomon on the 'quant ticket', hidden like an exotic pet in a windowless backroom. Rosenfeld would go straight onto the cacophonous trading floor, as a member of the bond arbitrage group. His smart ideas, if they worked, would translate onto his paycheque as a huge Wall Street bonus.

Over the next three years, a trickle of academics would follow Rosenfeld to Salomon. First there was Greg Hawkins, who was lured away from Berkeley and joined in 1985, also as a trader. Then came Bill Krasker, a colleague of Rosenfeld's from the Harvard Business School. Conforming more to the quant stereotype, Krasker was put in charge of building the group's models. However, Meriwether still wanted more traders. So he went and raided Liebowitz's bond research department, putting Haghani and Hilibrand on the trading desk next to Hawkins and Rosenfeld.

Meriwether treated all these new arrivals differently to the normal rough-and-tumble manner expected at Salomon. They were given their own area in the middle of the bond trading floor and were not subject to the suit-and-tie dress code expected from normal traders. According to Saman Majd, who joined the group in 1987, Meriwether respected intelligence: 'His style was to take smart people and expose them to the market, in the belief that good things would happen.'

One example of this in action was Victor Haghani. A British national who had a degree from the London School of Economics, Haghani was sent by Meriwether to work in Tokyo, with the famously abrasive arbitrage trader Shigeru 'Sugar' Miyojin. No shrinking violet, Haghani returned to New York with an abrasive streak of his own, and several good arbitrage ideas.

For the ex-academics, the siren call became irresistible. Majd recalls being at Yale University in 1986: 'I was disaffected with the pace of academia', he says. 'The option problem in my last paper took three weeks to solve, but two years to get into print.' Meeting Majd in 1986, Meriwether took a softly-softly approach. He suggested that Majd come to Salomon for short visits over several months, and simply observe the activity in different areas of the firm, from bond trading to traditional investment bank business like mergers and acquisitions. If he liked it, fine. If he didn't, that was fine too.

Majd liked it, and joined the arbitrage group. He never doubted making the right decision: 'If the academic literature was published, well understood and there were no trade secrets there; and if there were a large number of academics either consulting with or working at Wall Street firms in the early to mid 80s, why was it that one firm stood out head and shoulders above the rest in terms of application? I think the answer to that lies with Meriwether.'

5

The Warning

Experience was of no ethical value. It was merely the name men gave to their mistakes. All that it really demonstrated was that our future would be the same as the past, and that the sin we had done once, and with loathing, we would do many times, and with joy.

Oscar Wilde, *The Portrait of Dorian Gray*

The first sign that something could go horribly wrong with mathematical models of human behaviour came in October 1987. It was a foretaste of what was to come; just as in 1998, a firm that had made its name by applying financial theory came unstuck. Yet the Crash, which devastated the world's stock markets, seemed like an old-fashioned, populist event. For those who needed it most, the message didn't get through.

The 1980s had seen a striking revival in the US stock market, moribund since the early 1970s. Encouraged by Ronald Reagan and his libertarian Chicago school advisers, a wave of corporate takeovers and restructurings swept through America, masterminded by a few Wall Street firms. The resulting layoffs of employees caused great resentment, and lowered average incomes across the country. But share prices arced upwards.

Since its foundation in 1980, the portfolio insurance company LOR had proved an enormous success. To protect their recent gains in wealth, US pension funds and mutual funds had entrusted LOR with insuring billions of dollars worth of stock portfolios against a decline in the market.

The options needed to do this weren't available either on exchanges or over-the-counter, but Black, Scholes and Merton had said that options could be replicated by trading the underlying stock. Applying the theory, and continuously replicating put options that protected its client's portfolios, LOR provided peace of mind. It also spawned a number of imitators.

LOR's job had become even easier when the CME had launched futures contracts on the S&P 500 stock market index. Most of LOR's clients' portfolios imitated this index, and at the very least tried to beat it. Now, instead of painstakingly buying and selling dozens of individual stocks, LOR could trade a single contract.

The kind of replicating strategy used by LOR is called 'delta hedging' by options traders. In Chapter 2, the simple replicating portfolio we used to price an option was an example of a delta hedge. By owning one stock for every two options sold, when the premium we had received was taken into account, we broke even exactly.

And as we now know from the last chapter, that cartoon up-and-down stock market we used as a model is simply one branch of a tree growing in Stephen Ross's garden of forking paths. As the stock price zigzags through the tree, tracing out its path through time, at each fork an options trader works out how much stock to buy or sell to break even in the next time step.

Our example in Chapter 2 was for a call option – the right to buy a stock at a future date. A put option is the right to sell a stock, or in LOR's case, the right to sell the S&P 500 index at its current level. Adapting our example, instead of owning one stock for every two options, we now must sell one stock short. If our tree forks downwards, the gain on this short sale compensates for an increase in the value of the put option we sold. If it forks upwards, the loss on the short sale balances a decline in the option's value.

This delta hedge calculation was being done thousands of times a day on LOR's computers in the summer of 1987. The answer would appear on the screen, and someone would phone a broker in Chicago to sell the precise number of index futures contracts needed to replicate the clients' put options.

In the months before the Crash, LOR's fund manager clients might not have slept so soundly had they known what Mark Rubinstein and his colleagues had just realised: that they were flying with a faulty parachute. Delta hedging was flawed. The problem lay in the small print of Black, Scholes and Merton's theory – in other words, the assumptions behind it.

The ant and the flea

Every theory in science starts out with assumptions. When applying his laws of motion, Isaac Newton assumed that the world was frictionless. On Earth, this isn't a very realistic assumption in most situations. However, in space there is virtually no friction, and Newton could use his laws to calculate the motion of the planets – the first time this had been done.

That is how successful theories work – relegating the less important detail to the small print and focusing on the essentials. Up to Newton's time, followers of Aristotle had argued that the planets occupied a purer realm than the corrupted, imperfect Earth, and that different laws applied. Newton showed that the same laws applied to both, while friction could be brought in later on as an extra bit in the equations.

With their option formula, and more importantly the law of dynamic replication that allowed virtually any derivative on earth to be priced, Black, Scholes and Merton could claim to be the Newtons of finance. By leaving aside the details, they could take their idea from one market to the next: from options on stocks to the hidden option on crude oil prices that a company owns when it has oil drilling rights. It really was a universal law of finance.

And what about the details? There are three key assumptions behind Black, Scholes and Merton's theory. It is worth paying close attention to these details, because they would ultimately prove fatal to LTCM, as well as LOR. The first two, when Merton himself states them in his 1973 paper, resemble the small print of Newton: he talks of markets that are 'continuous' and 'frictionless'.

Friction in finance means costs. Every time you buy or sell something, whether a stock, a bond, or an option, you have to pay a brokers' transaction fee. When you sell a stock at a profit, you must pay capital gains tax. If you earn interest on a bond, you must pay income tax.

For individual investors, these costs are significant. But if you are a big dealer like Salomon Brothers or Goldman Sachs then you live in the friction-free world of Newton's planets. Dealing costs are virtually zero, and special trading accounts are tax exempt. So for the people who replicate options for a living, the assumption isn't a problem.

'Continuous' is more subtle. It doesn't mean that the market has to be open 24 hours a day; the theory allows for nights and weekends. But it does mean that when the market is open, you should be able to trade as often as you like – in principle, infinitely often. It also means that you can buy and sell the underlying stock or other asset in as large or small quantities as you like. To pay for this trading, you can borrow as much money as you need – and pay no more than the risk-free rate of interest.

As with frictionlessness, continuous markets are not as far from reality as they sound. The big dealing firms with their hundreds of traders have always been able to trade frequently during trading hours, and today individuals too can trade continuously over the Internet.

Nor is unlimited borrowing beyond the realms of the possible. For the retail investor, there may be problems. But investment banks are worth billions of dollars, and if they can't borrow from other banks there are always the central banks like the Fed ready to help them out. As long as you take 'unlimited' to mean 'larger than you would ever expect', then this part of the assumption seems to be fine.

What about buying and selling in any quantity? For the great multinational companies whose shares are traded on the world's principal stock exchanges, this, too, isn't far fetched. These companies have millions of shares in circulation, with total value measured in tens of billions of dollars. Every day, thousands of these shares change hands, and there seem to be plenty to go round.

This ability to buy and sell freely is called liquidity. It means that there is always someone out there willing to trade with you. Liquidity has been growing ever since markets began. A Bronze Age traveller living 20,000 years ago couldn't be sure that the tribe in a neighbouring valley would buy his goods. Today's trader of stocks in large multinationals swims in the most liquid markets in human history.

Because of the apparently limitless liquidity in the US stock markets, academics paid even less attention to the assumption of continuous markets than they paid to the assumption that markets were frictionless. There were a small number of papers on transaction costs and taxes, but these never had the glamour of mainstream option theory.

The third assumption, however, did attract some attention, perhaps because it lay at the conceptual root of modern finance. It was the assumption that stocks and other assets considered by option theorists followed a random walk.

As pioneers like Samuelson and Fama had shown, the random walk is closely connected to efficient market theory: the piranha-like ability of the market to devour new information means that the up and down moves of a stock from one time to the next are independent of each other.

The random walk gives stock returns a Normal distribution, that simple bell-shaped curve which captures patterns ranging from heights of animals to the outcome of coin tosses. Such beautiful simplicity was more than an assumption for the theorists; it was an article of faith. It also allowed clever mathematical devices like Ito's formula to be used.

In nature, the Normal distribution lives up to its name: it excludes the freakish and outlandish. For example, the heights of young adult Europeans have a standard deviation of about four inches, centred around a mean of about five and a half feet. Two thirds of this group occupy the zone in the middle, standing between five feet two and five feet ten inches, in other words, with heights only one standard deviation or less from the mean.

What about people shorter than four and a half feet? Such 'three standard deviation people' are about one in seven hundred. As for a 'six standard deviation person' – shorter than three and a half feet – you would only expect to see six people like this among all the five billion people living on earth.

The fact that 'little people' are commoner than this in real life suggests that the Normal distribution doesn't tell the whole story. Moreover, a Normal distribution of heights is just a description of a collection of people. It doesn't predict anything.

The random walk hypothesis, on the other hand, *predicts* that stock price returns have a Normal distribution. Instead of peoples' heights, there is a population of daily returns, stretching as far back in time as you choose. But as with human heights, freak events are largely excluded. A three standard deviation negative return happens only once every thousand trading days on average. That's about once every four years. As for a company like Microsoft's return going down six standard deviations in one day, you'd expect that only once in four million years of trading.

Sadly, this cosy picture isn't quite accurate. Freak events – namely, large daily stock price returns – do happen more often than the Normal distribution says. And why not? Traders and investors all know that important events like a takeover bid or threatened bankruptcy can make stocks leap up or down in a single day.

In the 1960s, a French mathematician, Benoit Mandelbrot, tried to point this out to the growing school of efficient marketeers. Instead of the simple random walk theory, a more sophisticated mathematical model was needed, said Mandelbrot. Unfortunately, his alternative of 'wild randomness' didn't have the intuitive appeal of random walks. To the efficient marketeers, he seemed like a temperance preacher at a drinks party. They threw him out.

The next generation of financial economists – Black, Scholes, Merton and the others – were more open-minded. In 1974, Merton came up with a simple way of looking at the problem. Suppose, said Merton, that a stock carries on happily following an ant-like random walk over time. But every now and then, something else kicks in and makes it jump unpredictably, like a flea. With this 'jump diffusion' model, Merton could describe reality better, but there was bad news as well.

Options couldn't be replicated any more. The random walk part was fine – the Normal distribution worked its magic as usual – but random jumps were different. The constantly adjusted balance between stock and option that was delta hedging could be thrown completely out of line by such a jump. While the other two assumptions mentioned above – friction-free and continuous markets – seemed to only have small effects, the violation of the Normal distribution assumption might be significant.

By 1987, this issue was nagging at Rubinstein. However, there were plausible reasons not to be bothered. Jumps happened to individual stocks, but LOR was trading the whole S&P 500 index. Averaging the 500 components that made up the S&P would surely smooth out any large individual moves.

What about jumps in the entire index? That hadn't happened since the Wall Street Crash of October 1929, when the Dow fell by 23 per cent over two days. The market had changed a lot since then. Rubinstein joked to his colleagues that only a Martian landing could trigger off the same kind of fall in the market.

In the end, the Martians weren't necessary. The stock market had been sluggish since September that year, and then in the week of 12 October, two items of bad news disturbed the market. First, on 14 October, the US Congress began debating new legislation to cut tax breaks for aggressive takeovers – a source of much wealth on Wall Street during the previous few years.

Then, Treasury Secretary James Baker reacted to some poor economic news by suggesting that the dollar was overvalued and should be allowed to weaken – a signal that foreign investors should pull their money out of US stocks.

The events of the next few days would not only prove that jumps in the entire market were more than the stuff of fiction. They would show that in addition to random walks, another Black–Scholes–Merton assumption was equally flawed. However, while the jumps got all the attention, this second flaw would remain obscure, until it wiped out LTCM in the summer of 1998. It was the assumption of continuous markets, in particular that of liquidity.

The two items of bad news don't seem that bad in retrospect, but for some reason, the market was disturbed. Confidence gradually evaporated that week, and growing sell-offs of stocks drove prices ever lower. By Friday 16 October, the Dow had fallen by 250 points – a return of minus 10 per cent for the week. That was already close to being a freak event in the population of index returns, and it was a sign that something was seriously wrong.

With each fall in the index, LOR and its competitors dutifully calculated an appropriate delta hedge. According to the tree model, they were sitting at a fork in the tree with two paths branching into the future – either the market could recover, or it could fall the same distance again. Since that distance was a large one, the model required the selling of enormous amounts of index futures contracts.

At that time, LOR had insured approximately $80 billion of stocks, and a decline in the market of 10 per cent required that about $12 billion of index futures were sold. However, by Friday evening, only $4 billion worth of the contracts had physically changed hands in the CME futures pit – and this was 15 per cent of the entire volume traded.

There were now $8 billion of index futures waiting to be sold on the Monday. If this was done quickly, then the clients of LOR and its competitors would be protected. Meanwhile, nervous investors all over the US – and also outside – sent orders to their brokers to sell stocks, and a large backlog built up over the weekend.

Mark Rubinstein was surprised when his partner Hayne Leland phoned him up – and suggested that Rubinstein watch the market news early on Monday morning. 'He'd never ever suggested that before' he recalls. So strong was the two men's belief in efficient market theory that they were usually happy to let their computers worry about the ups and downs of the index. But Rubinstein turned on his TV all the same. 'It was a disaster', he says.

On 'Black Monday', 19 October, the Dow dropped 200 points immediately after the opening bell rang on the New York Stock Exchange. Through the day, 600 million individual shares were traded, with a total value of $21 billion. The Exchange's computers were overwhelmed with the flow, and it was not until several hours after the closing bell that the extent of the carnage was fully known: 508 points off the Dow, a one-day negative return of 22.6 per cent. The S&P 500 index fell by 20.5 per cent.

Things were even worse in Chicago. There was already the $8 billion of S&P 500 futures waiting to be sold first thing in the morning. This caused the value of the future to drop 7 per cent as soon as the market opened. Then as the S&P itself fell that day, taking the downward path in the tree, a new delta hedge had to be calculated by LOR and the others. As a result of this, more sell orders arrived in Chicago, and through the day, $20 billion of contracts were traded. While 10 per cent of the day's selling on the NYSE had come from portfolio insurers, on the CME it was 21.3 per cent.

But the pressure was more than the futures market could stand. Although it was supposed to track the S&P 500, by the end of trading, the CME contract had fallen by 29 per cent – nine points lower than the actual index.

The effect was disastrous for the clients of LOR and its competitors. You want to sell futures to cover you against the index going down, but because of the discrepancy, you must effectively pay the 9 per cent difference before you get that protection. The clients thought they had paid for insurance, but now they didn't get it. Instead they lost millions of dollars.[1]

And then there were all the other investors who hadn't bothered with portfolio insurance – they lost too. Across the world, other stock markets followed America's downward plunge. The Brady Commission, set up by the US government to investigate the Crash, was blunt in its appraisal:

> From the close of trading Tuesday, October 13, 1987 to the close of trading Monday, October 19, the Dow Jones Industrial Average declined by almost one third, representing a loss in value of all outstanding United States stocks of approximately $1.0 trillion.
>
> What made this market break extraordinary was the speed with which prices fell, the unprecedented volume of trading and the consequent threat to the financial system.

The Crash also had disturbing implications for financial theory. At 20.5 per cent, it was a 20 standard deviation event on the S&P 500. According to the Normal distribution, a day like this wouldn't be expected during the lifetime of the universe – allowing for holidays. So jumps were for real.

The Crash wasn't good news for Markowitz's portfolio theory. Spreading your investment across the entire index was supposed to protect you because of diversification – the idea that different stocks would generally move in different directions, reducing volatility. That doesn't work when the entire index falls like a stone. Nor did buying foreign stocks help – they fell in price too.

And what about the elegance of random walks and efficient market theory? How did the flea get to vanquish the ant? It comes back to that other assumption – continuous markets and in particular, liquidity.

Most financial markets work in the same way. Buyers and sellers place orders, while the dealers in the middle – called 'market makers' – work to find a price at which a sale can take place. Once this is done, they take a commission, called a bid-ask spread. Historically, this was done face-to-face on an exchange; today it happens over computer networks.

In a normal market, if there are more sellers than buyers, market makers will mark down the prices to ensure a sale. The fall in prices attracts profit-hungry buyers into the market, and the balance of supply and demand is

---

1. There is still a debate over what was the right thing for the portfolio insurers to do. LOR stopped trading futures on 19 October, but its rival Wells Fargo Nikko continued and arguably lost less money for clients.

always restored. The willingness of these buyers, always looking for an easy profit, pumps liquidity into the market.

Liquidity is the lifeblood of any market. The futures speculators of nineteenth-century Chicago were initially welcomed because they provided liquidity in their eagerness to make a profit. The same speculators then became hate figures after greed got the better of them, and they started destroying liquidity with their dreaded 'corners'.

Liquidity depends on being able to buy and sell, but what if everyone decides to sell and no-one wants to buy? Sometimes, rather than seeing the decline in prices as an opportunity, the buyers see trouble. What if prices keep falling? So they sit and wait. Because there are no buyers, prices do keep falling – confirming the prophecy. By now, would-be buyers have joined the sellers and what started as a slight imbalance has become a rush to the exits.

As for the market makers, their books are suddenly full of unfulfilled sell orders. Normally, the exchange – whether for stocks, futures, currencies or commodities – will constantly monitor the imbalance between supply and demand for all the market makers, and adjust the price by the minimum amount, called a 'tick'. A tick is a single step in Bachelier's random walk.

But this is not a normal situation. A single tick isn't enough to account for the gaping hole in demand. When the price is finally marked down, it has jumped dozens or hundreds of ticks. On a time chart, the price looks like it has fallen off a cliff. What was a random walk has been turned into a downward jump by lack of liquidity. The flea has vanquished the ant.

That is what happened on Black Monday. If a market is the heart, where supply and demand sets prices in time-honoured Adam Smith fashion, and liquidity is the blood flowing through the heart, then Black Monday was a heart attack. The blood stopped flowing, and the heart stopped working.

This sudden loss of liquidity was bad enough for ordinary stock investors who could only sell at a large loss. In the futures market, it was worse. And for the portfolio insurers such as LOR whose business depended on being able to replicate options using delta hedging, it was disastrous.

One group of investors survived the Crash reasonably well. These were people who had actually bought the limited range of exchange-listed put options available at the time. Although the underlying stocks went down with the index, the option holders had a legal contract entitling them to sell at the original level. Ironically, LOR had just started a new strategy involving options before the Crash, but only three of its clients benefited.

Then the Brady report came out. It blamed the portfolio insurers for making the Crash worse, and recommended 'circuit breakers', to halt trading on both the stock and futures exchanges if the index fell too far in a day. With all the bad publicity, the aftermath for LOR and its competitors was a story of slow decline, as disappointed clients dropped away one by one.

As for Rubinstein, the thought that his computer program had crashed the global financial system sent him into a deep depression. He was unable to get out of bed for weeks.

The lesson was not lost on the wider investment community. From then on, they would demand contracts, not strategies, to protect their portfolios. In Europe, this would lead to the development of a great new market, and ultimately, one of LTCM's biggest trades.

How did financial theorists react to this event? Many treated the Crash as an inconvenience, and stuck to the assumptions that made their work easier. For others, 1987 sparked off a new wave of research into those monstrous events lurking in the tails of the Normal distribution. Yet the key lesson of the Crash – the problem of liquidity didn't sink in. That would have to wait another 11 years, until the summer of 1998.

Salad days at Salomon

Market crashes are like mass extinctions. Lines of business, and the characters that run them, disappear from the fossil record. New, formerly obscure areas rise into prominence. Just like the mammals that lived alongside the dinosaurs, these newcomers had always been there, but the decline of their rivals allows them to grow rapidly in size. That's what happened to John Meriwether and his followers.

It didn't seem like that on Black Monday. For the young academics Meriwether had brought onto the Salomon trading floor, the Crash was a terrifying experience. According to Eric Rosenfeld: 'I still remember sitting at the desk and wondering about the end of the whole financial system.' The panic in the stock market hurt the arbitrage group too. Its entire profit for the year – some $200 million – was wiped out in a few days.

John Meriwether was unfazed. He called his group into a meeting which went on late into the night. Rosenfeld recalls: 'He questioned you to the 10,000th detail about your positions.' Surrounded by the debris of take-away food boxes and coffee cups, Meriwether and his group worked out how to cut their loss-making trades. But Meriwether wouldn't stop there. He then told his bleary-eyed protégés to think up new trades, and make all that money back.

Traditionally, the bond markets do well when stocks tumble. And when a Judgement Day event like October 1987 happens, only the ironclad debt of the US government will do. Treasury bonds, with their topsy-turvy yields, may be a grey area most of the time, but in a crisis, investors seize them like life preservers. Much of this business was now flooding through Salomon Brothers. How could traders take advantage of the turmoil?

There are two sides to the story of what happened next. According to Meriwether and his protégés, Craig Coats Jr, arch-traditionalist and Meriwether's great rival, made the mistake of a lifetime. As head of government bond trading, it was up to Coats how Salomon should react to the crisis, and after conferring with Salomon's chairman, John Gutfreund, he did on a grand scale what everybody else was doing – he bought $2 billion worth of brand new 30-year Treasury bonds. As the bellwether of the US bond market, the 30-year had already gone up in price, and Coats expected this rise to continue.

Back in 1929, Coats's strategy would have been the right thing to do. After its initial crash in October that year, the Dow fell by even more over the next two years, ushering in the Great Depression. Unfortunately for Coats, this was 1987, and America had a secret weapon: Alan Greenspan. Today, the Fed chairman has a near-deity status in the financial world, but that October, he was an unknown quantity; he had been in the job only three months since replacing Paul Volcker in August.

After making a statement underlining the Fed's willingness to support the financial system, Greenspan quickly flooded Wall Street with money. Within a few weeks of the Crash, the panic subsided, setting the stage for a remarkable stock market recovery. The bad news for Coats – according to Meriwether – is that on-the-run Treasuries stopped rising in price and fell instead, resulting in a loss for Coats of $75 million.

Meriwether, however, had instructed his acolytes not to buy the sought-after new 30-year Treasury, but sell it short (a technique explained in Chapter 3) – while at the same time buying a matching quantity of cheaper $29\frac{3}{4}$-year Treasuries. This of course, was Meriwether's classic on-the-run/off-the-run trade. As an idea it was not new, but Meriwether now had such power at Salomon he was able to do the trade in a larger size than ever before.

Although the idea wasn't new, what made it different was the opportunity. The usual slight discrepancy between the prices of 30-year and $29\frac{3}{4}$-year bonds had ballooned in size. In the panic of Black Monday, there were few cool heads to reason that these two bonds were really worth the same. By the time prices converged again, Meriwether's group had made $50 million and would end the year with profits of $150 million.

The story told by Coats is very different. Coats says that he did buy $2 billion worth of Treasuries, but they had a variety of maturities and made a net profit for Salomon. The $29\frac{3}{4}$-year bond was being pushed up in price by Japanese investors fleeing their home market. A number of Salomon clients were short of this particular bond and now faced heavy losses. According to Coats, 'we used our capital get our clients out of his trade'. Sitting nearby, Meriwether's group learned what was going on and promptly bought the bond in order to 'front run' Coats's clients – or, in other words, exploit their misfortune.

Whatever actually happened, the episode was a watershed. There was now a wide-open rift at Salomon between Coats and Meriwether's protégés. Larry Hilibrand would later contemptuously compare Coats to a lab rat lost in a maze, while Coats would describe the group as parasites 'putting out tentacles' and exploiting privileged client information for their own ends. It was up to Gutfreund to choose between them and he supported Meriwether's group. Disheartened, Coats left the firm in 1988, complaining that Salomon was turning against its own clients.

The psychological effect on Meriwether's men was profound. They saw Coats's downfall as a vindication of their theories. Flaws in the assumptions of finance theory may have been disastrous for equities. The world's mightiest stock markets had stopped working, as liquidity vanished.

But the bond markets – in particular the trillions of dollars of ever-growing US government debt – remained a bottomless ocean of liquidity. Here also were the mathematically-exact relationships between bonds, from the simple ones Meriwether used to the far more complex connections that Eric Rosenfeld had noticed.

And now some of the liquidity that people took for granted in equities had drained out into the bond market, pushing prices in different directions. Mathematics would pull them back again. Meriwether's trade was a machine for extracting money out of this excess liquidity.

Over the next few years, with Gutfreund's support, the Salomon fixed-income arbitrage group would build a series of increasingly elaborate machines on Meriwether's foundations. These dazzling but invisible devices, when assembled together, were more than money-making machines. They were a money factory and they transformed Meriwether and his protégés into Wall Street legends.

In 1987, the core team was already in place. The head traders in Salomon's fixed income arbitrage group were Eric Rosenfeld, Larry Hilibrand, Victor

Haghani and Greg Hawkins, who had joined earlier that year from the mortgage bond trading desk.

After Coats's departure there was a round of promotions. Rosenfeld now became co-head of the bond arbitrage group. Working with Rosenfeld in a three-man triumvirate in charge of bond trading were Hilibrand and another Meriwether protégé, who took Coats's place, Paul Mozer. Together, they commanded a whole floor of traders.

It was a proud moment for Rosenfeld. Once he had been a hippie graduate student, now he was a star on Wall Street. One of the first things he did in 1988 was seek out his old mentor Robert Merton, and hire him as a special consultant to Salomon's chairman John Gutfreund.

While Merton had been Rosenfeld's mentor, Gutfreund had given Meriwether the crucial support he needed to rise at Salomon. Merton was flattered by the gesture:

> They made me an offer I couldn't refuse: unlike the simple model-building/product-design role of my past consultancies, this one also called for a role as trusted advisor (with technical skills) to the CEO on business matters of the firm and on the direction of institutional change in the global financial system. Over the next four years, I learned much about the operations and management of a global intermediary, and trust that I contributed something as well.

Hawkins and Haghani stayed on the arbitrage desk, along with Saman Majd and Bill Krasker. They continued to recruit new blood from the universities. As for Meriwether, he was already a board member, but now he became vice-chairman of Salomon, as well as being global head of fixed income and currency trading. There were now only two people above him in the firm – Thomas Strauss, Salomon's president, and John Gutfreund, its chairman.

Salomon had also recently acquired a new owner – the legendary investor Warren Buffett. A month before Black Monday, the Wall Street-driven takeover boom of the 1980s had finally reached Wall Street itself as corporate raider Ron Perelman prepared to make a bid for Salomon. Buffett stepped in at the last minute with a $700 million offer, becoming the firm's largest shareholder.

With his proverbial good timing, Buffett had taken money out of the top-heavy stock market and invested it in a company whose profits came largely from bonds. He supported Gutfreund, and in turn Gutfreund supported Meriwether. Meanwhile, the money-making machines were taking shape.

One such machine had been constructed by Greg Hawkins during his sojourn in the mortgage department. An expert on hidden options since completing his thesis with Merton on credit agreements, Hawkins started looking at mortgage-backed securities. Since Ginnie Mae began packaging home loans into bonds back in the 1970s, two more Federal agencies had joined the game: Fannie Mae and Freddie Mac. Taking advantage of this growing market, Salomon now ran one of the most successful mortgage bond trading desks on Wall Street.

Mortgage-backs work as a kind of funnel, transferring the monthly repayments from home owners into a coupon received by the bondholder. They are more complicated than ordinary bonds because some of the mortgages get repaid early, either when people move house, or when they refinance their borrowing.

Initially, issuers assumed that early repayments would happen at a constant rate, independently of the market, rather like how life insurance companies treat death rates. But when interest rates began falling in the early 1980s, home owners started taking advantage of their right to refinance at a lower rate. That unexpectedly lowered the value of mortgage bonds.

However, Hawkins had spotted a hidden option. He realised that the home owner's right to refinance was effectively an option on interest rates: if rates went up, they would stick with their current mortgage, and not exercise the option, but if rates fell, it would be in their interest to refinance. The premium of the option was buried in the coupon payment that went to the bondholders, to compensate them for giving home owners the right to prepay their mortgages.

Using the skills he'd picked up from Merton, Hawkins could price the options. But there was a snag – mortgage bonds might contain hundreds of individual mortgages which were all slightly different from each other. Taking over the Salomon mainframe computer, Hawkins priced all the options together and worked out what kind of coupon should be paid to bondholders.

However, in the real market these hidden options were overpriced. Not understanding the nature of the embedded options, investors demanded a much higher yield from the issuers than they needed to. Hawkins saw that his model could be turned into a money machine.

To construct his machine, Hawkins would buy up mispriced mortgage-backs, and replicate the bits and pieces inside them. Simplest of all was the interest rate exposure – the risk that a rise in interest rates would reduce the bond's value. To hedge the risk, Hawkins would sell Treasury bonds whose maturity matched the mortgage bond.

Then there was the danger of the yield curve steepening, which would also reduce the mortgage bond's value even if long-term rates stayed constant. Hawkins took care of this using interest rate swaps, which transformed some of the mortgage bond coupons into quarterly floating rate payments.

Finally, there were those hidden options to worry about. Since the owner of the bond had effectively *sold* these options to the issuer, the risk could be covered by buying Treasury bond options. Hawkins' computer model told him how many he needed to buy.

By now, Hawkins had created a mirror image of the mortgage bond, which hedged away all its hidden risks. The only thing left was the extra value – or *spread* – that investors demanded for holding the bond. So long as he didn't sell the bond too quickly, Hawkins could capture this spread as risk-free profit. This would become one of the group's most lucrative trades.

Another machine emerged from the fertile brain of Victor Haghani. Only 25-years old in 1987, and with no more than a Bachelor's degree from the LSE, what Haghani lacked in qualifications he made up for with sheer determination. After picking up the theory he needed from Rosenfeld and his old boss Martin Liebowitz, Haghani soon showed himself their equal.

His brainchild was conceived during his sojourn in Tokyo. A new type of bond had appeared in the early 1980s. Called a 'convertible bond', it had been invented as a response to the leveraged takeover boom that fuelled the pre-Black Monday bull market.

The takeovers worked on a simple principle: shareholder bribery. In return for backing the raider's scheme to seize control of a corporation, fire the management and strip out the assets for cash, the shareholders were rewarded with large dividends and skyrocketing share prices.

The takeover itself was financed with high-yielding debt, known as 'junk bonds'. Unfortunately, the new management in charge of some of these companies simply paid out all the assets to shareholders before going bust, leaving no assets left for the debtholders to claim after bankruptcy.

To keep nervous bond investors happy, the bankers came up with the convertible bond. A convertible started out looking like an ordinary bond, but after a certain time it could be converted into shares at a fixed price. Here was another hidden option – in this case a stock option which was embedded in the bond.

Convertibles quickly became popular in the US, but it was in Japan where Haghani saw the opportunity. On the surface, it was a leading free market economy, but underneath the surface Japan was different, driven by a culture of consensus and community. The Japanese government imposed strong restrictions on its leading companies, which were deeply enmeshed with each other through cross-ownership of shares.

With so much value tied up in mutual share ownership, a government priority was to keep share prices high. One way it did this was through keeping the supply of shares artificially low, by preventing companies making new issues. This posed a problem for the companies which wanted to raise equity capital. Convertible bonds were the answer.

However, the investor appetite for Japanese convertibles was tiny. The demand was swamped by supply, and the price fell. This is what Haghani noticed. Working with Salomon's Tokyo trading chief Sugar Miyojin, Haghani bought as many convertibles as he could get his hands on. He then broke the bond down into all its component parts.

The coupon paid by the bond would be stripped away using an interest rate swap, which transformed it into a floating rate payment. Since the bond had been paid for using borrowed floating rate money, this eliminated any interest rate exposure from Haghani's book.

Then there was that hidden option to worry about, which Haghani owned. What he did was sell an over-the-counter stock option exactly equivalent to the one embedded in the bond. On the open market, such an option would be priced using a Black–Scholes model which took into account the volatility of the Japanese stock. Haghani would receive fair value for this sale.

Meanwhile, the hidden option had not been priced at all. It was merely a giveaway designed to get round government rules. By now, Haghani had 'locked in' the free money in the convertible, and with his money machine he would make hundreds of millions of dollars for Salomon.

For Haghani's and Hawkins's money machines to work, they needed some seed money to start them off. The mispriced bond would have to be purchased before it could be stripped down and milked for profit. However, you might need to own billions of dollars worth just to extract a few million.

The most obvious way to buy bonds is to pay cash. That is how 'real' investors like pension funds purchase their assets, using their members' money. When a fund talks about having billions under management, it is talking about things it actually owns. These bonds will sit on the books until they mature.

But an arbitrage trader like Victor Haghani doesn't want to own bonds for twenty years like a pension fund. He wants to do a hit-and-run raid on a mispriced security, then dump it after he has squeezed out the profit. And Salomon Brothers only has a limited amount of dollars to throw around. It isn't in the business of sitting on bonds.

In the 1980s, an ingenious way of owning bonds without physically purchasing them was invented. It is called 'repo'. Short for repurchase agreement, a repo is a simple transaction between dealers at two different banks. It works like this. Imagine that Haghani wants to buy a billion dollar bond at an auction. He bids for it and gets it.

There is a small problem – he hasn't got a billion dollars. So he phones up Goldman Sachs' repo desk and asks the dealer if he can repo the bond. 'No problem' replies the dealer, who immediately wires a billion dollars to Haghani. Haghani then pays for the bond and promptly delivers it to Goldman. No actual cash or certificates change hands; the whole transaction is done electronically in a few seconds over computer terminals.

But what has actually happened? Through Haghani's trade, Salomon Brothers owns the bond, and receives the interest coupon payments from the issuer. As a result, it is exposed to the risk that changes in interest rates could lower the bond's value.

Goldman, on the other hand, has lent Salomon a billion dollars, but isn't worried because it holds Haghani's billion dollar bond as secure collateral. Since Goldman knows that it can sell the bond itself if Salomon goes bust, Haghani only has to pay a risk-free floating rate of interest for the loan.

Goldman doesn't bear any interest rate risk on the deal, because the repo agreement stipulates that it will receive its billion dollars back, plus interest. Since it is essentially a low risk lending business, repo is run as a separate business from bond trading proper.

The repurchase part comes when Haghani sells the bond: once he receives payment, Haghani then returns the billion dollars to Goldman, repurchasing his bond which he then immediately delivers to the buyer. Although it looks like a collateralised loan, a repo is legally a sale and repurchase, so repoed bonds in effect have more than one owner.

If Haghani wants to sell a bond he doesn't own, repo makes that easy too. He finds a buyer willing to pay a billion dollars for a bond. He calls Goldman again; this time they will lend a bond to him. Taking the buyer's money, Haghani wires it to Goldman, receiving the bond in return, which he delivers to the buyer.

Goldman doesn't worry about its bond going astray, because it is sitting on a billion dollars, and pays a floating rate of interest to Haghani for this privilege. At the end of the deal, Haghani buys the bond back again on the open market, and delivers it to Goldman, in return for his billion dollars – which he uses to settle this second transaction. From Haghani's point of view, this is called a 'reverse repo'.

Repo had a dynamic effect on the bond market, because it allowed dealers to control far more assets than they could buy with their available capital. In our examples above, the rise or fall in a bond's value between the time of purchase and that of repurchase accounts for all of Haghani's cashflow.

In other words, repo allows leverage. Of course, leverage is not new in banking and finance. A high street bank takes deposits from savers, and lends out most of the money to borrowers.

Futures are another example of leverage. Anyone capable of keeping up with the exchange's margin payments can control large quantities of assets, whether wheat or Treasury bonds. Although the physical assets are often not involved in the transaction, the leverage is still there.

However, high street banking and futures markets are different from repo because at least in the latter half of the twentieth century, they have been tightly regulated. We have already seen how the nineteenth century free-for-all in the Chicago pits was curtailed by legislation. As for high street banks, most governments protect their savers through deposit insurance: if a bank goes bankrupt, at least part of their savings will be paid back by the government.

Repo was different. It started out as a wholesale, over-the-counter business in Treasury bonds conducted between investment banks, and was essentially unregulated. Because it was in everyone's mutual interest for the system to work, it did. As more and more dealers used the system, it became possible for single bonds to change hands dozens of times.

In the example above, once Haghani had repoed his bond with Goldman, there was nothing to stop Goldman repoing the bond with another firm – say, Bear Stearns – and then using the cash to buy another bond. Bear Stearns could do the same thing. Several houses might have billion dollar bets on the same bond, and the effects of price changes were now magnified across Wall Street.

Swaps had the same effect. They allowed bets on whether floating rates would match longer-dated fixed interest rates without bothering to own a bond or deposit account at all. In this sense, they went beyond repo.

With tools like repo, swaps and futures allowing big trades to be done, Meriwether demanded equally big profits from his traders. Each one would have to make at least $60 million a year for the firm in order to keep his job. For those former academics used to living in an abstract world, the pressure was intense.

A bystander recalls watching Costas Kaplanis, a London-based arbitrage trader who had just joined Salomon from the London Business School. Kaplanis had designed a money machine to take advantage of the UK Gilt market, but on the morning he was due to actually execute the trade, he appeared sick with fear and could barely pick up the phone. Needless to say, the trade made the profit Kaplanis had predicted.

Arbitrage was having an effect on Salomon itself. By 1990, the firm's balance sheet swelled above $150 billion dollars in size, most of it in the form of repoed government bonds. Like an inverted pyramid, this balance sheet sat on top of only $4 billion of equity capital – the value of Salomon's shares, added together. But Salomon was more than just a factory for Meriwether's money machines.

As a leading Wall Street securities firm, Salomon did a great deal besides bond arbitrage: it had a global client business. There were many aspects to this business. Salomon issued new bonds for companies, and marketed them to investors. It traded bonds on its clients' behalf. Salomon also had an equities division, issuing and trading shares. Every week, it would send out research reports to clients giving tips on all these markets.

Unlike arbitrage, this was much more like an ordinary business. Salomon had to compete with its rivals on the basis of price and quality of service. While bond arbitrage only employed about 100 people worldwide, Salomon's client business had over 6000 staff spread across the globe.

By the standards of most people on the planet, any Wall Street dealer or analyst makes a fortune. But ever since hominids started banding together on the African savannah millions of years ago, relative status has been important. And Wall Street is a highly status-conscious place.

By 1990, Salomon's arbitrage business was generating the same earnings – about $1 billion a year – as its client business. In accordance with standard business practice, Salomon would deduct a fraction from these earnings – perhaps a third – to cover its overheads, then pay the rest as a dividend to shareholders.

On Wall Street, by far the most important overheads are salaries. You don't have to be Robert Merton to figure out that a third of a billion dollars divided between 100 people is going to seem a lot more impressive than the same fraction divided between 6000.

This arrangement was formalised by Meriwether in 1989, when he cut a deal with Strauss and Gutfreund to pay his arbitrage traders 15 per cent of their profits as a bonus. Since individual traders were by now making hundreds of millions in profits, the result was predictable. Mild-mannered ex-professors like Greg Hawkins were suddenly earning as much as Tom Cruise. In 1990, Hilibrand became famous for earning a $23 million bonus.

By 1992, Victor Haghani would celebrate his 30th birthday with a single $25 million payment – a reward for his Japanese convertible trades.

Among the client dealers and analysts who were 'only' making $1 million a year, this was a recipe for resentment. Hilibrand didn't endear himself to this faction when he campaigned to have Salomon's sumptuous dining room shut down on the grounds that it didn't contribute to his profits. But with the chairman firmly backing Meriwether, and the shareholders applauding the earnings squeezed from the markets by the money machines, the client employees could only mutter to themselves.

Yet the arbitrage traders needed the client dealers. The reason was information. It was all very well to scour the market for mispriced bonds and invent money machines, but a growing part of the market was largely invisible even to the most eagle-eyed arbitrage trader. This of course, was the OTC derivatives market, in particular the world of interest rate options.

Back in the early 1980s, swaps were a novelty, and interest options were puzzles best left to the likes of Fischer Black. By 1990, the market was growing at a dizzy rate. There were various reasons.

Loans had become deeply unfashionable, both internationally, because developing countries were defaulting on them, and in the US, where the S&L crisis was in full swing. The problems had become so bad that in 1988, an international conclave of central bankers, the Basle Committee on Banking Supervision, had stipulated that henceforth, all banks would have to stump up 8 per cent in reserve capital for every loan on their books.

Interest rate swaps, on the other hand, required virtually no capital at all. Because they were off-balance sheet, regulators were still largely ignorant. Tax authorities had no clue. Yet swaps allowed billions of dollars to be switched around at the drop of a hat. Corporate America was starting to get the message.

With swaps came options. In the US, interest rates had been falling ever since Paul Volcker's drastic inflation-cutting measures back in 1981. Companies who borrowed in this environment wanted to 'lock in' the existing rate, while taking advantage of subsequent falls. Options, in particular interest rate caps, fitted the bill.

For investors entering the market, declining rates posed another problem. Each year, Treasury bonds, the benchmark for the entire fixed income market, yielded less and less. The investors wanted a way of making their investments look prettier compared to what everyone else was buying.

The solution was to sell options at the same time as buying a bond. The complete package was called a callable bond, since the issuer had the right to buy it back at face value if interest rates went down below a certain level. The investor was compensated for granting this right by an extra-large coupon on the bond. As for the issuer, which would be a company like Ford or IBM, they weren't interested in owning such an option – called a swaption – and they would sell it on to the banks.

At Salomon Brothers, the head of derivatives marketing, Dick Leahy, was at the centre of this business, along with his star salesman, Arjun Krishnamachar. Neither man had an academic background; like Meriwether, both had come from business schools – Wall Street's version of vocational training. Yet because they met real customers – the ultimate supply and demand everyone depended on – they had some insights to share. Meriwether introduced Leahy to Eric Rosenfeld and his fellow professors.

The story Leahy told was simple. On one side, customers were demanding interest rate caps, pushing the price above what the Black–Scholes formula said it should be. On the other side, callable bond issuers were eager to sell off their swaptions, pushing that price down.

Many rival firms didn't see any connection between these two markets, and traded them separately. At Salomon, the only people that knew how to trade these options were Rosenfeld, Hawkins and other members of the arbitrage group. Acting on Leahy's tip-off, Rosenfeld gave the problem to Bill Krasker.

The solution to the problem lay on the cutting edge of financial theory. We have seen how back in 1977, Oldrich Vasicek found a way of integrating random walks into the yield curve, like tying a bluebottle to a piece of string. Since then, a succession of quants had improved on Vasicek's model.

Caps could be priced by these models. Being options on the short-term floating rate, you tied the bluebottle to the short end of the curve, and then summed over paths on a tree, in classic Feynman style. Swaptions were options on a longer-term rate, so you would tie the bluebottle further along the curve and let it buzz there.

But none of these models was good enough to handle the caps and swaptions at the same time, although some academics were getting close. What Krasker did was find a way of tying two bluebottles to the yield curve, which would now be influenced by two independent random walks.

The problem was incredibly complex. The tree needed to sum up the possible paths was so tangled and twisted that a new technique called 'Monte Carlo' had to be used, which involved programming the computer to throw a dice and pick out a few paths at random. Yet Krasker solved it, and found a way of replicating the two options simultaneously. Rosenfeld could then instruct his traders how to construct a money machine and make that all-important risk-free profit.

The moral was clear: talking to clients provided vital intelligence about what the market was doing. But to suggest – like Coats – that arbitrage traders were taking advantage would be untrue, according to Saman Majd:

> When I joined, all interest rate options were traded by the arbitrage desk. There just wasn't the expertise in other areas to trade government bond options, caps, swaptions, whatever it was. That's what I did as a member of that desk. I traded those things, I had a proprietary perspective on it. But I was also the place where salesmen would come to get a price on anything. So I would argue that the activities of the group helped build the customer franchise.

Scandal

By early 1991, John Meriwether could afford to relax at last. With his protégés earning billions a year for Salomon, Meriwether was being tipped as Gutfreund's successor for the top job. And if his protégés were earning movie star bonuses, Meriwether was getting even more.

He had married his wife Mimi Murray a few years earlier; she was a former Olympic-standard showjumper. The couple bought a 43-acre property in Westchester County, north of Manhattan, where they could keep horses, and Meriwether paid for a large covered paddock where Mimi could practice her skills. Then there was golf. Meriwether had come a long way since he had caddied as a twelve-year old.

He could now flash membership cards to some of the top country clubs in the US. Locally, he played at the Winged Foot and Shinnecock clubs in New York and, if the weather spoilt his swing, he would fly to the Cypress Point club near Pebble Beach, California.

But being a mere member was no longer enough for Meriwether. He decided to buy his own golf course, back in the 'old country' of Ireland. The place he chose was Waterville, a top-rated course with a Georgian clubhouse on the wild coast of County Kerry. Some of his colleagues at Salomon put in money too.

For the bond arbitrage group, a yearly ritual began. Every summer, Meriwether would fly the traders out to Waterville for a week of eating, drinking and golf. It was a chance to let the hair down, and Meriwether led the way. One story has the group visiting a local seafood restaurant, which had live lobsters in a tank.

On a whim, Meriwether bought up all the lobsters. Clearing a banqueting table, he then taped numbers to the lobsters' backs and organised a race. The Salomon traders were expected to place large bets on their favourites, while Meriwether called out the progress of the race in the style of a racetrack commentator.

But it would have spoiled the fun that day had Meriwether known what was about to happen. His career would suffer a near fatal blow, and he would be forced out of the investment bank that had treated him so well. The reason lay close at hand, in the form of Meriwether's number one bond trader, Paul Mozer.

The adjective 'aggressive' is common on Wall Street. It's considered a positive quality, particularly for traders. So when traders themselves universally describe Mozer as being aggressive, then something extreme is going on.

As a member of Meriwether's arbitrage group, Mozer appears to have enjoyed taking on the 'dirty' jobs, which required brawn but little brain. These jobs had a shady nature. It began back in 1986, when the head of Salomon's tax department, Saul Rosen, asked Mozer to help solve a tricky little problem.

A company earning billions a year would be expected, at first sight, to be paying many millions a year in taxes. The job of accountants and tax experts is to do their utmost to ensure that 'earnings' is as tiny a number as possible, usually by finding 'losses' to set against them. This was Rosen's task at Salomon.

However, what Mozer agreed to do was illegal. He created losses from thin air. Mozer did special deals with other firms, whereby Salomon would sell off certain Treasury bond positions at a loss. After a decent time interval, Salomon would buy the positions back again, getting compensation from the other firms for any price change during the time interval. By 1991 Mozer had concealed $168 million of earnings in this way.

But that was nothing compared to what Mozer would do on his own initiative. According to former colleagues, the problem started in 1988 when Mozer inherited Coats's old job. Far from welcoming the promotion, Mozer was infuriated at being excluded from the bonus bonanza being enjoyed by the arbitrage group. How could he fight back? As part of his new job Mozer was responsible for Salomon bidding at Treasury bond auctions operated by the New York Fed. Being the biggest bond house on Wall Street, Salomon invariably bought up the lion's share at these auctions. Now Mozer bought even more to try and work the market to his advantage. Given that half a trillion dollars worth of bonds passed through the auctions every year, there were high stakes involved.

The Treasury wasn't happy with this situation. Its job was to sell US government bonds at the highest prices possible. But with Salomon dominating the market, prices stayed low. In yield-goggle terms, that translates into higher interest rates that US taxpayers must pay on their debt. So in 1989, the Treasury stipulated that no more than 35 per cent of its bonds could be bought by a single buyer.

Mozer's response was to break the law again. He not only would bid for the entire 35 per cent he was allowed, but also submitted false bids on behalf of Salomon clients. Once the false bid had gone through, Mozer would transfer the bonds into the Salomon account.

By doing this, Mozer could increase profits and earn a bigger bonus. But there was another, more sinister side to Mozer's strategy. Dominating the Treasury auctions allowed him to manipulate prices in an attempt to drive Salomon's competitors – particularly Goldman Sachs – out of the arbitrage business.

Indirect evidence comes from the repo market. During 1989 and 1990, the repo market in on-the-run Treasuries was frequently 'on special', which means that a shortage of supply made physically holding the Treasuries particularly valuable. This usually happens when large numbers of players have sold Treasuries short, and the need to buy and deliver the securities creates a shortage and drives up the price.

Most bond arbitrage trades involve heavily shorting liquid, on-the-run securities, and by 1990 many firms were catching up with Salomon and doing just that. But by grabbing all of the available supply from the auctions, Mozer was able to squeeze Salomon's competitors who would be forced to buy from him at inflated prices, thus losing millions on their short positions.

Mozer did this during December 1990 and February 1991. After that second auction, things began to go wrong. The Fed asked why the British investment bank S.G. Warburg had submitted two bids; one for itself, and one through Salomon, that took it over the 35 per cent limit. Mozer told the Fed that the Salomon bid was a clerical error, and urged the Warburg traders not to tell the Fed anything. But the writing was on the wall.

In April, a panic-stricken Mozer went to Meriwether and told him everything. This meeting would change Meriwether's life. Hearing Mozer out, Meriwether told him that his actions were 'career threatening' and immediately brought the news to Gutfreund and Strauss.

What happened next has remained a mystery. Despite Meriwether's grim assessement, and despite being advised by Salomon's in-house lawyer to sack Mozer and immediately tell the Fed, Gutfreund and Strauss did nothing. They waited until the beginning of August before finally suspending Mozer and issuing a press release.

On 13 August, the New York Fed president Gerry Corrigan fired off an angry letter to Gutfreund demanding an explanation and hinting at possible sanctions against Salomon. Meanwhile, Salomon's share price started plummeting, and more disturbingly, investors started dumping the firm's debt. This meant that Salomon's huge edifice of repo trades and short-term debt might collapse.

As Salomon's biggest shareholder, Warren Buffett became involved. To save the firm, Gutfreund and Strauss were ousted, and Buffett agreed to step in as chairman. Meriwether was the next target. All those in Salomon's client business who had resented the gargantuan bonuses of the arbitrage group started urging Buffett to sack Meriwether. Buffett was unsure, but then Meriwether resigned anyway. He would never work at Salomon again.

Worse was to come from Corrigan. Not getting a satisfactory response from Gutfreund, he delivered a bombshell: Salomon would be banned from bidding in Treasury auctions. In the nick of time, Buffett managed to get the decision rescinded, and so saved Salomon from bankruptcy.

In the aftermath of the scandal, the SEC investigated the culprits. Mozer was fined and banned for life from working in a securities firm, along with Gutfreund and Strauss. Although he was charged, Mozer did not actually spend any time in jail for his crime. Today, the Fed downplays the crisis. 'All he did was lie on a government form' one official told me. Salomon itself had to pay $100 million in fines, and a further $100 million in compensation to shareholders.

Meriwether contested his case, and ultimately settled with the SEC for a three-month ban and a $50,000 fine. As a man used to being in control, Meriwether was devastated, and in a rare interview afterwards, he for once expressed his feelings. 'I'm a fairly shy, introspective person. But I became front-page news. I was in the wrong place at the wrong time. If you are in Alaska and you look to the right and see a bear cub and look to the left and see a mother bear, that's exactly how I felt. There's no weapon that will prevent you from going down.'

6

The Dream Team

When today's associate professor of security analysis is asked, 'Young man, if you're so smart, why ain't you rich?', he replies by laughing all the way to the bank or to his appointment as a high-paid consultant to Wall Street.
Paul Samuelson, introducing Robert Merton's *Continuous Time Finance*

Robert Merton had had a vision. Like something out of the Bible, it suggested an elaborate, invisible structure climbing upwards into the sky. Small figures worked tirelessly to build Merton's structure, which stretched not towards Heaven, but to Kenneth Arrow's complete market utopia. Merton called it the financial innovation spiral.

The vision was a testament to Merton's life's work. At the base of the spiral were Merton, Black and Scholes pricing options for the first time at the end of the 1960s. Then came the pit traders of the CBOE, putting their ideas into action.

On another part of the spiral were Merton's former students at Salomon Brothers, hunting for hidden options to make an arbitrage profit. Above them were the growing markets in interest rate options, thriving on the liquidity provided by the arbitrage desks. Remaining at the base of the spiral, allowing new derivatives to be hedged, the pit traders served as a foundation for these new markets.

The pattern on the spiral was always the same: a constant switching back-and-forth from banks and universities where innovation happened, to markets where the new products were 'commoditised', becoming cheaper and more accessible. The new markets then became the basis for a further generation of more sophisticated products, and the spiral would continue upwards.

As Merton first articulated his vision during the late 1980s, a further insight came to him. While the spiral's structure remained fixed, the figures who built it kept changing. The purpose of the spiral was to transfer risk in some way – to provide options to protect share portfolios, for example – but it left the issue of who provided this service wide open.

In the past, scholars of finance had assumed that specific institutions always provided certain services. As Merton pointed out, this wasn't necessarily true. In the 1960s, individual investors bought stocks directly from the market via brokers. In the 1970s, mutual funds took over this function. By the 1980s, exchange-listed index futures and options were transferring this function back to the market.

Merton called his idea the 'functional perspective' to distinguish it from the traditional 'institutional perspective'. What was important was the function, not the institution that did it. Today, with the Internet reshaping the business landscape, we no longer associate specific services with bricks-and-mortar institutions, but ten years ago, the vision was a prescient one.

The spiral of innovation was more than just a linking together of events in financial history. It was a philosophy of money machines. The inefficiencies, frictions and irrational sentiments that pulled prices out of line and made arbitrage possible were constantly getting ironed out with each turn of the spiral. Taking your profits, you then built new machines with the next generation of financial tools, and so on.

In other words, by hitching your wagon to the arbitrage horse, you would be pulled along by a force of history itself. You couldn't lose. No wonder that Merton's disciples believed in the spiral with quasi-religious fervour.

As for Merton, he had come a long way since his days as a drag-racing teenage tearaway. In 1988 he had left MIT and moved to the Harvard Business School, that seminary of US capitalism. Finding good case studies for his new students to analyse wasn't a problem – Merton could always hop on a plane down to Salomon Brothers to watch his ex-students in action.

On moving to Harvard, Merton proceeded to celebrate his own life's work with a book, *Continuous Time Finance*. A compendium of his most important papers, including his PhD work with Paul Samuelson and his key option pricing paper, the book also showcased Merton's new vision.

The book's painstakingly prepared bibliography showed Merton's place at the heart of the academic finance community. There were the obvious references to Samuelson, Fama, Black and Scholes, along with newer arrivals to the subject like Stephen Ross and John Cox.

But like a father recounting his children's accomplishments, Merton took particular care to list papers by his former students and disciples who were now making a name on Wall Street. Eric Rosenfeld and Greg Hawkins both made an appearance in the bibliography, together with Saman Majd. Other names such as Chi-Fu Huang and David Modest were obscure when the book was published, but by 1998 they would be unwillingly thrust into the limelight.

At the end of his book, Merton went for the high ground: policy issues like pensions and deposit insurance for banks were trawled for hidden options, and the shimmering vision of the financial innovation spiral was revealed. The social and economic problems of the future, suggested Merton, might better be solved by foregoing the cosy security of institutions in favour of shadowy new 'intermediaries' who could do the job more efficiently.

But who were these intermediaries? The underlying mechanism of Merton's spiral was, as always, arbitrage, which enforced cheap pricing. Unlike the angels on Jacob's ladder, the figures climbing up Merton's spiral were Larry Hilibrand and Victor Haghani. The cynical view was that by allowing Haghani and his cohorts to make $20 or $30 million a year, your grandmother might earn an extra $10,000 on her pension.

Among the economic mandarins who actually set policy, Merton's vision had the whiff of brimstone about it. Worse still, they didn't even take it seriously. Lawrence Summers, who would eventually become US Treasury Secretary, summed up this view when he referred to arbitrage as 'ketchup economics'. It was, he said, no more profound than saying that a bottle of ketchup equalled two half-bottles. 'Real economics' was equivalent to asking how the ketchup was made from tomatoes.

Such dismissals infuriated Merton. He wanted to prove how important his vision was, and demonstrate its power to the world. However, in 1991, Merton's best shot at the corridors of power suffered a blow. He was 'special consultant to the office of the Chairman' at Salomon Brothers; suddenly the chairman, namely John Gutfreund, along with Thomas Strauss and John Meriwether, had lost their jobs.

While Warren Buffett himself took over Gutfreund's title as chairman, this was only a back seat role. Gutfreund's replacement as CEO was Deryck Maughan, an investment banker in the classic British mould who had once worked at the UK Treasury. Neither Buffett nor Maughan were particularly interested in the oracular musings of a Harvard finance professor.

As far as Merton could see, the only senior banker who understood his vision was John Meriwether — who had sponsored him at Salomon. Where

Meriwether went, Merton would surely follow, and in 1992 he resigned from his position.

Myron Scholes was another case in point. A year before the Treasury auction scandal, Meriwether had brought Scholes in as yet another special consultant, this time to Salomon's fixed income division.

Since his discovery of the option pricing formula with Fischer Black all those years before, Scholes had taken the opposite path to Merton. While Merton increasingly cast himself as the visionary philosopher of finance theory, Scholes was worried about nuts and bolts. Stephen Ross describes Scholes: 'Myron is motivated by the real world he lives in, more than Bob is. Myron's not without his visions, but is much more interested in taking the vision and making it work. He's like an auto mechanic.'

But what was in Scholes's toolkit? Since moving from the University of Chicago to California's Stanford in 1983, Scholes had focused on one area of small print underlying his formula, namely the assumption of no taxes. But Scholes went far beyond merely tweaking his option formula.

Merton's mantra was 'assume markets are continuous and frictionless'. However, in the world of Scholes, taxes, like death, were inevitable. For investors maximising the gains on portfolios, and for companies raising capital with equity and bonds, the only possibility was to reduce taxes rather than assume they didn't exist.

We have already seen how the desire to avoid taxes at all cost helped to destroy the career of Paul Mozer. Scholes wanted to put tax avoidance on a respectable footing by deploying the benefits of financial theory. With such insights at your disposal, he reasoned, breaking the law should no longer be necessary to reduce your tax bill.

To distinguish his ideas from those of Mozer, Scholes talked of 'tax planning' as opposed to avoidance. And nothing suited Scholes's purposes better than the growing market in swaps and other OTC derivatives. With the ability to discreetly shift assets and liabilities off balance sheet – and back on again – income could become capital gains and vice versa. The possibilities were endless, and the tax authorities didn't have a clue.

From being rigid facts of life to be memorised by accountants, the tax treatment of different types of asset and cash flow now became 'inefficiencies' that could be easily by-passed with the help of a friendly client derivatives desk. These differences in tax treatment were often the sole reason for price differences between one type of bond and another. That attracted arbitrage desks (such as Salomon's) who in turn provided liquidity for the client derivatives business.

Working as a consultant at Salomon, Scholes was enthralled to see his ideas in action. As he put it in his own understated manner, 'My interests shifted back to the role of derivatives in financial intermediation.' Instead of remaining semi-detached, like Merton, in late 1990 Scholes accepted Meriwether's offer of a full time job as co-head of fixed income derivative sales and trading – although Scholes took care to hang on to his job as a Stanford professor too.

However, Scholes had not been in his new post for long when the Treasury auction scandal erupted, and Meriwether departed. In the days of the scandal, Salomon was one intermediary the world felt it could do without.

Not only did investors flood the market with unwanted Salomon bonds which they expected to go into default, but clients also wanted to cancel their derivatives contracts with the firm. With such high-profile swap clients on its books like IBM and the Kingdom of Denmark, Salomon faced a catastrophic decline in revenues.

Why did the clients want to get out? If Salomon went bust, the firm might renege on any derivative contract where it owed money. Such a danger is called counterparty risk. For futures and options traded on exchanges, this risk isn't a problem, because the exchange itself is on the other side of every trade. There is usually a special insurance policy in place to make sure that all contracts are honoured.

Over-the-counter derivatives offer no protection if one side of the deal goes bankrupt. As well as options, swap contracts, where payments were exchanged in both directions, could have a considerable value at certain times, depending on the level of interest rates. Although the big investment banks that devise derivatives contracts don't go bankrupt very often, a small amount of counterparty risk is always there.

Although the auction scandal soon passed, and the market regained confidence in Salomon again, Scholes pondered the issue. How could Salomon's counterparties be reassured? What they wanted was the promise of liquidity – the ability to turn their derivatives contracts quickly into cash if Salomon was in trouble. If that peace of mind was there, then Salomon would attract more customers to its derivatives business.

The riskiness of default is traditionally assessed by credit rating agencies such as Standard & Poor's or Moody's Investor Services, which after conducting extensive research into a company, assign letter codes to its debt. In terms of creditworthiness, the very best rating is triple-A, which is assigned to governments like the United States, and a few massively rich companies.

However, to win such a high rating, a company must be awash with capital at all times – not a practical proposition for a leveraged firm like Salomon Brothers. To protect its derivative clients, all Salomon needed was enough capital for them to cash in their contracts during a crisis. As Scholes would later comment after the LTCM crisis, this was equivalent to owning an option to supply liquidity and could be extremely valuable.

Ironically, such an option wasn't available on the market – it had to be created dynamically. Scholes's solution was to create a special entity, called Salomon Swapco, which was carefully ring-fenced from Salomon proper. Clients would do their deals with Swapco, which would always have just enough cash sitting in its accounts so that, in the event of Salomon losing its credit rating, the derivatives could be cashed out within two weeks. This was enough to convince the credit rating agencies to award Swapco the coveted triple-A rating it needed.

The creation of Swapco in 1992 – which was imitated by other firms – established Scholes's reputation as a doer as well as a thinker. Yet, like Merton, Scholes felt closer to Meriwether than any of the other Salomon apparatchiks. Both of them wanted to work with the man who understood their ideas better than any other senior figure in the industry. So what was Meriwether doing?

Brave new world

With his three-month SEC-imposed ban ending in December 1991, Meriwether at first seemed likely to return to Salomon. After all, he was Gutfreund's crown prince, and was highly popular within the firm. But Maughan didn't want him back. Determined to build his own power base within Salomon, Maughan would only offer Meriwether a post with diminished responsibility. Meriwether said no.

If there was one man who could have brought Meriwether back, it was Warren Buffett. While Meriwether has always insisted that Buffett had regretted his resignation in 1991, Buffett didn't lift a finger to bring Meriwether back to Salomon afterwards. As far as Buffett was concerned, the old vice-chairman's connection to Mozer made him tainted goods.

What about joining another investment bank? The problem was that Meriwether's style was too idiosyncratic. The Salomon bond arbitrage operation was a legend on Wall Street but where else could it fit in? Commercial banks couldn't trade bonds in the US – that ruled them out.

The other big securities firms apart from Salomon were Morgan Stanley, Merrill Lynch and Goldman Sachs. The first two were still some way behind in terms of sophistication. Goldman was catching up, due to the efforts of Meriwether's old classmate from Chicago Business School, Jon Corzine. By hiring people from Salomon, Corzine was starting to replicate what Salomon had been doing, but wanted to do it his way. So there was no place for Meriwether at Goldman either.

Moreover, Meriwether didn't want to be part of a big institution any more. Although the customer businesses at Salomon had been useful to the arbitrage desk, the responsibility of dealing with 6000 employees didn't entice him. Nor was he interested in socialising with important clients or any of the routine tasks expected from a senior investment banker.

Taking time to improve his golf during the summer of 1992, Meriwether started weighing up all the ideas and advice coming from his friends. There was Merton, saying that on his heavenly spiral, the function performed was more important than the institution that performed it. There was also Scholes, who had rolled up his sleeves and shown how to set up a special trading entity and protect it against liquidity.

Then there was James McEntee, who was Meriwether's constant companion on the green. Close friends since Meriwether's early years at Salomon, the duo spent that summer jetting back and forth between race meetings and golf courses, from New York state, to California, and then to Ireland.

A Bronx native, McEntee had started trading bonds while still taking classes at Fordham University, and at the tender age of 23 had formed his own government bond dealership, Carroll McEntee McGinley. Although dwarfed by the likes of Salomon Brothers, the company had been a highly successful niche player, and was eventually bought by Marine Midland bank, bringing McEntee a handsome profit.

McEntee played the court jester to Meriwether's prince. When Myron Scholes joined the pair that summer on one of his first ever golf trips, McEntee teased the bookish novice mercilessly, later commenting: 'Myron read 100 books about it to figure out the physics of the swing.' But the prince himself still lacked a kingdom. Yet, if McEntee could set up a thriving company from scratch, why not Meriwether?

By late 1992, Meriwether had thought up a plan of action. There would be no more dreaded 'customers' and no more corporate bureaucracy. Investors were necessary, but would be kept at arm's length. The tight-knit blood brotherhood that Meriwether had created at Salomon would be created anew. Meriwether had decided to set up a hedge fund.

The roots of hedge funds lie in an obscure law passed by the US Congress in 1940, called the Investment Company Act. The Act was mostly concerned with protecting small investors against being ripped off by crooked mutual fund managers claiming to be whiz-kids of the stock market.

With the Crash of 1929 still on everyone's mind in 1940, the foremost concern was to ensure that all mutual funds were tightly regulated by the SEC and other government agencies. But as an afterthought, the Washington lawmakers decided to make an exception to the rule.

If an investor was wealthy enough, reasoned the lawmakers, surely they didn't need the government interfering in what they did with their money. The lawmakers decided that by wealthy, they meant anyone with more than a million dollars to their name. Discreet fund managers who only dealt with fewer than 100 such investors and didn't advertise would be largely exempt from the rules, save for some cursory reporting requirements.

With the excitement of the Second World War diverting peoples' attention, it was not until 1949 that someone took advantage of this special loophole. That man was a journalist called Alfred Winslow Jones, and he called his investment company a 'hedge fund' because it would not just buy the stocks it liked, but it would also sell stocks short that it felt were overvalued. Since it was 'hedged' in this way, the fund was less susceptible to big market moves than traditional funds.

Jones didn't sell his investment skills cheaply. He stipulated that his wealthy investors would not only pay him and his fund managers a 1 per cent annual fee to stay in the fund, but would also pay 20 per cent of the profits generated. They didn't seem to mind. Jones commented: 'The way I like to put it, is that the investors get 80 per cent of the rewards, and that's made them happy.' These terms would become the standard for hedge funds.

After Jones had paved the way, hedge funds started popping up like mushrooms. By 1968, there were 120 of them. In the 1970s, chafing against banking restrictions and high taxes, many wealthy investors shifted money to offshore centres, such as the Cayman Islands in the Caribbean, where taxes and financial regulation were non-existent. Hedge funds began to move offshore too.

But it was not until 1992 that they first captured the popular imagination. And that was the doing of the most famous hedge fund manager of them all, George Soros.

A Hungarian emigrant who ended up in New York, Soros started the Quantum Fund in the late 1960s. As a result of Soros's knack for judging the behaviour of markets, the fund grew steadily over the following 20 years until it was worth billions of dollars. Soros had a particular genius for intuiting the economic factors underlying foreign exchange rates.

The burgeoning currency markets that sprang up after the end of the Bretton Woods system, along with futures and options derived from exchange rates, gave Soros the tools he needed. These markets were growing rapidly – in 1993, the daily amount traded in global currencies would exceed $1 trillion for the first time.

By the 1980s, the governments of continental Europe were fed up with floating exchange rates. For countries like Germany and France, which traded heavily with each other across their common border, the typical 20 per cent annual volatility of the deutschmark/French franc exchange rate was damaging. Even worse, the two currencies were separately at the beck and call of the mighty US dollar, which seesawed in value.

While there was no hope of returning to Bretton Woods again, something could be done to reduce the problem within Europe itself. Thus was born the idea of European Monetary Union (EMU) – which ultimately led to the European single currency.

For the first stage, the continental European countries, led by France and Germany, agreed to link their currencies together in what was called the 'Exchange Rate Mechanism' (ERM). Rather than allow their exchange rates to ebb and flow freely according to supply and demand, the countries agreed to keep the rates hemmed in within a narrow band.

This was to be done using the central banks of the member countries. For example, if the French franc-to-deutschmark rate strayed too low, and threatened to cross the band, the Banque de France would intervene in the currency markets, buying francs until the rate went up again. This meant spending taxpayers' money, but the benefits of reduced volatility were thought to outweigh the costs.

The problems started after German reunification in 1989. With the country facing huge spending requirements in its eastern territories, the German Bundesbank raised short-term interest rates to fight inflation. But this made deutschmarks attractive to international investors, because they could earn higher rates (adjusted for inflation) than in neighbouring countries. So money poured into Germany, strengthening the deutschmark against other currencies.

The other ERM members, including Britain, which had joined in 1990, raised interest rates too, but this was not enough to stop their exchange rates against the deutschmark falling perilously close to the edge of the band. So the central banks had to intervene in the currency markets. In September 1992, the UK chancellor Norman Lamont announced that he had earmarked $14 billion to keep the pound within the ERM band.

But George Soros, and other speculators, had smelt an opportunity. The high short-term interest rates which reached 15 per cent in the UK were proving a social disaster, because unlike in the US, the majority of Britons paid floating-rate mortgages, while many businesses had floating-rate loans. There was only so much the people could stand before the government would have to crack.

Trading with the big London banks, the speculators sold the pound short. This was done by borrowing in pounds, then entering into forward contracts to exchange those pounds for deutschmarks at a later date. However, rather than keep the pounds, they immediately exchanged them for deutschmarks. The bet was that when it was time to settle the forward, pounds would be cheaper and you could make a profit.

Speculators also bought currency options which gave them the right to sell pounds for deutschmarks at a rate that fell outside the ERM band. Believing that no government would allow the band to break, some European banks sold these 'out-of-the-money' options very cheaply because they assumed they couldn't possibly be exercised.

What did the Bank of England do? Because it had to buy pounds to drive up the price, the 'war chest' is best seen as being in foreign currency. Every time sterling drifted through the band, the Bank would hand over deutschmarks or dollars in return for pounds. By keeping this up for long enough, the Bank hoped to foil the speculators' plans.

It was all in vain. When the Bank had used up the $14 billion war chest, it was begging for mercy. On 'Black Wednesday', 16 September 1992, the UK – along with Italy – left the ERM, and the pound floated freely again, immediately plunging in value against the deutschmark. No longer needing to keep them high, the Chancellor allowed UK interest rates to fall to humane levels.

Soros's Quantum Fund is believed to have netted $2 billion – UK taxpayers' money given away by the Bank of England. Using the 20 per cent rule as a minimum, and bearing in mind the fact that successful hedge fund managers are usually heavily invested in their own fund, we can safely assume that about half a billion dollars of this profit went straight into Soros's pockets.

Less visible were the proprietary desks of some London banks. In particular, the chief currency trader at Salomon, Hans Hufschmid, did well out of the crisis and in 1993 he would receive a $28 million bonus. But it was

Soros who mesmerised Wall Street, and hedge funds were suddenly in fashion. Between 1992 and 1998, the amount of assets controlled by hedge funds would increase by 15 times.

The lesson was not lost on Meriwether. A central bank – namely the Fed – had brought about his downfall in 1991, due to its iron grip on the US banking system. Soros, as an unregulated entity outside the banking system, had brought about perhaps not the downfall but certainly the humiliation of another central bank. Meriwether now envisaged the mother of all hedge funds – Long-Term Capital Management.

The gathering

First of all he had to re-assemble his team from Salomon. But would they jump into the unknown with Meriwether? Eric Rosenfeld had been promoted rapidly after Meriwether's departure. Not only had he taken Mozer's old job as head of government bond trading, but he was elevated to Salomon's executive committee.

Maughan and the new Salomon grandees, who were desperate to hang on to him, didn't stop there. They put Rosenfeld in charge of the risk management and capital allocation committees too, and gave him 203,000 shares in the firm – worth about $10 million.

They hadn't reckoned with the closeness of Rosenfeld's relationship with the man who first saw his potential. Rosenfeld would never forget how Meriwether, alone on Wall Street, had trusted him with real power. In January 1993, Rosenfeld resigned from Salomon. From that point onwards, he would be Meriwether's right hand man in the running of LTCM.

As for the rest of Meriwether's old arb team, they were continuing on in spectacular style. In 1990, their money machines had made $485 million for Salomon. In 1991, it was $1.1 billion and in 1992 $1.4 billion. Between 1990 and 1993, they were responsible for 87 per cent of Salomon's profits.

Yet they were starting to push against limits. A colleague of Haghani recalls how his huge convertible bond trades led to friction from the equities department, which wanted a slice of the action. Haghani also had wanted to make some big bets in Europe, to take advantage of the disruption in the bond markets after the ERM crisis. The head of arbitrage in London, Dennis Keegan, forced Haghani to keep his bets small. Hitherto, every arbitrage trader reported to Meriwether, who had looked after his protégés' interests. Now they had to fight their own battles.

The thought of being given complete freedom in Meriwether's new venture was too enticing to resist. There was also a kind of fanatical loyalty involved. As Meriwether's old rival Craig Coats would waspishly comment, 'they love the guy. They worship the ground he walks on'.

After Rosenfeld, Haghani was first to jump ship. He resigned from Salomon in April 1993, and received a standing ovation as he left the New York fixed income trading floor for the last time. In July, Greg Hawkins made his exit, followed by Myron Scholes in August. Larry Hilibrand – now head of the New York arbitrage division – and Dick Leahy would wait until the end of the year.

By August 1993, LTCM consisted of seven 'principals' – Meriwether, Rosenfeld, Haghani, Hawkins, Merton, Scholes and McEntee. Their combined wealth amounted to $150 million, most of which belonged to the first four. A sum of $10 million, invested wisely in stocks and bonds, can earn you an income of about $1 million a year for the rest of your life. Rather than enjoy their wealth, these men invested all of it in LTCM.

Meriwether and Rosenfeld began scouting for property to base the new fund, and started looking for staff to help run it. In what was a symbolic fresh start, they avoided Wall Street completely, and decided to base LTCM in Greenwich, Connecticut, about 40 minutes drive north of Manhattan.

The apparent obscurity of this location would later add to the sense of mystery surrounding LTCM. Yet it was not a great surprise. With Manhattan increasingly overcrowded and expensive, financial firms had been moving into cheaper Connecticut well before LTCM. Indeed, LTCM's new home on East Weaver Street was the former office building of a Salomon Brothers subsidiary, Phibro Energy.

It was more than a matter of cost. Greenwich is quintessentially suburban. When I visited LTCM in April 1998, I arrived at the station on an empty off-peak commuter train and the cab driver only recognised the address as being near a car wash. The town has its own little harbour on Long Island Sound and is surrounded by golf courses. Rather than suits and ties, dress code is to wear slacks and polo shirts. For the LTCM's seven principals, with a median age of 46, it was an escape from the Wall Street rat race, on their own terms.

But the immediate priority was to find investors. Without their capital, LTCM wouldn't have the clout it needed to make Salomon–sized bets. An obvious candidate, who had the deep pockets required, was Warren Buffett. In July, Meriwether and Rosenfeld flew to Omaha, Nebraska, where Buffett presided over his management company Berkshire Hathaway.

Joining Buffett for dinner – his favourite dish of steak followed by ice-cream – the two men made their pitch. A famously canny investor, Buffett made his name by buying large stakes in undervalued companies such as Coca Cola and Gillette, and sticking with them. Rosenfeld's mathematical money machines didn't impress him, and he turned them down.

Clearly there was a problem. Despite their mythical profits, Meriwether and his partners were so institutionalised after working at Salomon Brothers that they needed help in selling themselves to the outside world. They found it at Merrill Lynch. As part of its huge brokerage business, Merrill had a team of salesmen who specialised in selling private equity stakes – including hedge funds – to wealthy investors.

Meriwether's contact at Merrill was Edson Mitchell, who ran the firm's debt markets division. They did a deal. Mitchell would put his private equity team at Meriwether's disposal, and in return, Merrill would get one cent in every dollar raised for LTCM by its salesmen. The service was cheap at the price. Typical US public equity offerings involve a fee of 6 per cent.

There is a well-worn technique to such 'private placements'. First, the company produces a prospectus explaining its business strategy, and then senior executives accompany a sales team on a 'roadshow', visiting potential investors. The investment house providing the sales service is expected to coach the company's executives in presenting their case.

LTCM's prospectus appeared in October 1993. Entitled 'confidential private placement memorandum', the document revealed the influence of Merrill's salesmen. The use of the word 'arbitrage' is an example. On Wall Street, arbitrage was still a lucrative and hence a glamorous activity. In the outside world, it was associated with the 1980s and the excesses of Ivan Boesky, who had gone to jail after illegally using inside information on takeovers to make arbitrage profits in the stock market.

The A-word only appears in the prospectus where it is needed to describe the principals' former job titles at Salomon. In the section on investment strategy, there is a single mention of 'classic arbitrage' but the most common phrases used are 'relative value' and 'convergence'. This affirmative language, suited to the kinder, gentler 1990s, was designed to calm investors, and remind them that the trades were more than outright bets on the stock market or the direction of interest rates.

Despite giving a few examples of strategies, such as Meriwether's classic on-the-run versus off-the-run Treasury trade, the prospectus was sparing with information, and left all avenues open. 'The exact range of markets and instruments . . . cannot be specified in advance' it said, adding 'the portfolio company is expected to develop new strategies'.

The prospectus admitted – prophetically as it turned out – that some trades were 'conditional on pricing models being correct'. At the same time, LTCM reserved the right to make simple, Soros-type directional bets which would be chosen 'opportunistically'. It hinted at great complexity, saying 'efficient implementation of such trades may involve a "chaining" together of more than just two securities'.

There was no attempt to hide the fundamental property of money machines – the fact that huge inverted pyramids of borrowed money were needed to extract a decent profit. 'It is expected that the portfolio company will be very highly leveraged', the prospectus stated.

One paragraph was especially significant. It began, 'LTCM intends to form strategic relationships with organisations with strong presences in specifically targeted geographical locations around the world.' The Merrill Lynch connection was one example of such a relationship; there would be many others to come.

Leaving his protégés to do the actual trading, Meriwether would play a central role in fostering these relationships. By building up a hidden network of friendly insiders, the idea was for LTCM to be much more like an investment bank than a mere hedge fund.

Interviewed the following year, Meriwether was keen to promote the idea of LTCM's secret network of money machines: 'They can be our window. We want to be global, and we want to have an ability to employ this technology in any country in the world.'

While the trading strategy seemed shadowy and complex, the structure of the fund was simple. The trading positions – whether through ownership of bonds or as a counterparty in derivatives transactions – would be held entirely by the Long-Term Capital Portfolio. This was the fund itself, which was to be registered in the Cayman Islands under the administration of Dutch financial services company Mees Pierson.

No flights to the Caribbean were necessary though, and Mees Pierson did little more than some basic accounting. The Cayman registration was only required to minimise taxes and regulation; all decisions about the fund would be made by LTCM itself in Greenwich, which was a US-registered limited partnership.

The prospectus ended with a list of the seven principals and some of their accomplishments. All of this talent came at a price, however. Instead of the

1 per cent annual fee and 20 per cent of profits rule established by Jones in 1949, LTCM asked for a 2 per cent annual fee and 25 per cent of profits. Investors happy with this arrangement would then have to stump up a minimum of $10 million to be allowed into the fold, and would not be able to withdraw any money for at least three years.

Having a good sales pitch was one thing. But making it happen was another. Meriwether and his partners wanted to recreate their Salomon business completely from scratch, without the unwanted baggage. However, sitting inside a global investment bank with 6000 employees had not been without its advantages.

Modern finance appears to consist of a handful of brainy, highly-paid people at their computers, sending trillions of dollars round the world each day. In this picture, old-fashioned paper is extinct, replaced by mouse clicks and the pulsing of electrons through networks of cables, weaving digital money patterns in space and time.

But this would be a naïve assumption. There may be a few figures like Meriwether and his protégés with great power, but they depend on more than computers. Thousands of people, mostly invisible, keep the system running. They are only noticed when the system breaks down. To appreciate what they do, consider a Greg Hawkins mortgage bond money machine.

As we saw in Chapter 5, this machine is a leveraged, top-heavy contraption containing not just the bond, but also Treasury futures, swaps and dozens of interest rate options, each of which click into action and out again at different points in time. Computer simulations on trees – the garden of forking paths back in Chapter 4 – tell you how to construct the model. But how do you keep it running properly?

In a car factory we separate the white-collar designers and managers who conceive and plan new cars from the blue-collar workers who actually build them. It is the same in finance. Suppose Greg Hawkins is at the apex of a pyramid. Who is beneath him?

Directly under Hawkins are those senior white-collar types who share his PhD-level education in finance, and perhaps have a trading background too, but are younger and less experienced. At LTCM, they were called strategists, and during LTCM's life, several of them would be promoted to principals. We can think of them as apprentice money-machine designers.

Under them, we find a junior white-collar level of traders, risk managers (we will discuss them further below) and software designers. The traders are the men who execute the trades; constantly on the phone, they wear headsets and talk in the slang of the Street. Greg Hawkins and his strategists tell them what to do each day; their job is to test the waters in the market and find the best deal on a swap, option or bond that meets the specification given.

Hawkins will not tell the traders everything about the money machine he has designed – particularly its size or timing. At this level, a lot of people change jobs regularly. It wouldn't do to have them take secrets to a rival firm. However, they do need a good understanding of the components of money machines. Indeed, many of these traders have PhDs, although often the subject is not finance, but physics or mathematics.

With the forking paths option pricing trick borrowed from Richard Feynman's quantum electrodynamics, graduate theoretical physicists in the early 1990s found that their skills made them especially valuable as options traders. A drying up of government funding for particle physics at the time encouraged many to make the move. The risk managers and software designers came from a similar background.

Below the junior trader level is the key white-collar/blue-collar divide. At the top of the blue-collar pecking order are the pit traders. In our analogy, they are like skilled machinists on a car production line. The pit traders don't get to speak to Hawkins or the strategists. Their point of contact is a junior trader who gives them orders over the phone.

While the junior trader in the office knows at least something about the money machine he is helping to operate – the privilege of being a white-collar employee – the pit trader knows next to nothing. He is simply told to sell a billion dollars of Eurodollar futures over three days, or perhaps to buy 100 options on the FTSE index over a week.

The pit trader doesn't ask questions, and he probably doesn't even have a college degree, let alone a PhD. Instead of a boiler suit, he wears a stripy blazer with his firm's logo on it. His job is to execute the order he is given at the best possible price. Because he is further down the chain of command, he has some additional freedom. With a big order to fill, he can use it to work the market to his advantage, and make some extra profit on top of his commission.[1]

In nineteenth century Chicago, pit traders had wealth and status. In Frank Norris's novel *The Pit*, the hero has his own box at the opera. While increased regulation skimmed off some of the riches once available to pit traders, today's wafer-thin margins are a result mostly of relentless

---

1. Pit trader Nick Leeson would take this freedom to its logical conclusion in late 1994 when his unauthorised trading losses bankrupted Barings Bank.

competition and growing efficiency. The pit trader's decline to blue-collar status is an example of Merton's spiral in action.

Below the pit trader in the hierarchy – who has his own team working for him – is a much larger layer of people who know virtually nothing about money machines, although their role is no less important. They are the workers who do the most repetitive production line jobs.

Known variously as clearing, settlement or operations, the unglamorous status of this bottom layer is summed up in an expression often used, 'the back office'. If you stand on Wall Street at 5pm, most of the people pouring out of bank lobbies and into the subway stations are back office employees.

Paid far less than traders and investment bankers, back office staff ensure that the money machine keeps working down to its tiniest details. Take a ten-year swap contract, for example. Over its ten-year life, the swap involves 50 separate payments in different directions. In the back office they make sure that no payment is made incorrectly or missed out. When the white-collar trader enters into a swap, he says 'done at a hundred million' down the phone. In the back office this verbal agreement is turned into 20 pages of legal documentation, in which every line is checked.[2]

When Hawkins was at Salomon Brothers, every person sitting under him in this pyramid was an employee. The pit traders worked for the firm's subsidiary Plaza Clearing Corporation. The back office lurked in the bowels of Salomon's lower Manhattan skyscraper, and accounted for a good fraction of Salomon's staff.

At LTCM, Meriwether decided, the pyramid would be cut off at the base of the white-collar level. All blue-collar jobs would be outsourced, or done by outside companies. The decision fitted in with his 'no baggage' philosophy. But who would place their blue-collar workforce at Meriwether's disposal?

In Meriwether style, the solution was a second 'strategic relationship' along the lines of the one he had already forged with Merrill Lynch. The link was provided by a former member of Meriwether's Salomon arbitrage group, Vincent Mattone, who was now head of repo operations at US securities firm Bear Stearns.

Bear Stearns, along with Merrill Lynch and other houses, had already forged close relationships with the fast-growing hedge fund community. It hinged on a service known as 'prime brokerage'. The securities firms knew that their large workforces that carried out financial blue-collar work made them

2. The corporate lawyers who ultimately oversee this process are, of course, well rewarded.

the equivalent of a Detroit car plant with spare capacity. Why not rent out this workforce to the hedge funds, and earn a profit?

For the early hedge funds that made simple bets on stocks, the firm would make available its staff who worked on the relevant stock exchange. The hedge fund would never need to physically trade shares; the bank either bought on the hedge fund's behalf or supplied what was needed from its own extensive inventory. The hedge fund's assets would then be held in a special account within the firm. With the rise of futures exchanges and international currency markets, hedge funds could use the banks to bet on these markets too.

The advantage for hedge funds was that they avoided the onerous capital and legal requirements for trading on exchanges; the advantage for securities firms was that by facilitating in this way they greatly increased trading revenue and also earned interest for any security they lent out.

As privately negotiated contracts between banks and their counterparties, over-the-counter derivatives were different because they were largely unregulated; the obstacle for hedge funds was their low credit quality, and the back office capacity required to process these contracts. By doing a facilitating job here as well, the Wall Street firms played a key role in opening up the OTC derivatives market to hedge funds.

So what LTCM needed, Bear Stearns was ready to provide, in the form of pit brokers and back office staff. Trying to compete in the prime brokerage business against giants like Merrill, Bear Stearns CEO James Cayne couldn't believe his luck when Mattone introduced him to John Meriwether. The biggest and smartest hedge fund in history had landed in his lap!

With its highly-leveraged portfolio, LTCM would eventually earn Bear Stearns about $25 million a year in fees. So excited was Cayne that he immediately made a personal investment of $10 million in LTCM, proudly telling *Business Week* 'There's no such thing as "the fee's too high" if the returns justify my investing'.

Meanwhile, in late 1993, the LTCM principals and the Merrill Lynch salesmen were on the road. The salesmen had prepared an itinerary. There were the obvious targets – 'high net-worth' individuals, such as Hollywood movie stars, sporting celebrities and various tycoons. One was Larry Tisch, the co-chairman of the Loews cinema chain, who put $10 million of his money into the fund.

Then there were university endowment funds – the means by which private universities in the US manage their wealth. With the strong academic background of LTCM's principals, it was straightforward to convince many such universities that their money would be safely invested. St John's University in New York and the University of Pittsburgh were two that took the bait.

But by far the most significant investor in LTCM would be the financial industry itself. Not all meetings went well. When managers at Conseco Capital Management, part of an insurance company based in deepest Indiana, expressed scepticism about LTCM's strategies, Scholes berated the Midwesterners for being hicks, saying 'as long as there continue to be people like you, we'll make money'. To the embarrassment of the Merrill salesmen, the meeting quickly ended without a deal.

However, once the principals learned to curb their urge to score intellectual points, investor capital started rolling in, as Meriwether exploited his mystique for all it was worth. US management consultants McKinsey invested $100 million. US investment firm PaineWebber put up $100 million, and its chairman Donald Marron personally contributed $10 million. The well-known private banker Edward Safra followed suit, and so did Swiss private firm Bank Julius Baer, along with Germany's Dresdner Bank, which took a $100 million stake in the fund.

By Christmas 1993, Merrill's salesmen had helped Meriwether raise $1 billion dollars, which would grow to $1.5 billion in early 1994. Edson Mitchell was so pleased with the new relationship that he persuaded Merrill to invest its $15 million fee in the fund. At this stage, even if the fund didn't make any money for three years, LTCM was already guaranteed an income of $20 million a year during this period.

Joining the seasonal festivities at Greenwich were Bill Krasker, Larry Hilibrand and Dick Leahy, just departed from Salomon. Hilibrand had been so eager to join his old comrades in arms, that he had walked out on a highly-profitable mortgage bond trade that was about to earn $500 million. Hilibrand's number two on the Salomon arb desk, Robert Stavis, would receive a $35 million bonus for this trade.

LTCM now had over 100 employees, busy preparing to start trading in February. An office in London was being opened by Victor Haghani, and a Tokyo office was in the pipeline. While Meriwether worked his charm on Wall Street investors, Rosenfeld and Merton brought in a crop of crack finance PhDs to run LTCM's research efforts.

Starting in the late 1980s, Salomon Brothers had regularly set up a recruitment booth at the December annual conference of the American Finance Association. In December 1993, LTCM's booth took pride of place, attracting a throng of graduate students and young lecturers.

Some key names who joined the fund as staff had already made an appearance in the bibliography of Merton's *Continuous Time Finance*. Foremost was Chi-Fu Huang. Working with John Cox at MIT, Huang had gained a reputation in the 1980s as being the world's expert in the mathematical subtleties found in the garden of forking paths.

Jon Corzine then enticed Huang to Goldman Sachs, where he built models for the new fixed income arbitrage group which were so complicated that even Fischer Black couldn't understand them. However, Corzine had kept Huang well away from the trading floor. The possibilities at LTCM, where the boundaries between research and trading were intentionally blurred, were too much for Huang to resist.

There was also David Modest. A native of Boston, Modest had been a colleague of Greg Hawkins at Berkeley after completing his PhD at MIT, where he had worked as a teaching assistant for Merton. Focusing his research on equities rather than interest rates, Modest had missed the boat at Salomon, but now Rosenfeld hired him to LTCM, where his skills as an analyst of stock markets would be deployed in developing new strategies.

As LTCM began gearing up for its first day of trading early in 1994, there was one more principal left to join. As a regulator, he had been instrumental in spreading a new doctrine through the markets – the idea of risk management.

The man from the Fed

At the end of July 1993, while John Meriwether was starting to woo his investors, the great and the good of the OTC derivatives industry gathered in Manhattan. The occasion was the summer conference of the International Swaps and Derivatives Association (Isda).

Formed to thrash out standard legal contracts for swaps in the early 1980s, Isda had developed into a talking shop and lobbying organisation for the industry, which was growing at a rapidly accelerating pace. Isda's annual conferences were a chance for the top dealers on Wall Street, and now London, to come together over dinner and exchange war stories.

As vice-chairman of the Federal Reserve Board in Washington DC, and number two to Alan Greenspan, David W. Mullins Jr was a hot keynote speaker for Isda. There might have been some apprehension, however.

After all, the former head of the New York Fed, Meriwether's nemesis Gerry Corrigan, had made no bones of his suspicions of Wall Street and the derivatives industry in particular. Back in 1991 he had complained about the astronomical salaries being earned on Wall Street. During a speech in 1992 he lambasted the swaps dealers for shady practices, ending with the words, 'I hope this sounds like a warning, because it is.'

The dealers needn't have worried. Rather than deliver invective, Mullins took care to flatter his audience, saying:

> When one assesses this field, I think it is not hyperbole to suggest that the development and growth of financial derivatives constitute one of the most dramatic success stories in modern economic history. In the short space of 25 years, financial derivatives have sprung from conception to global prominence, spanning the world's financial markets and institutions, permeating the global financial system.

Why the change in tone? The answer lies in the sea change in the attitude of the financial establishment to the flourishing new architecture of derivatives. Corrigan, a six-foot-four Irish-American with a brusque turn of phrase, had spent his career in the Fed since the early 1970s. He had a conservative's distrust of the new developments.

Mullins, on the other hand, was an academic insider. Born in Memphis, Tennessee in 1946, Mullins had grown up on a cotton plantation in the Mississippi Delta region of Arkansas. His father, then a young graduate student at Columbia, had bought the land with the help of government tax concessions. Concerned that he wouldn't land a job in academia, Mullins Senior decided to be a farmer if things didn't work out.

In the event, he was successful and eventually became President at the University of Arkansas. As for Mullins, his childhood days helping his father clear the land and set up the farm appear to have been idyllic. But he would not remain long in the land of the bottleneck guitar. Winning an under-graduate place at Yale, Mullins went on to do a PhD in that hotbed of finance theory, the Sloan School at MIT. There he met Merton.

From MIT in 1974, Mullins took the well-travelled walk up Massachusetts Avenue to Harvard, where he became professor at the Business School for the next 14 years. Closer to the economic mainstream than Merton or Scholes, Mullins was a popular teacher, punctuating his classes with humorous asides. He also ran a special external programme, coaching senior executives in management skills.

A passionate free-market Republican, Mullins stood apart from both his Arkansas Democrat roots and the left-leaning atmosphere of Harvard, but the affiliation did provide a route to the corridors of power in 1980s Washington. In 1987, Mullins was invited by Treasury Secretary Nicholas Brady to manage the Brady Commission, set up to investigate the carnage of Black Monday.

In a subsequent interview, Mullins acknowledged that the Brady Commission was a watershed event in his career: 'Running the Brady Commission was not only an interesting intellectual and managerial experience, but it also gave me insight into the Federal Reserve. It was the first time I worked closely with Chairman Greenspan, and I got to see how the Fed responded in a crisis situation.'

The ink on the report was barely dry when Mullins began working full time for Brady – as Assistant Secretary to the US Treasury. There, he helped make the decisions that Salomon traders depended on: how much money the United States needed to borrow. Once the Treasury had decided on the size and maturity of the bonds it would issue, the order was dispatched to the New York Fed which would then hold one of its auctions.

But the real moment of glory came for Mullins in 1990, when President George Bush appointed him to the Federal Reserve itself, for a four-year term as vice-chairman. As one of the inner conclave of bankers who set US interest rates, Mullins was now a figure with global power.

Immediately dubbed the Fed's 'resident intellectual', Mullins was its first senior figure with a background in financial theory. So it was no surprise that three years later, in July 1993, Mullins came to the Isda conference to deliver the paean to derivatives quoted above.

Yet, the subject of Mullins's speech was not just derivatives. After all, his audience was expert on that already. The subject was a report that had just been completed by a Washington think-tank called the Group of Thirty entitled 'Derivatives: Practices and Principles'. What interested Mullins, as a regulator, was the report's focus on risk management.

Derivatives were invented as a means of transferring risk from those who didn't need it to those who were prepared to take risks to earn a profit. The 1987 Crash had shown that replicating strategies such as portfolio insurance weren't good enough – they let customers down. People wanted contracts for swaps and options, and firms like Salomon, Goldman, JP Morgan and the others were freely providing them.

These 'swap shops' built and sold derivatives in the same way that General Motors manufactured and sold cars. It was just another business. However, for all the advantages of cars, one thing every car buyer wants to know is how dangerous the vehicle is to drive. Car manufacturers, meanwhile, want to know what can go against them as part of running the business. Both customer and producer are interested in risk management.

For the banks selling derivatives, life was complicated by the fact that those with big proprietary desks – Salomon Brothers in particular – were customers as well as being producers. But overall, two questions remained: what was the risk of owning a derivative, and what was the risk associated with running a derivatives business? Regulators wanted an answer to the second question, so they could tell banks how much capital to keep in reserve.

At the simplest level, the problem was one of accounting. Where did derivatives appear on the annual report? Not on the balance sheet with other assets and liabilities – that was a reason why they were so popular in the first place. For most customers at this time, derivatives appeared as a cashflow – sometimes positive, sometimes negative – and easily hidden inside other cashflows.

That kind of accounting wasn't good enough for bank regulators, and nor was it good enough for senior bankers trying to understand this new business. The investment houses that traded derivatives needed to value their own positions.

The traditional method was to use 'book value' accounting – in other words, write down the amount of money changing hands in the original deal. For example, when a company buys a building, the purchase price of the property becomes its book value. For a bank making a loan, the book value would be the size of the loan itself. When the asset or liability is removed from the firm's books, a profit or loss suddenly makes an appearance.

A slight improvement, from a banking perspective, is to use 'accrual accounting'. For the owner of a bond, this means including the expected future interest payments as well as the face value. For the owner of a share, dividends are taken into account.

This kind of bottom drawer accounting may be easy to do, but it brings killer surprises. The S&L banks in the 1980s ran their books in this way. On their balance sheets, their assets – namely loans – were balanced exactly by liabilities – mostly deposit accounts. When the loans defaulted, the banks were underwater, but no-one who read their published accounts ever knew. Eventually, billions of US taxpayers' money was needed to bail out the depositors. Recently, the same thing has been going on in Japan.

The large firms that traded derivatives already understood this, and had developed a new technique called 'mark-to-market' accounting. It could be applied to any asset that had a market value. The idea was simple in principle. Rather than use the original sale or purchase price as a guide, the bank uses the current market value. In other words, how much would you get if you sold it immediately?

Pit traders had done this for years. The reason was self-preservation. Back in the nineteenth century, when grain prices swung widely, Chicago pit traders would go bust as the market went against them. This would leave dozens of fellow pit traders with useless futures contracts.

A system called margining was invented to protect against such dangers. A futures trader today, when taking a position, leaves a sum of money called a margin with the exchange. Typically, this amounts to a few percent of the contract's value.

At the end of every trading day, the future is marked-to-market. If the trader is in luck and prices go in his favour, the exchange gives some of his margin back. If prices go against him, the exchange makes a 'margin call' on the trader. If he can't pay, the futures contract is 'closed out', or terminated.

During their early years as gentlemen's agreements between large banks and their corporate clients, over-the-counter derivatives such as swaps hadn't been marked-to-market. Deals were monitored on a quarterly or annual basis, whenever payments were exchanged, and blue-collar practices such as margin calls were unheard of. But with the explosion in derivatives portfolios across currencies and interest rates, and with hedge funds entering the picture too, there was now much more at stake.

The effect of the new system on senior bankers was profound. Under the old accounting regime with derivatives, they had been on dry land that ever so often was afflicted by inexplicable earthquakes. Now, marking-to-market, they suddenly found themselves trying to keep their feet on a boat in a stormy sea.

Every type of position was buffeted by different risks. If it was equities, then the value rose and fell daily with the index. If it was bonds, then every twitch of the yield curve could make a billion dollar difference. This newly-perceived hazard had a name: market risk.

Marking-to-market didn't work for everything. There had to be a liquid market out there which gave a daily price. That wasn't a problem for the more common derivatives such as swaps or currency options. However, the newer, exotic options that were being devised and sold weren't available on the open market. To work out their value, a quant had to sit down at a computer and work out the replication cost over time by summing over the garden of forking paths. This was called marking-to-model.

There were also the proprietary positions to worry about. How did you value a Greg Hawkins money machine? A quant had built it, but you also needed a quant to monitor it. There were hundreds of moving parts involved.

So an arms race began. The trading desks were hiring PhDs to price and deal options; now management needed its own PhDs to keep track of what was going on. These new arrivals were called risk managers, and became important members of the junior white-collar hierarchy.

This happened at all levels. Humble junior traders reported to a senior trader, whose job involved marking his subordinates' positions to market at the end of a day's trading. Tired of leaving work at 8pm every night, the senior trader would hire a risk manager to do the job. Senior traders reported to a divisional head, who hired his own risk manager, and so on up to board level.

The chairman of the investment bank, sitting in his oak-panelled office, suddenly found himself overwhelmed with pages and pages of computer printouts. He was the captain of the ship, but he couldn't navigate through the storms of market risk without a navigator.

Two CEOs, Dennis Weatherstone of JP Morgan and Charles Sanford of Bankers Trust, took the initiative. Not only did they want a radar system, and thus see the forest for the trees, but they wanted to use risk as a tool for controlling the firm's business. How could it be done? Some time in the late 1980s, each man assembled a team of hand-picked former traders and quants to work on the problem. To solve the problem, both teams went back to the roots of financial theory.

Rethinking risk

The JP Morgan team, led by Til Guldimann and Jacques Longerstaey, focused on the radar system. Their inspiration was Harry Markowitz's 1952 portfolio theory. As we first saw in Chapter 1, Markowitz made two key contributions. Firstly, he got people to think about risk in terms of volatility – in other words, stocks with more volatile returns were riskier. Secondly, he showed that the risks of a portfolio of different stocks could be less than the sum of its parts.

This miracle happened because of correlation – the tendency for one stock to go down when another went up, cancelling out some of the risk. What Guldimann's team did was show how to apply portfolio theory to the hundreds of trading positions held by a bank, and come up with a single volatility for the entire firm.

That wasn't quite enough. A bank chairman doesn't want volatility, given in percentage terms. He wants a dollar figure. Guldimann and Longerstaey went back to basics again. Financial theory treats an investment such as a stock purely as a population of returns, day-by-day.

Like the sizes of people or animals, this population has a statistical distribution. As we know from Chapter 1, we can describe this distribution using the mean or average return, and the standard deviation or volatility – which says how spread out the returns are around the mean.

But there is another way to look at the distribution. Suppose we have a collection of people of different heights. Rather than the mean or standard deviation, we are interested in one question only: if a single person is picked at random, what is the smallest they can be, nineteen times out of twenty?

In financial terms, the question is, what is the most we can lose on an asset, nineteen days out of twenty? The answer to the question in both cases lies in the shape of the distribution. For a Normal distribution, with its well-behaved nature, the answer is simply related to the standard deviation or volatility.

If its returns are normally distributed, the greatest percentage loss in a stock's value nineteen days out of twenty is the volatility itself, multiplied by 1.65. For example, if you own ten thousand Microsoft shares, which have a daily volatility of 2.39 per cent, the greatest daily loss would be 4.83 per cent.

If you multiply that by the dollar value of your holding in Microsoft, then the result is the most you can lose, nineteen times out of twenty. If Microsoft stands at $140 per share, on most days, your $1.4 million stake could go down by no more than $67,600. Guldimann and Longerstaey's stroke of genius was to give this last number a name. They called it 'Value-at-Risk' or VAR.[3]

Now consider again the problem faced by the bank with its thousands of positions. What Guldimann and Longerstaey did was take Markowitz's portfolio approach to adding the risks together, at the same time as multiplying them by the sizes of positions. The result was a combined VAR figure for all the trading positions in the firm, which was first calculated in 1989.

This was the magic radar system that Weatherstone and other bank chairmen had been waiting for. They could now employ their own firm-wide risk manager whose job was to tell them – rather like a Roman slave

---

3. The choice of nineteen out of twenty comes from the statisticians who traditionally describe an experimental relationship as 'significant' if it is violated in no more than one out of twenty tests.

whispering to the Emperor that he was mortal – how many millions of dollars the bank could lose that day, nineteen times out of twenty.

Guldimann and Longerstaey surrounded their new toy with caveats. For a start, the Normal distribution couldn't be trusted – 1987 had shown that. An improvement was to take the historical distribution of returns, perhaps for the previous year, and use that instead. This incorporated the 'fat tails', namely the chance that rare events would happen more often than the Normal distribution would predict.

But the *really* rare events – such as 1987 – weren't captured by this approach. So the next stage was to use 'stress testing'. More folklore than financial theory, stress testing was akin to gathering campfire stories of mythical monsters and Biblical floods in the markets, and trying to imagine how you would deal with them.

Another issue that was completely ignored at this stage was liquidity. If you get into financial problems and are forced to sell your Microsoft shares too quickly, you may depress the market, and lose much more than VAR predicts. However, the currency and interest rate markets that were Guldimann and Longerstaey's initial concern appeared too liquid for this to be a worry.

For the senior bankers and risk managers who seized upon VAR, this was all small print and minor detail. The main thing was that magic number. Even better, the Markowitz portfolio trick said you could take two risks for the price of one – for example, if stocks and bonds were negatively correlated, their volatility cancelled out.

Over at Bankers Trust, the focus was on using risk to make business decisions. The team formed by Sanford went back to research done by Markowitz's successor, Bill Sharpe. One of the questions Sharpe had asked in the early 1960s was, how should an investor allocate his or her money to a group of different stocks?

The fraction of total wealth that the investor allocates to one stock is called the 'weighting' of that stock in the investor's portfolio. Sharpe wanted to know what the optimal weighting was for each possible stock.

What Sharpe did was to take the returns of the whole portfolio, subtract the risk or volatility, and find the set of individual weightings which made the return as big as possible. It turned out that the weighting was the return (above the risk-free rate) divided by the volatility. This became known as the Sharpe ratio.

As an example, recall the two stocks we considered in Chapter 1 – Microsoft and Netscape. With its 149 per cent returns in 1998, Netscape seemed like a better bet than Microsoft which returned 114 per cent over the same period. But the Sharpe ratio tells a different story. Because of its higher volatility, Netscape's Sharpe ratio is 1.43, while Microsoft's is 3.02. According to Sharpe, you should therefore allocate more than twice as much money to Microsoft than Netscape.

What Sanford's team did was transfer this thinking out of the stock market into the banking business. While Sharpe's investor spends money on stocks, a senior banker allocates capital to traders and other managers in his firm. Whether they use this capital to make loans, issue bonds for clients or delta-hedge options that they have sold, the traders earn a return on this capital.

If you measure the volatility of each trader's return, then you can calculate a Sharpe ratio, to work out how to best allocate capital to them. Thus, a trader may earn a high return on capital, but be so volatile that he isn't worth the capital. Sanford's team called this approach 'Raroc', short for risk-adjusted return on capital.

Over the next few years, the radar system – VAR – and the control system – Raroc – slowly gained ground among Wall Street and European banking firms. Both approaches required marking-to-market, so one side-effect of their popularity was an explosion in computer technology and data gathering, which was also driven by increased trading volume.

As regulators became aware of OTC derivatives in the early 1990s, the leading banks could point to VAR and Raroc as signs of their responsibility in controlling this expanding business. To make things more rigorous, they introduced a technique called 'backtesting' whereby if a VAR limit was breached too often – say three days out of twenty rather than one – then more capital could be allocated to a position.

The regulators, in particular the Basle Committee, took the bait, and signalled that they would permit the use of 'internal models' in allocating capital for a derivatives business. In other words, the biggest banks would be able to regulate themselves. And it was in this spirit that Mullins addressed his soothing words to the Isda audience in July 1993.

The new developments were not lost on John Meriwether and the LTCM principals. Their October 1993 prospectus contains a section on risk management, which says: '... the Portfolio Company will focus on investment strategies with high expected-return-to-risk ratios and intends to employ continuous monitoring and disciplined risk management techniques to achieve this objective.'

In other words, LTCM would use VAR and Raroc as if it were an investment bank with regulatory approval. Even more tantalising was the suggestion that by using its risk management skills to hedge unwanted risks, LTCM would then bring in untold profits through carefully-applied leverage:

> The reduction in the Portfolio Company's volatility through hedging could permit the leveraging up of the resulting position to the same expected level of volatility as an unhedged position, but with a larger expected return.

It is worth examining this statement carefully. An investor would make a comparison with the S&P index, which had a given return and volatility. Eugene Fama had said that the efficiency of the market made this index impossible to beat without increasing risk. Yet here was LTCM, saying that its combined genius could guarantee the impossible.

Indeed, Meriwether seemed deadly serious about this claim, as he spent $20 million setting up a state of the art computer system, together with crack software engineers to run it. There were also dozens of PhDs with backgrounds ranging from theoretical astrophysics to algebraic set theory that he and Rosenfeld hired as risk managers and traders. For investors who visited the Greenwich offices and felt the buzz, the claim really did have the ring of truth.

And what about David Mullins? A few months after his Isda speech, he, Alan Greenspan and the other Fed chieftains began raising short-term interest rates, which had stood at 3 per cent. In the space of a year they would double. In yield-curve goggle land, this was very bad news for the fixed income market.

In the derivatives business, firms like Bankers Trust had been helping their corporate customers take advantage of the benign low interest rate environment using complex swap transactions. While the swaps enabled them to lock-in very cheap borrowing levels, what these corporate treasurers didn't realise was that they were effectively making massive bets that interest rates wouldn't rise.

So eager were the Bankers Trust salesmen to help that some very questionable trades were done. For example, BT entered into an interest rate swap with soap manufacturer Procter & Gamble where the floating rate paid by P&G depended on the difference between two US Treasury rates multiplied by 17 times. When rates began to rise, this swap suddenly left P&G $190 million underwater.

Led by Procter & Gamble, furious clients sued Bankers Trust for selling them dangerous products that they hadn't understood. Unlike the banks, these customers hadn't yet learned how to mark-to-market, and left the complex positions lying on their books until the inevitable blow-up occurred.

Amidst the blaze of lawsuits, Charles Sanford was forced to resign as chairman of Bankers Trust. It was ironic, because Bankers Trust had completely hedged itself against the interest rate moves, and its risk managers were among the best on Wall Street.

However, the architect of Raroc had missed one crucial risk – that of allowing his salesmen to destroy the firm's reputation by exploiting the ignorance of clients. Once the leading US derivatives player, Bankers Trust would slowly decline until it was eventually taken over by Deutsche Bank in 1998.

Out at the long end of the yield curve, the bond markets were devastated as the curve lurched upwards. Many hedge funds that were betting on bonds went out of business. For LTCM, which frowned on outright directional bets, the crisis was a marketing opportunity. The October prospectus had said: 'returns are generally expected not to exhibit significant systematic correlation with the returns on global stock and bond markets'.

From now on, the hip phrases to drop during Wall Street meetings would be 'convergence' and 'relative value'. Everyone wanted to be immunised against swings in the stock market or the Fed. Not that Mullins was pulling the strings any more.

In February 1994, Mullins left the Fed. His four-year term was about to end, and as a Republican, he didn't expect President Bill Clinton to re-appoint him.

Rather than return to academia, however, Mullins became LTCM's newest principal. Back with his old cronies from MIT and Harvard, Mullins now had a ringside seat in the greatest experiment finance had ever seen. On 24 February, with $1,011,060,243 of investor capital, LTCM began trading.

7

Out of Control

Any fool can commit murder. Any half-trained operative can arrange a suicide.
But only a craftsman can stage a convincing natural death.
Lavrenty Beria, head of Stalin's secret service

On Saturday, 28 October 1995, a group of darkly-dressed figures crossed Harvard Yard, a tree-shaded eighteenth-century quadrangle at the heart of the University. They entered the Memorial Church, an imposing structure fronted by Doric columns, towering over a cluster of nearby undergraduate dormitories.

Inside the church, plaques commemorate Harvard graduates who fell in both World Wars. The University shows even-handedness to its dead – there is even one German graduate who died fighting for Hitler.

To the sound of a harp and flute duo playing Bach, the arrivals took their places among the pews, exchanging quiet greetings as they sat down. The man they had come to commemorate had died two months earlier. Twenty-seven years before that, he had made the world-changing journey across the Charles River to MIT. He was Fischer Black.

Diagnosed with terminal throat cancer a year before his death, Black had kept working as Goldman Sachs' chief quant as long as he could. According to his close collaborator Emanuel Derman: 'He neither hid it nor announced it, but told the necessary people. He didn't complain to anyone I knew at Goldman Sachs, and he spoke about it in a fairly detached, almost objective sort of way. I never heard him complain.'

A massive operation gave Black hope for a while, and he was full of praise for his surgeon. But the cancer returned, until one day, Black confided to Derman 'things are looking kind of iffy right now'. Too ill to make the daily journey to his office, Black continued working from home until the end. He was 57. A private funeral had been arranged by his family, but this memorial service would be for the entire financial community.

After a reading from Ecclesiastes – 'a time to live, and a time to die' – and more music, this time Pachelbel's Canon, the remembrances began. Two former academic colleagues of Black, Doug Breeden and Michael Jensen made short speeches. Then the towering figure of Jon Corzine – by now co-chairman of Goldman Sachs – took his place at the lectern. Next came Robert Merton, followed by Merton Miller. Black's daughter read a speech by Myron Scholes, who was unable to attend.

In the congregation were many other notable figures from mathematical finance. Black's frequent collaborator from Goldman, Emanuel Derman, was there, along with a large contingent from LTCM. After the memorial service ended, everyone made their way to the cordial surroundings of Harvard's Faculty Club for a reception.

Outside the sombre atmosphere of the Church, the mood lightened. Everybody seemed to have a Fischer Black story; some fond memory of a quirk in the great man. There were his famous two minute silences, and his penchant for programmable calculator watches. Derman himself recalled how Black detested the computer mouse, preferring old-fashioned keyboards instead.

But Black's death raised some deeper questions. It was the end of an era. Black had a strong attachment to equilibrium – the idea that the returns on an asset compensate investors for the risk of holding it. This idea, in the form of the CAPM had driven Black's original quest for an option pricing formula.

Always suspicious of Merton's replication argument, Black couldn't hide his pleasure when Derman simulated option replication on a computer and apparently found an error in the price (the 'error' was due to a programming glitch). But while CAPM and other equilibrium arguments have faded in their power over time, replication and no-arbitrage thinking took over Wall Street like a religious movement.

There were cultural questions too. Black loved quantitative finance, and became a role model for quants who took pride in their work. However, when it came to using models for trading, Black took a sober, restrained attitude. Models were there to be guarded carefully by quants – like military ordnance – until they could be explained to traders in simple terms. Often, Black's research papers contained no equations at all.

Black's worst nightmare was an idiot savant trader who made money using a model without understanding or explaining why. As Derman recalled: 'He suggested traders at banks should be paid for the plausibility story they told behind the strategy they used, rather than for the results they obtained, thus rewarding intelligence and thinking rather than possible luck.'

In the world according to Black, a strict barrier was needed between quants and traders – a sort of analogue to CP Snow's Two Cultures of science and the arts. But the Salomon arbitrage revolution had changed everything. Starting with Rosenfeld, Meriwether allowed the quants themselves to trade, with spectacular results. LTCM was the logical conclusion of that.

Now, Jon Corzine was jumping on the bandwagon too. The head of Goldman's fixed income trading division, Jacob Goldfield, had set up an arbitrage unit and was following LTCM's footsteps scouring universities for mathematical PhDs who wanted to trade. Economics faculties and business schools were unable to produce graduates fast enough, but anyone sufficiently mathematical would do – a string theorist from Princeton perhaps, or maybe a logician from Berkeley.

Other banks were doing the same. After the Bankers Trust débâcle, customer business dropped away, and resources were shifted into proprietary trading. Although these firms retained their traditional quantitative research departments, apart from a few shining exceptions, they began to lose their lustre. If you're so smart, the quants were asked, why aren't you trading?

And surely these PhD traders were too clever to be idiot savants. Hedged against all possible market moves, their money machines were engineered to extract slivers of money from the irrationality of investors and the inefficiency of tax laws. What could possibly go wrong?

In the Fischer Black worldview, believing too fervently in your own model was dangerous, because of the hidden assumptions involved. For example, when Emanuel Derman and another Goldman quant, Iraj Kani, discovered a way of incorporating information from market prices of options into the tree pricing model, Black insisted the model was flawed because it didn't account for jumps. Recent research has shown that Black's reservations were justified.

Yet many quants ignored such flea-like behaviour in the market because it didn't have the nice mathematical properties of Brownian motion. For those hired from ethereal subjects like string theory, such mathematical purity would always come before the messy imperfections of the real market.

However, the real danger was more insidious. The culture of quants resembled science: it thrived on openness, constructive criticism and a sense of intellectual equality. Trading was different – it was obsessively secretive, to prevent competitors from gaining the slightest advantage.

The quants that did well as traders became wealthy, and other firms would attempt to poach them. It was hard to criticise these stars of the trading floor when they were doing so well. No less hard was it for successful traders to criticise themselves or the science underlying their success. After all, if they were making ten million dollars a year, the models had to be right. It couldn't just be sheer luck.

Goldman Sachs, Credit Suisse First Boston and other firms leaping on the arbitrage bandwagon created by John Meriwether encouraged such self-belief. While at LTCM, traders belonged to a rigidly controlled pyramid structure, and were allowed only limited autonomy, at Goldman and the others it was different. The old-fashioned managers on the vast trading floors of these firms were believers in the 'parable of the rat'.

An age-old pest control method in Eastern Europe, the parable instructs you to put a dozen rats in a barrel with nothing except water. After several days, the rats begin to devour one another until only one is left. This last rat is then let loose, striking terror into its brethren, who flee your farmyard.

Allocating his firm's capital to a dozen or so prop traders, the senior trader would apply a similar principle. The winnowing mechanism was quick and dirty. Many stock market investors instruct their brokers to sell whenever the price of a stock they own falls below a certain level. This is known as a 'stop-loss'.

In the same manner, a prop trader who lost more than a specified amount, say $50 million, would be fired, and their positions liquidated. The remaining traders would carry on regardless. During market turmoil, it was not unknown for successful traders to trade against their weaker rivals – in accordance with the ancient parable.

However, this wasn't scientific enough for the new generation of risk managers, and the board-level executives who sponsored them. For a start, how did you decide where the stop-loss level should be in the first place? Traditionally it went up with your track record, but the new quant traders argued that they should be given priority because they took fewer risks.

The new regulatory climate provided another impetus for risk managers to monitor traders. After intense lobbying by the industry, international regulators, in particular the Basle Committee, had allowed banks and brokers generous terms for their capital reserves in return for giving risk managers important policing powers.[1]

1. The new rules, in the form of an amendment to the 1988 Capital Accord, appeared in 1996. Strictly speaking, in the US they only applied to commercial banks and not securities firms like Salomon Brothers. But in practice, VAR was adopted as a risk control mechanism by all the leading OTC derivatives dealers.

Using VAR, the risk managers took a 'top down' approach, starting at the level of the firm as a whole. As we saw in Chapter 6, these risk models highlighted volatility as an evil to be avoided at all costs, and rewarded diversification. From its initial use as a passive radar system, the risk managers transformed VAR into an active tool intended to replace the stop-loss limit.

If the bank breached its 'VAR limit' – in other words, lost more in a day than it was expected to, on average, 99 days out of 100 – it would have to reserve additional capital against market risk, to keep the regulators happy.[2]

At the next level down, if a trading division (such as fixed income) breached *its* VAR limit, it would have to find more capital in turn. As it percolated downwards through the firm, this use of VAR would ultimately run up against the opposition of a senior trader who favoured his own stop-loss limits.

But if this trader's boss was a believer in VAR, then that senior trader could be ordered to reserve extra capital whenever he breached the VAR limit that had been calculated for him. But the only way to find that extra capital was to liquidate positions. So VAR limits effectively became a new kind of freely-floating stop-loss limit linked to volatility.

As we will see, it wasn't until 1997 and 1998 that people realised how dangerous this system could be. When they first became popular in 1995, VAR limits appeared capable of catching any mistakes in models before they could do real damage. Risk-adjusted-return-on-capital (Raroc) was another failsafe. Traders whose positions were too volatile in relation to the returns they were making, found themselves starved of precious capital.

And yet, both VAR and Raroc raised very subtle questions about statistics and measurement – for example, when calculating their volatility, should you monitor traders for days, months or years? And how important was stress testing – those monster events lurking in the tail of the distribution?

But these questions were brushed aside, as it became clear that the sort of arbitrage trades favoured by LTCM and its imitators had very low volatility indeed. A Raroc computer program, created to optimise the process of allocating money to different types of trades, would instruct you to pour money into relative value. And during the first years of LTCM's existence, that's exactly what people did.

---

2. Strictly speaking, the bank's risk managers would 'backtest', or first check that the number of VAR limit violations during a set time period was more than would be expected for the return distribution in their risk model. At desk level, traders liked this because a single limit violation was no longer grounds for disciplinary action. In the summer of 1998, the quick succession of multiple limit violations – clear evidence that the models were flawed – made backtesting largely superfluous.

Yet, the kind of quants who had thought up VAR and Raroc were also the ones doing relative value and arbitrage trading. Was it possible that smart people could engineer their way round the failsafe mechanisms? Was it possible to fool VAR or Raroc and take hidden risks?

These awkward questions were far from everyone's mind in 1995, on that October afternoon in the Harvard Faculty Club. Once upon a time, Black had told Derman 'One of the things that limits my influence is the fact that I always tell people the truth, even if they don't want to hear it.' Now Black was dead, the difficult questions would remain unasked.

They weren't being asked at Goldman and the big investment banks. For very different reasons, they weren't being asked at LTCM. The Basle Committee had teeth because its members were central bankers and national regulators — such as the New York Fed. In each national jurisdiction, regulators could send 'risk cops' to check a local bank's VAR models.

As a hedge fund, LTCM was beyond the reach of the Basle Committee. It could decide for itself how much capital to reserve against its positions. The only US regulator whose authority LTCM recognised was the Commodity Futures and Trading Commission, which oversaw futures exchanges. However, when it came to hedge funds, the CFTC's role was largely ceremonial in nature, because most of them — including LTCM — receive special exemptions from its oversight.

Not that this lack of regulatory control meant that Meriwether and his partners had ignored risk management. But they thought they had one huge advantage which made Basle-type regulation unnecessary. The fund was committed to 'term financing of positions' — once LTCM had decided to make a bet, nothing could make it throw in its cards early. There were no stop-loss rules at LTCM. So the name Long-Term Capital Management really meant something.

It was Myron Scholes, practical as ever, who helped make this possible. He had protected Salomon Brothers from counterparties by setting up Swapco, which as a separate entity was always kept topped up with sufficient capital to maintain its all-important triple-A rating. Now, Scholes repeated his trick for LTCM. This time, however, credit rating agencies wouldn't be necessary.

At first sight, counterparty credit for hedge funds looks like an insurmountable problem. When two public companies enter into a derivatives contract, each does a credit check on the other, to make sure that it can bear the risk of the other defaulting on the contract. If a bank has too much exposure to a certain company, then its credit officers will turn down any new derivatives deals.

The starting point for a credit check is a credit rating, which summarises how much capital the company has available compared to its outstanding debt. A highly-leveraged company with huge debts will have a low credit rating, and faces problems trying to find derivatives counterparties. And no-one is more leveraged than a hedge fund like LTCM!

When I put this to Scholes in April 1998, a twinkle appeared in his eye, and he replied, 'you gotta post collateral!' Instead of setting up an entity like Swapco, Scholes was saying, why not set up thousands of tiny Swapcos, one for each contract you did? The trick was to post ironclad collateral – typically US Treasury bonds – against each contract.

If a swap, for example, goes against you, more collateral could be delivered to the counterparty to keep them happy. With collateral in his hands, the counterparty would be protected against the risk of you defaulting, because the collateral could always be sold.

The trick that Scholes used to LTCM's great advantage was that if one swap goes against you, there is probably another in your favour. If the counterparty for that contract has to post collateral to you, then the *net* amount of collateral you need is relatively small.

So LTCM's *modus operandi* was to ensure that every swap agreement it did was a 'two-way mark-to-market collateral arrangement' – in other words, it was symmetrical. Once these contracts were in place, all LTCM needed was a sophisticated computer system which monitored all the contracts at once, and shifted collateral rapidly around the world. With such a system in place, LTCM seemed unshakeable.

So it wasn't surprising that the mood lightened at the Harvard Faculty Club. Indeed, here was Merton, with a new spring in his step, full of pleasure in his new role as LTCM partner. For although LTCM had many secrets, with its dozens of investors on Wall Street, there was one secret that was impossible to keep. LTCM was making enormous amounts of money.

The 1994 bond market turmoil had been good for LTCM. Larry Hilibrand had exploited the distortions in prices to construct a mortgage bond money machine that reaped big profits. A dollar invested in the fund in February 1994 was now worth $1.61 net of fees – a good return in less than two years.

People got the message. Since the beginning of trading, the fund had attracted another $2 billion from investors. The total assets owned by the Long-Term Capital portfolio had just reached the staggering level of $100 billing, and that doesn't include off-balance sheet positions such as swaps. But one of LTCM's biggest trades was only just beginning to take shape.

The Italian job

Two weeks before Fischer Black's memorial service, David Mullins had preceded Merton's Cambridge trip with one of his own. Rather than Harvard, Mullins went to MIT, to speak at a prestigious twice-yearly conference called the World Economy Laboratory (WEL).

Big name economists like Paul Krugman and the IMF's Stanley Fischer would be in attendance, along with top central bankers. Rubbing shoulders with former colleagues from the Fed and other Washington insiders, as well as the academic community, Mullins was LTCM's eyes and ears in the corridors of power. He was given a warm welcome. To his old friends, Mullins' move to the private sector was of little consequence.

He himself had joked, while Fed vice-chairman, that working for the government had made him 'poor enough' to get married. After his years of public service, who could begrudge Mullins a decent income?

Anyway, with its academic star roster, LTCM seemed more like a think tank than a money factory. Mullins did nothing to dispel that notion. If pressed, he could always say that he was making the markets more efficient – it sounded like public service. Back in Greenwich, Mullins would then boast to investors that he could 'get inside the mind' of the Fed.

On this occasion, Mullins had been invited to introduce the star speaker: Jean-Claude Trichet, governor of the Bank of France. The title of Trichet's speech was 'French monetary strategy on the way to Emu'.

European Monetary Union has produced more pages of economic analysis, and more keynote speeches than almost any other economic topic. 1995 was no exception. After the embarrassment of the 1992 ERM crisis, the main drivers of the project, namely Germany and France, became determined to prove that it could succeed.

Earlier in the year, at the WEL Spring conference, Mullins had introduced the head of the German Bundesbank, Hans Tietmayer, to talk about 'Stability and prosperity'. These two words summed up the case for Emu. But for many it seemed like wishful thinking. There was no more obvious example than Italy.

In September 1992, Italy was drummed out of the ERM along with Britain. But while Britain could take or leave Emu as an idea, being excluded from the fold of 'core nations' rankled in Italy. After all, not that long before, Italy looked like an economic basket case. With chronically high budget deficits – the legacy of government spending based on patronage – Italy was miles away from the Tietmayer's bourgeois German ideal.

In August 1995, Mullins' busy diary had taken him to Jackson Hole, Wyoming, where the Federal Reserve Bank of Kansas City organised a regular summer conference. Although a speech by Alan Greenspan got most of the attention from the assembled policymakers and pressmen, Mullins was more interested in a talk given by an Italian academic. His name was Alberto Giovannini.

One of Europe's most influential economists, Giovannini was a prolific author of academic papers, and by 1995 had nine textbooks in print. Earlier in his career he had worked at MIT, and fallen under Merton's spell. He had also befriended Eric Rosenfeld and Mullins. Now he was a professor at Columbia University, and had a special position as advisor to the Italian Treasury.

Giovannini's talk focused on a central area of his research – the role played by debt in controlling government deficits. And this problem lay at the heart of Emu convergence. Back in 1992, before the crisis broke, the members of the European Exchange Rate Mechanism had sat down in the Dutch town of Maastricht to work out a roadmap to creating a single currency.

The main problem was to agree on what economic yardsticks should be used to measure convergence. How could you tell if Germany and Italy were ready to share a currency? Everyone agreed that deficits – the difference between a government's spending and its income through taxes – had a central role to play.

The Germans wanted high-spenders like Italy to rein themselves in before they could join the new currency. In the Maastricht Treaty, a deficit target would have to be met for a country to qualify for Emu. To ensure that big and small countries were treated equally, the target was a ratio: deficits could account for no more than 3 per cent of a country's Gross Domestic Product (GDP) or the amount of wealth it produced per year.

But Giovannini was among those responsible for a further yardstick – debt. A country that spends more than it earns from taxes must raise money somewhere or else go bankrupt. Countries like Italy had traditionally paid for their deficits by borrowing money; in other words, they issued bonds.

By issuing debt, a country could cheat on the Maastricht criterion and simply use the cash raised from bonds as 'income' to cosmetically reduce its deficit. In an influential 1990 paper, Giovannini had urged that this be prevented by limiting the amount of debt as a fraction of the deficit. The Maastricht Treaty took this recommendation on board, and set the debt/ deficit ratio at 60 per cent.

Italy had signed the treaty, and after the fuss over the ERM crisis had died down, it rejoined ERM again. But meeting the two criteria in time to join Emu's 'first wave' in January 1999 seemed like a tall order.

Reducing the deficit was hard enough. Italian tax collection was notoriously inefficient, and went hand-in-hand with high debt levels. It was a standing joke that Italians would evade tax only to lend the government the money instead.

In the past, with such a high deficit, Italy had to issue plenty of bonds. Because they were so plentiful, they were cheap, and when viewed through yield goggles, that meant Italy had to pay high interest rates on its bonds to get the financing it needed. In 1993 and 1994, the benchmark Italian government bond, called a BTP,[3] paid between 12–13 per cent interest every year.

Unfortunately, the cheapness of its bonds kept Italy trapped in a vicious circle. Because the bonds were so cheap, the government had to pay high interest. But the high annual interest payments drained the government coffers which meant more bonds would have to be issued. Life would be much better if Italy could get a high price for its bonds and pay a low rate of interest.

As Giovannini would later comment in his talk at Jackson Hole, 'the success of a financial stabilisation policy for a country that has accumulated a large stock of debt depends crucially on the ability of that country to minimise the cost of government debt.'

In June 1992, Giovannini was appointed Chairman of the 'Council of Experts' advising the Italian Treasury – which issued the bonds. He was given a mandate to manage Italy's debt and get the country into Emu. However, when the ERM crisis broke only three months later, the flood of foreign money out of Italy lowered bond prices and drove up interest rates. Giovannini faced an apparently impossible task.

At the time, a cosy system operated in the Italian bond market. The Bank of Italy would regularly auction its bonds, which would be bought exclusively by retail investors and domestic banks. They liked the bonds being cheap and they liked earning high interest. There was also steady demand – Italian pension funds, insurance companies and hundreds of tiny

3. Buoni del Tesoro Poliennali.

savings banks were legally required to invest in the bonds and would buy them from the largest dealers.

To get the job done in the short time available, the Treasury would have to bring in a huge influx of foreign money into the Italian bond market, to drive up prices. The first step towards achieving this was to gradually abolish a rule whereby foreign investors had to pay withholding tax on their bond coupons. Because it took up to two years to reclaim this tax, foreign investors had been reluctant to buy.

The abolition of the tax rule did jump start the decline in Italian interest rates, but it wasn't enough. Most foreign investors such as mutual funds and pension funds were wary of a market with such a bad track record, and few believed that Italy would make it into Emu.

What happened next is the subject of some debate. The question is, did someone with great influence in the Italian Treasury and the Bank of Italy strike a devil's bargain for their country?

If the market couldn't be sold as a bright prospect, it could be pitched as inefficient and ripe for the kill. The Bank of Italy and the Treasury would encourage the world's most ruthless hedge funds and arbitrage desks to squeeze the bond market in Milan for profit. Local insurance companies and pension funds – 'widows and orphans' in Wall Street parlance – would be thrown to the wolves. Among these domestic players today, who were forced to buy bonds at inflated prices, there is still great bitterness that this was allowed to happen.

According to some observers who prefer to remain anonymous, the Bank provided LTCM and certain leading US investment banks with market access and privileged information denied to Italian banks – which would yield a massive profit. In return, LTCM – and a handful of others – would engineer the convergence of Italian debt, and help get Italy into Emu. Through an affiliate, the Bank also invested in LTCM – effectively front-running the population of Italy.

Pointing out that he left the Italian Treasury in the summer of 1994 for a teaching post at Columbia University, Giovannini denies any involvement with LTCM at this stage. However, Robert Merton is an enigmatic figure in the fund's Italian adventure. Italian finance academics – including Giovannini – had taken him into their hearts in 1993 when they awarded him the prestigious *Accademia Nazionale Dei Lincei* prize. This award has a long history, going back to Isaac Newton's predecessor Galileo. It was an early step in canonising the 'Newton of finance', which would lead him to Stockholm four years later.

1994, Merton began regular meetings with the mandarins of
y. Over fine food and wine, underneath the frescoed ceilings of
issance-era head office, the Palazzo Koch, Merton would have
is vision of the spiral of innovation. He would have told them
LTCM was, and how Italy could be part of the magic too.

This is not to suggest that Merton was a conduit for inside information
from the Treasury, or that LTCM did anything illegal. An innocent
explanation of Merton's presence in Rome is that he was Meriwether's
salesman, merely exploiting his intellectual status while touting for investors.

If this explanation is correct, Merton can take credit for persuading the
Bank of Italy to invest directly in the Long-Term Capital Portfolio. If
LTCM was to help engineer Emu convergence, this was a logical step for
the Bank – if it owned part of the fund, then LTCM was more likely to
deliver on its promise. The Bank could also share in some of the profits.

For Meriwether, it was another 'strategic relationship'. Rather than by
the Bank itself, the investment of $100 million was made in October 1994 by
the Italian Foreign Exchange Office (UIC), a separate but closely related
entity that intervened in the currency markets on the Bank's behalf. It would
be a lucrative deal on both sides.[4]

The plan was orchestrated from London, by the $23 million man,
LTCM's Victor Haghani. In LTCM's offices on Conduit Street – a stone's
throw from Salomon Brothers' trading floor in Victoria Plaza – Haghani
had constructed a mini-empire. That year, Meriwether had hired a fellow
principal to work with him – Hans Hufschmid, the Salomon currency trader
who did so well during the 1992 ERM crisis. But Haghani was in charge.

As LTCM's youngest co-founder, along with his former Salomon
research sidekick, Larry Hilibrand, Haghani's coolness under fire was
legendary. While Hilibrand was said to dabble in far-right libertarian politics,
Haghani had no outside interests. He was a living arbitrage machine. LTCM
counterparties found his character chilling.

According to one of London's top swaps dealers, working for a US
investment bank, 'Long Term had a real arrogant streak. Victor seems like
the politest, gentlest guy on earth, but the message is crystal-clear. I've never
heard Victor sound even slightly perturbed. But that said, when something

---

4. The UIC also made relative value investments in early 1994 with three Wall Street firms, Merrill
   Lynch, Salomon Brothers and JP Morgan. All three firms had large proprietary trading divisions
   and were active in the Italian market. Including LTCM, the UIC invested a total of $500 million.

upsets him, its clear to the person he's talking to. He's actually a very nice guy. Almost too mellow – you wonder if it's for real.'

Although its execution would be aggressive in the extreme, LTCM's Italian bet was no less grounded in finance theory than any other Salomon bond arbitrage play. By using the over-the-counter derivatives market, LTCM could also avoid detection. The key element was that in Italy, two yield curves were out of line.

As we saw in Chapter 3, a yield curve is simply the market price (seen through yield goggles of course) of the time value of money, ranging from a very short-term borrowing, to a debt of 30 years or more. In the United States, the yields of Treasury debt trace out the benchmark yield curve.

Since the 1980s, an alternative benchmark had established itself among the world's biggest debt markets. Called the swap curve, it traces out the price of interest rate swaps lasting for different periods of time – where a price of a single swap represents the market value of a series of floating rate interest payments made for a specified number of years.

Unlike government bonds, swaps are derivative contracts traded by big investment banks in (mostly) London and New York. In the US, banks are seen as more risky to do business with than the government, so the swap curve sits on top of the Treasury yield curve like a layer of foam on a wave. The thickness of this foam layer is called the *swap spread*.

But in 1994, receiving Italian Lira swap payments from an investment bank in London was seen as being less risky than making a loan and getting bond coupons from the profligate Italian government. In other words, the Italian Lira swap curve, as it was called, was valued more highly by the market, and through the yield goggles that means it sat *under* the Italian government bond yield curve.

There was a further factor at work. The fixed rate side of a swap is the value of all the future floating rate payments lumped together. As we saw in Chapter 4, if floating rates are expected to fall in the future, that pushes the current swap rate down.

In 1994, the market knew that within five years – if Emu went ahead – Italian floating rates would have to be identical to Germany's, since both rates would then be set by the European Central Bank. The fixed rate paid on a Lira swap fell in anticipation of this. Meanwhile the interest coupon on BTPs stayed high as investors remained shy of Italian government debt.

Haghani, along with other hedge funds and prop desks who followed in his wake, could use a simple money machine to take advantage of this difference. Firstly, he could order his traders to buy BTPs on repo through another bank, such as Morgan Stanley. The deal would work like this. The Italian Treasury holds auctions of BTPs every three months in Milan. LTCM could place orders through banks that were entitled to bid. As soon as LTCM received its allocation of BTPs they would be transferred to Morgan Stanley which would then pay the Treasury in cash.

At this point, LTCM – as the bond's owner – would receive BTP coupons from the Italian Treasury while paying Lira Libor (the London interbank offer rate) to Morgan Stanley which held the bond as collateral. Haghani's traders would then construct the second half of the money machine by entering into a Lira interest rate swap contract with a completely different bank, perhaps Deutsche Bank.

On this deal LTCM would receive Lira Libor, cancelling out the payment it was making to Morgan Stanley, while paying Deutsche the fixed swap rate. The overall effect was for LTCM to earn the difference between the BTP and swap rates until they moved closer together. At this point the swap would be terminated and the BTP sold onto the market.

An essential part of this trade, and a hallmark of LTCM, was that each interlocking component of this money machine involved a different bank as counterparty. That way, LTCM could try and prevent any rival from learning about and copying its trades. Like the parable of three blind men standing next to an elephant and identifying it differently according to whether they touch its tail, trunk or side, LTCM kept its counterparties in the dark.

However, this trade, although it would prove immensely profitable for some, was not done in great size by LTCM. The reason lay in Greenwich, Connecticut, with John Meriwether and Eric Rosenfeld. Both men were convinced that Italy was a terrible credit risk, and that Italian government bond prices could plunge at any time. This happened briefly in 1995, when the Lira fell against the dollar.

With a BTP repo trade on its books, LTCM would be exposed to this credit risk when it needed to sell the BTP at a future date. When Haghani suggested the trade at a partners' meeting in Greenwich, he was told to go back to London and think again.

How could Haghani reap the benefit without taking the risk? A solution came from a variant of the interest rate swap which had been invented around 1990. Called the asset swap, this contract allowed the owner of a bond to exchange his fixed rate coupons for a floating rate.

The bond's owner would keep the credit risk of the bond, which would now effectively pay him a floating rate. Asset swaps were popular with European domestic banks which had floating rate liabilities due to their customer deposit accounts. By purchasing an 'asset swap package' these banks quickly could match their liabilities and avoid getting in trouble with bank regulators.

Where LTCM could come in was as a provider of such a package in Italian government bonds. First buying up the bonds in the auction, LTCM would then sell the asset swap package, getting the credit risk off its books and receiving the BTP coupons it wanted via the asset swap.

The interest rate swap in the original trade would work the same as before, and LTCM would pay a fixed rate to a different counterparty. Rather than own any bonds, LTCM now had two off-balance sheet derivative transactions – an asset swap and an interest rate swap.

This was a smart idea, but there were several catches involved. First and foremost, why would anyone want to take on the Italian credit risk? The reason lies at the door of that conclave of central bankers, the Basle Committeee on Banking Supervision.

In its wisdom, when the Committee decided in 1988 that banks would have to allocate 8 per cent capital against their loans, they exempted loans made to European governments. Italian government bonds required no capital and this more than compensated European retail banks for taking on the credit risk. On top of this, many European investors were keen to take on the risk as an outright bet that Italy would make it into Emu.

The second catch was harder to overcome. Selling asset swap packages to European domestic banks required a large, locally knowledgeable salesforce – something which Meriwether had ruled out from the start. Also, smaller banks didn't have the ability to manage collateral which was required since LTCM didn't have a credit rating. Meriwether needed an investment bank as go-between. However, he didn't have to look far to find one.

Under the nose of Deryck Maughan, Meriwether and his former sales chief Dick Leahy had maintained a close relationship with his network of loyal ex-subordinates at Salomon Brothers. Many of them openly despised Maughan for not re-hiring their hero. Now they would play a vital role in LTCM's plans.

There was also Deutsche Bank which had recently poached Edson Mitchell from Merrill Lynch and Meriwether's protégé, Saman Majd from Salomon. Deutsche was the envy of Wall Street because of its dominant position in the lucrative German market.

Salomon's and Deutsche's salesmen would provide LTCM with liquidity, selling on the Italian bonds that LTCM provided in asset swap packages to their customer base, taking a slice of the profit in the process. The two firms would do a swap with each customer, backing this up through an identical swap with LTCM. It was yet another of Meriwether's strategic relationships.

The money machine was now much more sophisticated. It needed Italian government bonds flowing through it to work. They would be sucked up at Bank of Italy auctions in Milan, and spat out in asset swap packages to German retail banks. Salomon Brothers' and Deutsche Bank's function was to be a sort of water pump that increased the flow.

At first sight, this new machine was less immediately profitable than the first one, because the buyer of the asset swap was supposed to receive an extra bit (called an asset swap spread) in addition to Lira Libor in its floating rate payment. This cut into the meat of the trade – namely the difference between BTP yields and Lira swap rates that LTCM would earn as profit.

To make the machine worthwhile, Haghani had two choices. He could make the bonds entering the machine cheaper, or he could make the bonds leaving it more expensive. The second choice meant finding buyers who were prepared to pay more for the asset swap package than it was worth.

According to the top London swaps dealer quoted above, this was a quintessential aspect of LTCM's style: 'I think there were two kinds of people they wanted to deal with. One was people who were as smart as they were but who just had a different mindset about the way they used their brains; who were just going to give liquidity.' Salomon Brothers (post-Meriwether), Deutsche Bank and JP Morgan fell into this category.

The second category was different. 'The other people Long-Term liked to deal with were the idiots, who could be picked off routinely', continues the dealer. So we can imagine Haghani ordering his traders to spend long days phoning, phoning and phoning German Landesbanks and Hypobanks until they found someone who would naïvely misprice a BTP asset swap and be 'picked off' by LTCM.

The other method open to Haghani was even more dubious. If the flow of BTPs elsewhere in the market could somehow be blocked, then would-be buyers would be forced to come to LTCM and pay higher prices. This would have required taking the BTPs out of the market at source – in other words, squeezing the Bank of Italy bond auctions.

As one Italian dealer now working for a US bank puts it, 'Squeezing auctions is a dirty business.' The usual reason for doing it is to go for the jugular of competitors. Many dealers take short positions before a bond auction. Sometimes it is because they expect the increased supply to lower prices. It may also be a bet on bad economic news, or an attempt to short a liquid security in an arbitrage play.

Back in the nineteenth century, Chicago futures speculators had 'cornered' markets in this way. On Wall Street in the late 1980s, Paul Mozer had caused exquisite pain to Salomon's rivals when he squeezed the US Treasury auctions. After the Fed imposed the 35 per cent bidding rule to quell the practice, Mozer's inability to change his bad habits turned him into a felon.

But there were no 35 per cent rules in Europe. If you bid a high enough price, it was possible to take an entire issue out of the market. Arguably, had Paul Mozer been posted to Europe, he might still be a top investment banker today.

The precise role of some of Mozer's former colleagues at LTCM and Salomon Brothers in the Italian bond market will probably never be revealed, but among domestic Italian bankers, the date of 1 August 1994 is famous.

Prior to the BTP auction held that day, several of the biggest Italian banks had taken large short positions, betting that problems experienced by the incumbent Berlusconi government would translate into falling bond prices.

However, Salomon Brothers is said to have muscled in and bought up the entire auction, driving up prices and causing massive losses to the shocked Italians. It was like the Furies descending. Wall Street had arrived in Italy.

As Salomon's main source of bidding orders, LTCM joined in the turkey shoot at this auction, and several subsequent ones. Driving up prices wasn't difficult since hundreds of small Italian banks had promised BTPs to their private clients. Desperate to guarantee supply lest they lose these valuable clients, the banks were forced to go cap in hand to Salomon, and Haghani's traders at LTCM, paying high prices for the bonds. Insurance companies forced by law to invest in the bonds also fell victim to the squeeze.

It is interesting to place Haghani's strategy in the context of finance theory. As we have seen throughout this book, arbitrage and relative value depend on being able to replicate one security with something very close to it.

'Inefficiency' – perhaps an irrational demand for liquidity, or a tax law which treated the two securities differently – would move the prices apart. Buying one and shorting the other would yield an arbitrage profit. The inefficiency was always something extrinsic, that existed out there in the market and could be exploited.

But squeezing auctions went beyond this. It was making the market inefficient so one could make it efficient again. Some would call this cheating, and it isn't surprising that Italy's 'widows and orphans' feel bitter about how they were treated.

Haghani's BTP money machine did well in 1994 and early 1995, but it soon began to run out of juice. Other prop desks and hedge funds had smelt the opportunity and were piling in. The spread between BTP yields and Lira swaps began to narrow. But the money machine was too good to waste, and the Italian government had another bond in circulation which could be fed to it instead. It was called the CCT.[5]

The CCT was a floating rate note, which meant that rather than pay a fixed rate decided at the time of issue like a normal bond, it would pay a short-term rate, adjusted every few months. However, CCTs didn't pay Libor, the benchmark floating rate, but a different rate dependent on yet another Italian government bond, short-term Treasury bills called BOTs.[6]

Here Haghani struck pay dirt. The small Italian banks offering retail deposit accounts were excluded from the London Libor money markets, and instead bought BOTs for their customers. With this captive market, the Bank of Italy had long been able to sell these bonds expensively – making their yields about 0.5 per cent less than Lira Libor.

CCT investors knew this and demanded a premium on the floating rate to compensate them. Typically this premium was 30 basis points, or 0.3 per cent more than the BOT rate. However, CCTs had a maturity of seven years, taking them well into the Emu era.

Haghani and a few others made an observation: with a single currency, Italian banks would be free to look elsewhere in Europe for short-term government bonds, so the BOT yields would have to rise. However, the CCT promised the premium for its entire life. It looked like free money and it was.

The money machine was simpler this time. LTCM, with Salomon Brothers' help, bought massively in CCT auctions, then sold the equivalent asset swap package to German and other European retail banks with the assistance of Deutsche Bank. Receiving the overpriced CCT rate and paying Lira Libor, the resulting position was known as a 'CCT basis swap'.

Even if they extracted the full 0.3 per cent premium for the entire life of the trade, for someone physically holding the bond it was a negligible profit. However, CCT basis swaps, as an off-balance sheet derivative, permitted LTCM to leverage up the trade over 100 times, and earn 30–40 per cent return on capital.

5.   Certificati di Credito del Tesoro.
6.   Buoni Ordinari del Tesoro.

To take such a large position required an enormous temporary position in the physical bond. So while the total amount of CCTs outstanding was $408 billion in 1996, it is believed that 25 per cent of this market passed through LTCM's money machine during a two-year period. Needless to say, stories abound of the squeezing of CCT auctions as well.

Few other investment banks had even an inkling of what was going on. Nor did they have Haghani's magic ability to conceal his traces. In one notorious case in 1996, Credit Suisse First Boston, a firm known for its brashness, was caught red-handed trying to arbitrage Italy's post office savings bonds, and was pressurised into handing $80 million of profit back to the Italian Treasury. LTCM, with its secret network of inside contacts, never had such problems.

However, the huge flow required by the CCT trade eventually tested LTCM's relationship with Salomon Brothers to the limit. Haghani had a nasty fright when his former colleagues decided to stop providing him with liquidity. Without the credit rating needed to deal directly with Salomon's customers, Haghani's money machine was filling up with unwanted bonds that he didn't want. Something had to be done fast.

At this point he met with the leading swap dealer we met above. The encounter is a revealing one. The venue was a high-class London brasserie called Quaglinos. The dealer takes up the story . . .

It was a cordial lunch, and we talked about three or four things we'd done together, and the markets. Then we got to the subject of CCT basis swaps. We had purchased in that market only peripherally. We hadn't made a big investment in it, we had looked at it analytically and asked, how would you hedge this thing, as opposed to the way you could have looked at it, which was to see it as a commodity and try and find both sides.

As a result we were not present in it, and we definitely missed the opportunity to make some money.

And in what otherwise had been a very cordial lunch, Victor came out and said, 'you guys, you're just a joke in that market.'

So I went, 'well, why do you care?'

'It's just, you must be stupid. There's money sitting there on the table for you to take. I can give you the phone numbers of the people to call, from whom you can generate a handy profit. All you have to do is commit a little bit of capital to it. It's money for nothing.'

He came on so strong, that it was very obvious to me that they'd gotten themselves into a huge position, and that nobody was providing them with liquidity.

They were getting all their liquidity from Salomon Brothers, who was quite happy to put them through to the handful of pension funds and insurers on the other side. And when it came time for Long-Term to look for some liquidity in terms of exit, it wasn't there.

I could be wrong. It could be that they really did think we were just morons, and said how could we be so dumb not to figure this one out? And he was doing me a favour. But we looked at that market every week for the year before that and the year after that, and never found it to be a viable market. But we knew that Long-Term had the position on up to the eyeballs. They were huge, huge, huge.

Although this dealer did not follow the suggestion to phone the potential victims, luckily for Haghani, another bank soon did and the trade worked according to plan. Perhaps it is only a coincidence, but in June 1997, the LTCM partners and a group of senior Deutsche Bank executives celebrated their relationship with a golf outing in the Scottish highlands.

Between 1994 and early 1997, Haghani's Italian trades earned a significant proportion of LTCM's profits. By the end of 1996, a single dollar that had been invested in the fund back in early 1994 was now worth $2.40 – after LTCM had taken its 25 per cent cut. Italy's Foreign Exchange Office received a $122 million return on its investment.

Over at the Italian Treasury and the Bank of Italy, the mandarins were pleased. The interest being paid on Italy's debt had fallen by nearly half, contributing to the decline in the deficit. With the bonds now so much more expensive, fewer needed to be issued, helping the debt/deficit ratio. To the disbelief of the Germans, Italy had met its Maastricht target.

One man was unable to join in the celebrations at the Palazzo Koch in early 1997. That was Alberto Giovannini. No longer chairman of the Treasury's council of experts, he was about to start work as an economist working in LTCM's London office. His new boss was Victor Haghani.

The Swiss connection

While the Italian trade was perhaps the pinnacle of LTCM's success in the fixed income world, in some ways it was a retrograde step. Although yield curve models – those strings with bluebottles attached – were used to find out what BTP and CCT prices *should* be, to a large extent the trade relied on brawn rather than brain. Haghani had to push the bonds through the money machine to make a decent profit.

For the founders of option theory, and their disciples, it was slightly disappointing. Why weren't they using their incredible talents to the full? There were some options trades on LTCM's books, to be sure, mostly involving bonds with hidden options such as convertibles or callables.

In particular, Haghani himself made a nice profit courtesy of the Belgian government when it issued a badly mispriced option-laden bond nicknamed the 'Philippe'. But these trades were sideshows compared with the huge bond and swap deals LTCM was doing in Europe and the US.

But that was about to change. In 1997, options would take centre stage at LTCM. Not in interest rates, though, but in the old-fashioned stock market.

Carefully nurtured by Eric Rosenfeld, a team of strategists led by David Modest had been scouring the world's stock markets for opportunities. This had been an area forbidden to Rosenfeld and his colleagues when they were at Salomon. Soon they would be ready to plunge into the market. One opportunity the strategists noticed was in long-dated stock index options.

We last saw this kind of option back in Chapter 5, when Mark Rubinstein and Hayne Leland used the idea of replication in Black, Scholes and Merton's original theory to invent portfolio insurance. Their dream crumbled when the assumptions behind the theory broke down in the October 1987 crash.

A mere strategy that imitated options clearly wasn't good enough. After that débâcle, people wanted the real thing. There was a gap in the market waiting to be filled. However, in the US, the fund managers who had used portfolio insurance started using exchange-listed options instead. These markets were liquid and widely used. There were precious few opportunities for LTCM there.

The take-off in over-the-counter stock options would happen in Europe. And to a large degree, this new market was pioneered by the Union Bank of Switzerland (UBS). The story of this bank's rise and fall not only shows how LTCM found the option deal of a lifetime, but also takes us into John Meriwether's most fateful strategic relationship.

Back in the early 1970s, while Black, Scholes and Merton were putting the finishing touches on their theory, Ramy Goldstein was a lieutenant in a crack unit of Israeli paratroopers leading highly secret cross-border missions into Arab territory. Finishing his military service just before the October 1973 Yom Kippur war, Goldstein studied economics in London before making his way to Yale University where he became one of Steve Ross's first PhD students.

Ross remembers his student as being 'full of testosterone' and with a taste for combat in his blood, Goldstein was too restless for the pace of academia. After completing his finance PhD in 1978, he spent three years advising telephone company AT&T on portfolio management, but then entered the financial war zone as a self-employed trader doing bond and options arbitrage.

While today the layers have become more rigid, there is a well-trodden path from the blue-collar world of exchanges to white-collar investment bank trading desks. Particularly for options, being a self-employed 'local' on an exchange is a good way to learn the tricks of the market – especially liquidity – without risking too much money to do so. Daily margining ensures that.

In 1986, Goldstein decided to go for the big money, and he began visiting the Wall Street firms. This was the heyday of the Salomon arbitrage group, and Goldstein naturally paid a visit to Meriwether. However, the two men didn't hit it off, and instead, Goldstein ended up at the investment bank First Boston.

Rather than work in the fashionable area of interest rate derivatives, Goldstein took his chance in equities. Portfolio insurance flourished before the Crash because investment banks wouldn't sell index options. Unsurprisingly, Goldstein found First Boston's equities division was completely ignorant about derivatives. 'They had no idea about volatility' he recalls.

Over the next five years, Goldstein honed his skills, moving to the UBS in 1990. According to Goldstein, UBS had a 'pathetic reputation' in equity derivatives at the time, and was notorious for losing $20 million on a single warrant deal in Switzerland.

Emerging as a top dog in the age-old Swiss private banking tradition, UBS, along with its rivals Swiss Bank Corporation (SBC) and Credit Suisse, was breaking out of private banking, which depended on a dubious passion for secrecy, and becoming a global investment bank. Rather than hide Nazi gold like it had done in the past, UBS wanted to join the fun on Wall Street.

So when Goldstein proposed setting up a new global equity derivatives (GED) division, he found willing backers. Armed with a business plan, and deep Swiss pockets behind him, Goldstein began hiring and deploying his team. While his US and Japanese traders would do well enough, Goldstein hit the jackpot in Europe, with the invention of what he called structured products.

Structured products are no more than a means of packaging equity index options. The idea is to offer retail customers a chance to invest in the stock market without the risk of losing their money. In their simplest form, they consist of a long-dated index call option and a government bond. If the index falls, the option will expire worthlessly, but the government bond guarantees that you get your initial investment back.

Way back in the 1970s, Merton and Scholes had tried to launch structured products in the US, but had failed. The willingness of ordinary Americans to take risks on the stock market probably played a part in this. Buying options was like chickening out.

Europe is different. Until a few years ago, most investors (and the pension funds who invested on their behalf) largely avoided stocks in favour of their local government bond markets. Safety was an important reason among traditionally cautious northern Europe, while in inflation-ridden southern European countries such as Italy, government bonds paid high rates of interest. Investment and tax regulations also played a role.

However, even before LTCM descended like a banshee on Italy, interest rates were already declining elsewhere in Europe in the run-up to Emu. Earning less on their investments, Europeans were forced to look elsewhere. Equities looked appealing, especially since a wave of privatisations put huge amounts of affordable stocks on the market.

Structured products were the answer to everyone's prayers – the index call option gave an exciting equity kick, with a government bond attached as a comfort blanket. They made a lot of sense for older investors approaching retirement, and anyone worried about dipping their toes in the stock market.

People didn't actually buy the products direct from investment banks like UBS. Insurance companies and retail banks would buy them wholesale – usually in amounts of a few hundred million dollars at a time – then package them up with shop-window displays and brochures. Starting in Britain, the business quickly spread all over Europe.

The early products typically promised all of the upside on an index like the FTSE 100 after five years, with a guarantee that investors would get at least 100 per cent of their money back.[7] Unlike the US mutual funds that used portfolio insurance in the 1980s, the European insurance companies had legally binding derivatives contracts with the banks to ensure that they in turn could meet their obligations to the customers who bought these products.

But what about the investment banks providing the products in the first place? How did they hedge themselves? The government bond was simply sold directly to the insurance company – there was no risk there. But the index call option was a different story. Goldstein and his GED traders went

---

7. There would be penalties for early withdrawal, and the retailer usually took a 5 per cent fee which was non-returnable.

back to the basics of option theory to handle the problem. They started out
with delta-hedging.

Recall from Chapter 4 the tree model that Steve Ross invented together with
Rubinstein and John Cox. After the index chooses to go up or down at a
particular fork in the tree, an option trader must then buy or sell an
appropriate amount of the index so that the replicating portfolio – the option
plus underlying – is immune from the random outcome of the next fork.

When delta-hedging a call option in this way, the dealer is having to play
catch up – buying the index after it has risen, and selling after it as fallen. The
strategy always loses money over the life of the option – as it must, because it
is simply the option's mirror image. By the law of no-arbitrage, this loss,
when added up over the entire garden of forking paths, must be equal to
the premium charged for the option.

But as Rubinstein had learned to his cost, delta-hedging isn't enough
when the index makes big jumps. Such jumps can rapidly increase the value
of the option after it has been sold. This is because options are 'nonlinear' –
they offer unlimited upside in return for limited downside. However, an
index portfolio is linear – it goes up or down in proportion to the level of
the index itself.

So delta-hedging is like trying to trace out a curved shape using straight
lines. When the curve bends sharply – because a jump in the index makes the
option change its value rapidly – delta-hedging breaks down. The answer is
to include some curves in your hedging toolkit; in other words, buy some
options. The curviness of an option portfolio is called gamma, and protecting
against it is called gamma-hedging.

Emanuel Derman describes it well: 'The greater the curvature – gamma
– of the track the option rides on, the more sharply the options driver must
turn the steering wheel to keep the hedge on track as the index moves.'

So how big is the option premium? The Black–Scholes formula lets you
calculate the answer, but the garden of forking paths lets you actually *see* it.
When the index has high volatility, the branches of the tree are spread out like
a cedar, then the dealer has to pay more to catch up with the index after each
move. That makes the option expensive. When the index volatility is low,
the branches are bunched together like a cypress, and the option is cheap.

Index volatility, as we have seen, is defined as the standard deviation of
index returns. To find this, we take the daily returns for the last month, or a
year, or perhaps ten years, and work out the answer (as described in Chapter
1). However, if we used this number, called 'historical volatility' by option

traders, to price an option that we were selling today, we could be making a grave error.

The volatility in the Black–Scholes formula, that determines the spacing of tree branches, is the volatility *realised* during the life of the option. That lies in the future. As we saw in Chapter 2, Black, Scholes and Merton lost money when they used historical volatility – which looks back in time – to price warrants.

What option traders do in practice is take the price of options in the market, and turn the handle of the Black–Scholes formula backwards to find out what the market *expects* volatility to be in the future. This is called 'implied volatility', because it is *implied* by option prices in the market.

When Ramy Goldstein started selling five-year call options on European indexes, there wasn't a market that existed already, which would allow implied volatility to be used. Instead, Goldstein's quants used historical volatility as a first guess, then refined the guess by simulating the tree model inside a computer. They would also extrapolate the volatility of short-dated options which were already traded in the market.

It wasn't that bad an idea to use historical volatility. Because the options had such a long lifetime, the realised volatility over five years or so would probably be close to the long-term average historical volatility for the index – which was about 15 per cent a year. This reasoning was similar to that used by insurance companies – the number of insurance claims might go up or down every year, but in the long term, accidents or deaths happened at predictable rates.

Once the options had been sold, Goldstein's traders would hedge them using index futures, and also by buying portfolios of the underlying stocks. This was cheap because, as a large bank, UBS was constantly dealing shares for its clients already. To gamma-hedge their positions, the traders bought short-dated index options that were traded on European exchanges, buying new ones (called 'rolling over') as the old options expired.

As the market in structured products grew, and more banks entered the game, a market in long-dated index options started to take shape. The insurance companies no longer had to depend on a single bank, but could phone around for the best price. Among the small network of dealers involved, a new number was bandied about: the implied volatility for long-dated index options.

This implied volatility was greater than the equivalent five-year historical volatility. It had to be. Historical volatility might reflect how much it cost to replicate an option during its life using delta-hedging. In the real world, the dealers also had to gamma-hedge, and make a profit too.

This difference between implied and historical volatility encouraged newcomers into the structured products market. After all, statistics showed that the realised volatility over the next five years would very likely be similar to the previous five years' historical volatility. In other words, the future would be like the past.

By receiving an option premium based on a higher implied figure, and then delta and gamma-hedging their positions, dealers should be able to 'release' the difference between historical and implied over five years. Indeed, between 1992 and 1996, Goldstein's GED reported 'three digit million' profits every year.

However, there was another meaning to implied volatility. Because options are more valuable when volatility is high, owning them is like having a stake in volatility itself. In the street slang of dealers, selling options is called 'selling volatility'. By making a sale, you have staked your belief that the current level of implied volatility is a fair price.

But markets move on, and circumstances change. What if you change your mind? Now you need to buy the volatility back, and cut back on your exposure. Gamma-hedging doesn't help here, because that is done using short-dated options. Here you are committed to a contract lasting five years.

So if an options seller wants to get out of the business, he must find someone willing to sell that volatility back to him. On the open market, implied volatility is effectively the price he must pay. That is why seasoned options traders call implied volatility the 'cost of reinsurance'. It's just like the way insurance companies buy insurance against the risks they don't want from reinsurers.

Following the principle of marking-to-market discussed in the last chapter, each day, Goldstein's GED traders would construct a grid of implied volatility. Like a yield curve, it always stretched out into the future, away from the present. Close at hand, there would be short-dated index options traded on exchanges. Further out, the prices of long-dated options would be fed into the grid. When the implied volatility was plotted as a height above this grid, then the resulting landscape was known as a 'volatility surface'.

The nearby hills and valleys of this surface were familiar territory. The options here were so heavily traded that prices were reliable. Further away, the landscape appeared solid. But no-one would know until they walked upon it, or in other words, tried to buy reinsurance against their long-dated positions.

Before late 1997, Goldstein and the other players in European structured products hadn't given this question much thought. It was a booming, growing market after all. That year, about $20 billion worth of these products would be issued. But the party at the GED division was about to end.

It was around this time that LTCM forged its largest, most fateful strategic relationship of all – with UBS. In a pattern we have seen before, the catalyst was a former subordinate of Meriwether's who had joined the firm's fixed income division. His name was Ron Tannenbaum, and he was responsible for forging contacts between UBS and hedge funds.

The chief executive of UBS at this time was Mathis Cabiallavetta. As the leading member of a small clique of UBS managers originating from the same Romansch-speaking canton in southern Switzerland, Cabiallavetta had spearheaded UBS's attempt to compete with Wall Street. He was especially proud of Goldstein's GED.

But it wasn't enough for Cabiallavetta. For him, the pinnacle of Wall Street mystique was John Meriwether. The exploits – and profits – of Salomon's bond arbitrage group were legendary, and now they were doing it again at LTCM. Cabiallavetta envied those insiders like Merrill Lynch or the Bank of Italy who had the privilege of a 'strategic relationship'.

What particularly irked Cabiallavetta was that in 1993, before UBS made him CEO, Meriwether had invited UBS to invest, but the firm had said no. Now, in 1997, Meriwether had closed the fund to new investors after reporting 40 per cent plus returns for two years in a row. So eager were investors to get involved that a 'grey market' in LTCM shares had sprung up, with a 10 per cent premium being demanded per share.

Hans-Peter Bauer, UBS's head of fixed income thought he had an ace in the hole – Ron Tannenbaum. So in 1996, Bauer sent Tannenbaum to visit Meriwether in Greenwich to sound him out about the possibility of a UBS investment. This time, it was Meriwether's turn to say no.

One reason for Meriwether's response might have been the brush-off he'd received from UBS back in 1993. But more important was the need to keep control of the fund. Meriwether faced a classic problem experienced by every growing company. As a company grows, it needs additional capital to expand. But how do you raise money without diluting the equity ownership of the founders? The solution is to borrow money instead.

So LTCM started to solicit loans. In April 1997 the Bank of Italy's foreign exchange office lent $150 million. Around the same time, Chase Manhattan put together a syndicated loan facility totalling $900 million. More complicated than simply handing over the cash and earning interest, this worked like an enormous overdraft, which LTCM could draw upon if needed. Rather than work on its own, Chase put together a group of banks (the 'syndicate') which made funds available to LTCM.

But this wasn't glamorous enough for Cabiallavetta and Bauer. They wanted a piece of LTCM. What could UBS do? What ultimately made a deal possible was the schizophrenic nature of LTCM itself. For Meriwether and his partners, the fund was two different things. It was a business – a money machine factory – and they were its managers. But it was also their private pension fund.

When they founded LTCM in 1993, these men had sunk all their wealth – which was substantial – into the fund. Eric Rosenfeld had even boasted that his children's money was invested as well. As LTCM took flight, they became bewitched by their own success.

Hans Hufschmid, when he joined in 1995, not only invested all the money he had earned at Salomon Brothers, but borrowed $14 million from French bank Crédit Lyonnais to increase the size of his stake. In 1997, Larry Hilibrand went further and borrowed $24 million – doubling his investment.

The mood of excitement spread downwards to LTCM's employees. Many of the strategists and traders also invested their life savings in LTCM. By allowing them to have a stake, LTCM's principals cemented their loyalty. Working at investment banks before joining, some of these employees had earned hundreds of thousands or even millions of dollars a year in bonuses, but that didn't have the thrill of owning part of LTCM.

As the management company running the fund, the high fees meant that LTCM's profits from the fund were outstripping those of the ordinary investors. While investor net returns in 1995 and 1996 were around 40 per cent, LTCM's own return for those years was 63 per cent and 57 per cent respectively.

Most of this profit was reinvested in the fund. The main reason for this was taxes. Until the principals took their profits as income, they wouldn't be subject to income tax. As long the money remained offshore in the fund, the US government couldn't touch it.

Under US tax law, this is called a 'deferral' and is supposed to encourage long-term saving. By deferring income from an investment until retirement, investors not only build up a larger nest-egg, but can then be taxed at a lower rate because they are no longer earning a salary.

In LTCM's accounts, deferrals began to outstrip direct investments in 1995, and by the end of 1996 the deferral was $819 million, compared to $579 million in income-earning investment. Of course, LTCM's total stake was these two figures added together, and this was growing rapidly.

The effect of this growing stake was like a slow buy-back of shares over time. When the fund started up in 1994, LTCM had owned 10 per cent, but by the end of 1996 it had over a quarter for itself. But none of the LTCM partners – except for Scholes, who was now 56 – was likely to retire soon. How could they get their hands on the money without paying top income tax rates on it?

As LTCM's resident tax expert, Scholes pondered the question. In the US, like in many other countries, income tax is much higher than capital gains tax, which is only paid when you cash in on an investment such as a share. While deferrals merely put off the day of reckoning, if LTCM could turn its income into capital gains, the principals would save a fortune.

Scholes had been preaching the answer to that problem for years: use derivatives! The idea was to turn LTCM's deferred stake in the fund, which would pay a definite income, into something that *might* bring in a profit in the future – and that could be treated as capital gains. For this to work, some other institution would have to own the stake, at least temporarily. Here, at last, was a role for UBS. Scholes phoned Tannenbaum.

The deal Scholes cooked up for Tannenbaum was audacious. And appropriately for the man whose name graced the most famous formula in finance, it involved an option. The reason was simple. If UBS were simply to hold onto LTCM's deferred stake for a few years and then hand it back, there wouldn't be any risk involved, and the tax authorities might smell a rat.

However, if LTCM bought an option on the value of the deferred stake from UBS, giving it the right to buy back the stake at its current value in the future, then it would only be worth anything if the value went up. There was an element of risk involved, which would satisfy the taxman.

So in April 1997, Scholes proposed that UBS sell LTCM an option on its own performance. The size of the stake underlying the deal would be $800 million – roughly the same size as LTCM's deferred reinvestment. After seven years, the option could be exercised and LTCM would buy back the stake (which was expected to soar in value), at its original price.

If the deal went ahead, LTCM would pay a $300 million cash premium for the option. To hedge the option it had sold, UBS would buy a $800 million chunk of LTCM – if only for seven years. It would borrow about $300 million to fund this transaction, and the option premium would compensate UBS for doing this. This was the carrot that Scholes dangled in front of Tannenbaum. And it worked – Bauer and Cabiallavetta were delighted.

Ironically however, this option that Scholes had cooked up involved very little option theory. As we have seen in earlier chapters, the great leap in finance theory was that options could be hedged dynamically. By buying and selling a certain amount of stock at each up or down fork in the price, the seller of an option could replicate it and be almost perfectly immunised against risk.

For dynamic hedging to work, the underlying stock must be bought and sold frequently. That's why the small print of the Black–Scholes formula says that markets must be 'continuous and frictionless'. But the last thing Meriwether wanted was for LTCM shares to be traded in the market each day. That would involve marking-to-market and would invite the sort of public scrutiny which made life so difficult at Salomon Brothers.

So rather than protect itself by delta or gamma-hedging according to daily price movements, UBS would sit on the entire value of the share in LTCM until the option matured. This is known among option dealers as a 'covered write' or 'covered call' and is considered by some traders to be a rip-off.

Why? If the share goes up in price, all of its upside is paid out on the option. If the share value plummets, the option loses its value, but the covered call holder is exposed to the full decline in share price. Compare this with delta-hedging, where if the stock goes down, the holding in that stock is gradually sold off.

Tannenbaum might have raised this as a concern, because Scholes added a sweetener. If the LTCM stake did go down in price, UBS could, after a year, convert its holding into a seven-year floating rate loan. The rate LTCM would pay on this loan would be 0.5 per cent more than Libor – the same kind of rate paid by major investment banks.

The economic effect of this clause was insidious. If LTCM got into trouble, UBS could do nothing except replace one kind of exposure, market risk, with another, credit risk. For Meriwether and his partners, the clause transformed what looked like a call option into a put option – the right to sell their deferred stake at its current price.

LTCM would receive $800 million in cash immediately from UBS, and if the stake then declined, the worst that could happen would be that the partners would have to pay the sum back after seven years at an incredibly generous rate of interest. What isn't clear is how much profit UBS could earn on the $800 million stake before the option expired.

According to former UBS executives, there was a plan to package it up for outside investors, together with other hedge funds. This 'fund of funds' package would take the risk off UBS's books and allow it to earn a fee instead. However, nothing came of this plan. Meanwhile, no other investment bank would do a similar deal, except for Credit Suisse, which took a smaller stake of $100 million.

At least UBS would have the $300 million option premium to fall back on – reducing its total exposure to $500 million. But it seems clear that risk was not at the forefront of peoples' minds. So keen was Cabiallavetta in owning a piece of Wall Street legend that UBS invested $266 million of this premium as an additional direct investment in LTCM. Unlike the $800 million hedge, UBS would get the full upside on this stake.

In dollar terms, this was Meriwether's biggest strategic relationship of all. It was also the most advantageous. For UBS it felt like the deal of the century, and many of Bauer's team wanted to invest their own savings in LTCM, but were turned away. But as the deal was put together in late 1996, Meriwether wanted more. He took time to entertain the starstruck Cabiallavetta, inviting him on golf trips, along with other UBS executives and LTCM partners.

One topic kept cropping up during conversations. Meriwether and his partners would complain about the large numbers of counterparties they were forced to do business with. It made it harder to keep details of LTCM's money machines secret, which meant that rival prop desks were jumping in and taking profits that should rightfully be theirs.

It would be nice, said the partners, to do business with UBS. And one area they were now particularly interested in was equity derivatives. 'That's one of our strongest areas' replied Cabiallavetta, who went on to recount how Ramy Goldstein was king of the structured product market. 'We know that' said Meriwether. 'We'd like to see him.'

So that autumn, Goldstein was asked to join Cabiallavetta and Bauer when they flew to Greenwich to visit LTCM's lair. In a conference room overlooking Long Island Sound, Meriwether and the other principals held a long meeting with the UBS executives. Only Merton was absent. Haghani was busy trading, but briefly entered the room to shake hands with the guests.

As Meriwether talked of wanting to 'deepen his relationship' with UBS, Goldstein recalls asking himself, 'why is this happening?' On the table in front of them was a briefing document containing details of the $800 million option deal. Mullins then spoke about Fed interest rate policy, and Rosenfeld urged UBS to 'execute with LTCM' if index volatility went out of line.

Afterwards, driving in a limousine with Bauer back to the airport, Goldstein said the meeting had been 'a waste of his time'. But then he had an insight. As Goldstein now recalls, it was the 'body language' between Cabiallavetta and Meriwether that lodged in his mind.

They behaved like firm friends. Meriwether's game, thought Goldstein was subtle. 'I realised that Meriwether wanted to be able to rely on

Cabiallavetta if it ever came to a crisis. He wanted to be able to phone up and be able to ask for $300 million.'

Back in London, under pressure from Tannenbaum, Goldstein's dealers executed a trade on the Japanese Nikkei index for LTCM. However, Goldstein was unimpressed: 'Why should we help them make free money in the market? LTCM to us was a competitor and so I told my desk to avoid them.'

Other London dealers had been getting calls too. Bernard Oppetit, the head of equity derivatives at the investment bank Paribas – a leader in the French structured product market – was even invited to Conduit Street to meet Hans Hufschmid. Since Hufschmid was notorious in London for his huge Salomon bonuses, Oppetit recalls being slightly in awe as he met his host, but recalls him as being 'not striking in any way'.

Hufschmid and LTCM's head equity trader Vladimir Ragulin then proceeded to fire questions at Oppetit: 'They were interested in having a picture of supply and demand in long-term volatility. They were asking who was buying and selling, why, how much and so on.' However, LTCM didn't trade at this point.

What was going on at LTCM? In Greenwich, strategist David Modest had been investigating the new guaranteed product market, and had reached two conclusions. First, the long-dated index options being sold to insurance companies were overpriced, when compared with the cost of physically hedging them for four or five years.

Second, the banks that sold these options wouldn't want the trouble of keeping these positions for such a long time. They had sold long-dated volatility, but soon they would want to buy it back again. In particular, if implied volatility went up, mark-to-market losses for the sellers would go up too. Under the Basle market risk rules, some would have to cut positions.

What LTCM could do was then step in as a reinsurance company, taking on the risk that others didn't want. Comfortably outside the Basle regime, LTCM would secure the long-term financing needed to sell long-dated index options to the banks. A money machine could then be constructed which would guarantee a profit.

Merton had played a role in thinking up this new venture. For him, the structured product market was a textbook story from the financial innovation spiral. Ever since his PhD thesis, Merton had looked at how investors should best save money amid uncertain markets.

The great thing about options, said Merton, was that they allowed ordinary investors to forget about buying and selling stocks. By paying to receive only the upside on the index, all the dirty work could be left to a sophisticated trading firm which was best qualified to do it.

The future, Merton said, would be full of these smart 'financial gadgets', the convenience of digital mobile phones, and today's guaranteed products were the first stage. The price of long-dated index options was high because only a few firms were selling them. As the new market became 'commoditised', prices would come down. By selling the options now, LTCM would not only hitch a ride on the spiral of innovation, but could help build it by reducing some of the risks in the market.

It was a compelling argument, and in a principals' meeting that spring, Eric Rosenfeld approved Modest's strategy. Haghani and Hufschmid had then hired two traders to scour the London market for opportunities. And that is what Goldstein and Oppetit were noticing.

However, LTCM wasn't ready to trade, because it wasn't sure whether long-dated option prices had peaked yet. Soon, however, events would convince Haghani's traders that the time was right. The most important event that that changed their thinking was the downfall of Ramy Goldstein.

The central bank of volatility

Trouble started heading Goldstein's way early in 1997 when a hiccup in the Japanese convertible bond market began causing heavy losses for his Tokyo traders. At over $100 million, the losses would look bad, but since UBS was reporting record profits for the first half of the year, the problem wasn't noticed.

But Goldstein's aura really slipped in July. The UK New Labour government had been in office for only a month when the Chancellor Gordon Brown unveiled his first budget. Buried inside was the abolition of an obscure tax break which had allowed pension funds to claim back taxes paid on share dividends. This was disastrous for Goldstein.

Why? Investment banks like UBS had taken advantage of the tax break too. As we have seen, anyone selling long-dated options on the FTSE index needed to hold the underlying stocks as a delta-hedge. The tax break made the stocks more profitable, and UBS had passed this bonus on to customers.

However, Goldstein's traders had assumed that the tax break would continue indefinitely. Suddenly it was gone. The UBS losses exceeded $70 million, and were widely reported in the press. Already, the profits of the GED group for the year had been wiped out.

But worse was to come. Since 1994, equity markets all over the world had risen steadily. Nowhere was this more spectacular than in the emerging economies of South East Asia. In the US, President Clinton fostered a policy encouraging these nations to allow foreign investment. Clinton's standard bearer for the new policy was US Treasury Secretary Robert Rubin, the former chairman of Goldman Sachs whom Clinton appointed in 1995.

That year, a total of $77 billion flooded into Asia, rising to $93 billion in 1996. These nations – Thailand, Indonesia, Malaysia, South Korea and the Philippines – tied or 'pegged' their local currencies to the dollar using central bank intervention, rather like the European Exchange Rate Mechanism.

This meant that Western investors could earn higher returns on their local currency investments in these high-flying economies, then cash out back into dollars. Meanwhile, the high interest rates on offer in these countries also encouraged many Western investment banks to make dollar loans to Asian companies. Collateral for these loans was in local currency.

For three years, the 'Asian Tigers' enjoyed an extraordinary boom. Glittering skyscrapers and shopping malls sprang up where once there had been jungle or rubber plantations. Asian entrepreneurs made fortunes, and one Thai billionaire made it into the record books when he spent $100,000 on a wedding for his favourite two cats. In China, two tycoons had a dollar bill burning contest, to see who was richer.

But by early 1997, the Thai stock market, which had grown on a real estate bubble, was declining. Dollar loans, however, were still being made. Hedge funds, in the same manner as George Soros had done in 1992, saw an opportunity. As the Asian bubble burst, Western investors would want to withdraw their capital and change local currency back into dollars. This would put downward pressure on exchange rates.

Just like in 1992, hedge funds and prop desks began a speculative attack. They picked on Thailand as the first target. Selling the Thai Baht short using forward contracts – the funds took on the Thai Central Bank which had $30 billion in dollar reserves. Forcing the Bank to spend all its dollars to buy back Baht, the funds and prop desks finally drew blood on 1 July, when the dollar peg was abandoned. Malaysia, the Philippines and Indonesia soon followed Thailand as targets for hedge fund attacks.[8]

---

8. It is misleading, however, to paint the hedge funds as villains and the Asian nations as innocent victims. Real estate prices in some parts of Australia doubled during the crisis due to an influx of Asian money.

In September, the International Monetary Fund held its annual conference in Hong Kong. Malaysia's Prime Minister, Dr Mahathir Mohammed, had been booked to speak, and used the opportunity to rail against foreign speculators. At the same time, UBS held a reception nearby where Cabiallavetta spoke of his relationship with LTCM, and toasted Meriwether in champagne.

In Europe, no-one seemed that concerned at first. But, as one Asian economy collapsed after another, nervousness spread. Like invisible smoke spreading outwards from a distant fire, volatility started rising in European stock markets too.

What no-one expected, least of all Goldstein, was that the effect would be so dramatic in the European index options market. In early September, the prices of short-dated options began to rise sharply on European exchanges. Cranking the Black–Scholes formula backwards, the volatility anticipated over the next three months by option dealers jumped by 25 per cent.

Suddenly, all the long-dated option sellers had a problem. To gamma-hedge, they had to buy these short-dated options to avoid being exposed to jumps in the market. But the high cost of gamma-hedging began to eat into profits. However, the prices of long-dated options (expressed as implied volatility) represented an estimate of the costs of this hedging. So five-year implied volatility for index options went up too.

As the cost of reinsurance went up, the traders started feeling a sick sensation in their stomachs. If they had to get out of the market now, they were doomed to pay more than what they had received in the first place – in other words, they would have to 'lock in' their losses. These men who had been earning millions a year were suddenly one step away from being fired.

Unfortunately, they would not receive much sympathy from their management. The radar system of VAR had become universal, ever since it had been anointed by regulators. When long-dated index option positions were marked-to-market – in other words, compared with the cost of reinsurance – the equity derivatives traders were breaching their VAR limits.

For Goldstein, there was another problem to deal with. He had developed a particularly big line of business selling an exotic type of structured product involving the correlation between different indexes. Now he found that his London-based quant, Tim Mortimer, had mispriced this product. Goldstein would have to rebalance his books, and rehedge his positions.

Cabiallavetta was already nervous about Goldstein's losses earlier that year. Now this had happened. For some unknown reason, Cabiallavetta decided to go public and hold a press conference, revealing that UBS had a 'model problem'. To this day, Goldstein remains bitter about the consequences:

> There was no point in revealing that because rivals who knew roughly what our positions were could reverse engineer and work out what positions we would have to take in the market to make our hedging adjustments. So we would find that whatever we needed to buy went sky high, and whatever we needed to sell went through the floor. Tipping the market off was just about the worst thing they ever could have done.

It was now October, and the growing turmoil in the stock markets peaked on 27 October, when the Dow Jones Industrial Average fell by 550 points. Earlier that year, JP Morgan had estimated that the investment banks active in the London structured products market had sold so many index options that for every single percentage point rise in long-dated implied volatility, they stood collectively to lose $400 million.

Long-dated implied volatility, which had been at 16 per cent for months, jumped above 20 per cent for the first time, and rose to 24 per cent in November. Assuming that JP Morgan's reckoning was accurate, the collective mark-to-market losses in London were now over $3 billion.

Cabiallavetta had had enough, and ordered Goldstein to cut his positions. With the cost of reinsurance now so high, it was like asking Goldstein to cut his own throat. Goldstein says: 'If Mathis hadn't panicked, we would've ridden with it. All you're doing by reducing exposure is ensuring that the money won't come back.'

UBS would acknowledge losses of $420 million in 1997, and on 17 November, Goldstein was dismissed. Today, he feels that he was stabbed in the back by a 'fair weather friend'.

Elsewhere, a similar story was played out. Senior management at Barclays, Natwest, Salomon Brothers and Bankers Trust all decided to bite the bullet and get out of long-dated index options at once. To do that, they would have to buy back the volatility they had sold. But who from?

At LTCM's London office, Haghani's traders swept into action, offering precious volatility to all who needed it – at a price. So eager were they to trade that LTCM acquired a nickname among London's equity derivatives traders: the Central Bank of Volatility.

Of course, from LTCM's point of view, it was free money. The data showed that historical volatility in European markets was close to 15 per cent. LTCM was being paid good money on the expectation that it would be 23 per cent or 25 per cent. And with term financing, there was no chance of positions being closed down before they made a profit. LTCM's positions would be marked-to-market at the cost of reinsurance, but any changes either way were backed by ironclad US government collateral.

Over at the investment banks, the panicky CEOs and risk managers were delighted that LTCM was stepping in. By January, over $100 million of the $400 million exposure reported by JP Morgan had been absorbed by LTCM. Other hedge funds were encouraged to sell volatility too, and some desks even invented a new derivatives contract, the 'volatility swap' to enable them to do it in a simple way.

A couple of months earlier in the US, it was Merton and Scholes' turn to drink champagne, when on 14 October, they were awarded the Nobel Prize in economics for their work on option pricing. Scholes was not at LTCM when the news came through. Having become an avid golfer, he was in California playing at the Pebble Beach course – a Meriwether favourite – when his brother phoned from his car after hearing about the prize on the radio.

Merton was in Boston when journalists knocked on the door of his apartment at 6a.m. to tell him the good news. Emerging bleary eyed, Merton was persuaded to don a suit and be photographed on the banks of the Charles River.

Then came the trip to Stockholm to receive the prize itself. It was a sweet moment for both men. For Scholes it was the summit reached after a long journey out of childhood adversity. For Merton, not only had he equalled his sociologist father in stature, but firmly quashed for good all those naysayers who claimed that he wasn't a 'real economist'.

In an autobiography he provided to the Nobel Foundation, Merton depicted LTCM as the climax of his career: 'It was deliciously intense and exciting to have been a part of creating LTCM. For making it possible, I will never be able to adequately express my indebtedness to my extraordinarily talented LTCM colleagues. The distinctive LTCM experience from the beginning to the present characterises the theme of the productive interaction of finance theory and finance practice.'

Both men were now multimillionaires, thanks to their stake in LTCM. And they had changed since the days of being obscure academics. Both had divorced, and had found new partners. Scholes was seeing a California lawyer, Jan Blaustein. They planned to get married and build a house together near Stanford.

As for Merton, he had separated from his wife June in 1996, and braving a storm of gossip, began dating a much younger, fellow professor at the Harvard Business School, Lisa Meuhlbroek. He also bought a sports car, and ex-students noticed that his hair had somehow changed colour from a distinguished grey to a lusty shade of chestnut.

But amid all the festivities and self-congratulation that took place in the closing weeks of 1997, there was a deadly serious debate going on within LTCM itself. It boiled down to some fundamental questions – what was LTCM's purpose? Where was it going?

Without question, LTCM had proved itself to be the world's greatest money machine. The world's biggest investment banks held it in awe. Governments treated it as a valued partner, to be used whenever markets weren't efficient enough to achieve macroeconomic goals. It was global – even the communist-run Bank of China was a strategic investor – and was untouched by turmoil in the markets, and the whims of risk managers.

However, the core fixed income markets in which LTCM had flourished seemed to have yielded their riches. European Monetary Union was now virtually a certainty, and mispriced bonds were getting harder to find. In the US, mortgage bonds were trading at record low spreads to Treasuries.

The firm was branching out into equities, and David Modest was rewarded for his efforts with a coveted partnership in January. Meanwhile, Greg Hawkins was exploring possibilities in Russia, which seemed to many like the largest potential free market ever seen. But could LTCM keep on winning on its bets?

According to some of the principals, it was time for a change. LTCM was an impressive brand name, and now it needed to branch out and become a real investment bank. By going into markets such as client derivatives or asset management, LTCM could hope to find additional liquidity, as well as a sizeable ballast of capital to protect against swings in its core proprietary trading activity.

The downside was all the things that Meriwether and Rosenfeld had hated at Salomon: 6000 employees, pushy shareholders and tough regulators like the Fed breathing down their necks. LTCM's hardcore traders, in particular Haghani and Hilibrand, didn't want to belong to that culture any more.

Something would have to be done, because LTCM's annual returns would soon have to be announced. While the sheer amount of cash earned by LTCM in 1997 was $0.95 billion, only a third less than the $1.64 billion earned in 1996, the amount of capital underpinning it was considerably larger.

Since returns are calculated as the earnings divided by capital, the 1997 returns, unlike 1995 and 1996, were distinctly less impressive than before. Investors would receive a net return of only 17 per cent. Not bad compared to US Treasury bonds at 6 per cent, but dismal compared to the S&P 500 which was returning 31 per cent – not including dividends – for the same level of risk.

So it was already getting harder to earn the kind of mythical returns of the past, but making it harder was the size of LTCM's capital balance, which at the beginning of December 1997 stood at $7,065,341,077. This was too much capital on which to earn high returns. Either some would have to be invested somewhere completely new – such as buying up or building an investment banking franchise – or it would have to be given back to investors.

It was the LTCM's newfound role as the 'Central Bank of Volatility' which tipped the balance. Why go to the trouble of starting a new business when such an unbeatable bet was now sitting on LTCM's books? LTCM should take advantage of its unregulated status, give back the capital it didn't want and wait for the bet to pay off.

So that December, Meriwether wrote to about half of his original investors and told them that they would be getting their money back, with no further opportunity to invest in LTCM. A total of $2.7 billion was returned in this way. There was nothing the investors could do except complain.

Like a warship with decks stripped clean for action, LTCM began 1998 with a pared-down capital balance of $4,667,953,483. Just enough to fuel the vast money machines humming away at Greenwich and Conduit Street. LTCM was less than nine months away from disaster.

8

The Song of a Martingale

*Why did I gamble? I did not need to, for I had all the money I wanted to satisfy
my wishes. Why did I gamble when I felt my losses so keenly?*
Giacomo Casanova, *History of My Life*

Venice, 1754. It is the time of the annual Carnival, and masked revellers are
everywhere. Renowned womaniser Giacomo Casanova is conducting an
illicit affair with M.M, a noble-born nun, who wants to raise money to
escape her convent and elope to Paris. Casanova attempts to increase his
mistress's capital at the gaming tables.

> She made me promise to go to the casino for money to play in partnership
> with her. I went there and took all the gold I found, and, determinedly
> doubling my stakes according to the system known as the martingale, I
> won three or four times a day during the rest of the Carnival. I never lost
> the sixth card. If I had lost it, I should have been out of funds. In this way I
> was increasing my dear M.M's little capital . . .

Surprisingly, Casanova's colourful escapade takes us into the mathematical
heart of modern finance theory. The game he played – wearing a mask under
Venetian law – was called faro, similar to roulette, in that gamblers place
chips on a numbered baize table. Rather than use a spinning wheel, however,
the croupier draws playing cards from a shuffled pack.

Supposing that Casanova is betting on red (diamonds or hearts), then he
has a 50–50 chance of doubling his money on each draw of a card.[1] How does
the martingale work? If the croupier draws red, Casanova takes his winnings
and quits the game. If black comes up, Casanova doubles his stake and bets
again.

---

1. In roulette, the presence of zero on the wheel gives the casino an in-built advantage; in faro, the house
    wins whenever a pair is drawn in succession.

He starts out betting a single gold coin. Losing that, he puts down two coins, then four coins, eight coins and finally sixteen coins. Four black cards have come up in a row, and it is now the fifth card – luckily a red one. Casanova wins sixteen coins, plus his sixteen coin stake. However, he has already lost fifteen coins. So his total winnings consist of only a single coin.

The allure of the martingale as a betting system lies in its promise that you will win eventually, as long as you have enough capital to keep doubling your stake. Unfortunately, you might just go bankrupt before that happens. For example, in the unlikely event that the 26 black cards in the pack appeared in a row, Casanova would have needed to stake 67 million gold coins to win just one.

Even in a 'fair' casino which doesn't have a built-in advantage, the random order of the cards can go against you. In a real casino, the martingale is even more hazardous, as Casanova later found out to his cost:

> At this same time I was being ruined at cards. Playing by the martingale, I lost very large sums; urged on by M.M herself, I sold all her diamonds, leaving her in possession of only five hundred zecchini. There was no more question of an elopement.

His luck running out, Casanova was soon arrested and imprisoned by the Inquisition; he then escaped and made his way to Paris, where he founded the national lottery. Today, the martingale is banned from most casinos, but has found its way into finance theory.

For mathematicians, the term martingale is used to describe any process subject to chance where the expected future outcome equals today's outcome. Casanova expected – in an ideal world – to win one coin regardless of whether the game ended at the first card or the fifth. Mathematicians found it useful to consider a sort of idealised game in which Casanova would always win.

Finance is full of chance and randomness. Some compare it to gambling – so perhaps we can reproduce Casanova's betting system by investing. However, the return on a stock today – as brokers are supposed to warn their clients – is no indication of its return tomorrow. Stock price returns are not martingales. Nor are options.

But in 1979, two finance theorists, Michael Harrison and David Kreps, showed that the replicating portfolio of a stock *and* an option was a martingale. In other words, if you kept delta and gamma-hedging to match the break-even price of the option, the net value of your portfolio could never change.[2]

Martingales put Cox, Ross and Rubinstein's theory of trees on a rigorous mathematical footing. Harrison, Kreps and a third academic, Stanley Pliska, proved powerful theorems stating that if a martingale existed, no-arbitrage had to follow, while the ability to hedge meant that derivative prices were unique. As quants grew in power on Wall Street during the 1980s and 1990s, these martingale theorems gave them even more confidence in what they were doing.

In love with leverage

Meriwether's protégés at Salomon were no exception. The subtext of martingales was that if the strict mathematical conditions were violated — because of a mispricing in the market — then you could build a money machine. And here was a theorem which said you had to make money! No wonder Scholes felt able to berate the Midwesterners who doubted him. Indeed, most of LTCM's bets were essentially martingales.

However, the small print of martingales — which had wiped out Casanova in 1754 — was that while you were assured of profit in the long run, there was no limit on the amount of capital you needed to put on the table in the meantime. LTCM's bets depended on some irrationality in the markets being ironed out over time by the spiral of innovation. But there was nothing to say the markets couldn't get more irrational before they got rational.

LTCM had a big advantage over Casanova — leverage. Using its inverted pyramids of repoed bonds and swaps, Meriwether and his partners could lay huge amounts on the green baize table. One reason for this was that most money machines are to some degree, self-financing — if one component, such as a swap, declines in value, another bit, say a bond, will be worth more. Once the machine has been constructed, it hardly needs to be fed any more cash to keep running.

A further failsafe was supposed to come from LTCM's diversity. If one machine broke down badly and lost money, the others working in different, unconnected markets should carry on making a profit. Most important of all, no bank could pull the plug by cutting credit lines. With dozens of collateral

---

2. Strictly speaking, the portfolio's growth at the risk-free interest rate must be factored out.

accounts – like 'tiny Swapcos' – everyone could feel secure at all times. As long as sufficient collateral was there, legal agreements prevented banks from reneging on contracts.

These collateral accounts were dynamically managed, topped up with just enough Treasury bonds, but no more. If too much collateral was sitting in one counterparty's account, it would automatically be called back and put to use somewhere else. An influx of Treasury bonds, perhaps borrowed as part of a short position, might briefly be directed into another collateral account if needed.

A large part of LTCM's white-collar workforce was devoted to keeping the system running 24 hours a day by constantly shifting collateral between the firm's dozens of counterparties. One of the principals, an ex-Salomon trader called Robert Shustak, worked as LTCM's full-time chief financial officer (CFO) overseeing this process. Running it on a day-to-day basis were two key staffers – head of operations, Ira Rosenblum, and his European deputy, Murray Chatfield.

Underlying the whole pyramid was LTCM's equity capital base which by April 1998 stood at $4.87 billion. As LTCM would later say, it had a 'large fraction of equity capital held as excess liquidity due to working capital discipline'. What this means is that most of this total existed in the form of cash or short-term US Treasury bills sitting in LTCM's clearing account at Bear Stearns. And with investors' money locked up for three years, they couldn't touch it.

If a money machine became jammed, some of this liquid capital could be poured in to get it working again. If a collateral account couldn't be supplied fast enough from LTCM's other positions, some of the $4.87 billion could be instantly transferred to keep the counterparty happy. And if that wasn't enough, there was always Chase Manhattan's $900 million standby loan facility.

Underlying everything was the assumption that no money machine could misfire so badly, and no counterparty could ever demand so much collateral, that the $4.87 billion would not be sufficient to keep things going. So strong was Meriwether and his partners' belief in this assumption that – as we have seen – they forced their investors, under protest, to take back $2.7 billion.

But how good was the assumption? How could LTCM be sure of not suffering the same fate as Casanova back in 1754? It came down to risk management. Like JP Morgan or Bankers Trust back in the early 1990s, LTCM needed a global radar system for the entire fund. It needed what is now called firm-wide risk management.

When LTCM started trading in February 1994, this system didn't yet exist. Each money machine was finely engineered; its dozens of moving parts forming a beautiful, interlocking whole. For example, the Italian CCT money machine was adjusted to give an optimal performance given the various risks present in the Italian market. LTCM risk managers would express this in terms of Italy's swap curve – what if the curve rose, steepened, flattened and so on?

Statistical analysis on a computer would identify these risks or 'factors', and the risk managers would then use them as control dials, to maximise profit against the amount of collateral and borrowing costs that Victor Haghani had allocated to the trade.

What wasn't so well thought out was how different money machines interacted with each other. Could a sudden twist in the Italian swap curve affect the German curve? Could a jump in US mortgage bond yields affect long-dated implied index volatility? An important part of LTCM's sales pitch had been that this interaction was negligible, because correlations between different markets were low.

The purpose of a firm-wide risk management system is to constantly check such assumptions. So in 1994, after discussing the issue in their regular Tuesday morning risk management meetings, LTCM's principals began building such a system. They called it the 'Risk Aggregator'.

The Risk Aggregator has been the subject of much debate. As is now clear, it either didn't work properly or was misused by the LTCM partners – none of whom will now accept responsibility. One of Haghani's former lieutenants gave the following account of how it was supposed to work:

> The Risk Aggregator was a layer that collated those exposures across asset classes. It started with very few links to the existing risk management systems. The main goal was to be complete, and the only way to be complete was to start with a spreadsheet and manually record all your exposure. Eventually we built the links back to the systems that tell you how you're exposed to certain market conditions and so on. But the Risk Aggregator was there just to look at the overall portfolio risk and return.

Running on its own computer, separate from the money machines, the Risk Aggregator produced a VAR number for LTCM. In April 1998, it was telling the partners in the Tuesday morning meetings that the daily volatility of the fund was $45 million.

Translated into VAR terms, and using the Normal distribution, LTCM's capital – which then stood at $4.87 billion – would decline by no more than $45 million, two days out of three. Nineteen days out of twenty, it could decline by no more than $105 million.

It's more useful to translate the figure into monthly terms, since daily figures aren't available from LTCM. Scaling the daily figure up over the 21 trading days available in a month, LTCM's monthly VAR was $339 million.[3]

However, between February 1994 and April 1998, LTCM made a mean return of 1.96 per cent, which on $4.87 billion of capital, means a monthly profit of $95 million. The difference between this profit and the VAR number – $244 million – is the monthly loss, under standard risk management procedure, that was supposed to set alarm bells ringing.

Of course, LTCM's partners were much too sophisticated to assume that the Normal distribution was an accurate description of LTCM's daily or monthly returns. So once the Risk Aggregator had delivered its VAR number, Tuesday mornings became a campfire session of market monster stories – in other words, stress testing was done.

David Modest later recalled the flavour of these meetings: 'We spent time thinking about what happens if there's a magnitude ten earthquake in Tokyo, what happens if there's a 35 per cent one-day crash in the US stock market. We certainly spent hours and hours thinking about it.'

These nightmare scenarios were fed back into the Risk Aggregator, which would calculate the amount of capital LTCM could lose in each case. The very worst case possible, according to Modest, was that the fund could lose $2.5 billion – or over half its capital.

However, this unpleasant possibility was never taken very seriously. Even after losing half its capital, LTCM would still have the other half left to keep the money machines running. Moreover, the stress test assumed that the all-important collateral management system wouldn't be affected.

But the main reason that monster events were treated like fairy stories was because no-one knew how often they happened. Markets under normal conditions had a distribution, where daily returns belonged to a well-behaved population, just like a group of dogs or cats with different heights.

Monster events were badly behaved *by definition*. Where did they fit in? If you knew how often they happened, you could say how much you might expect to lose. Modest and the other principals couldn't agree on this.

So in the end, everyone in the Tuesday morning meetings felt that their time was better spent discussing VAR, which seemed much more useful

---

3. The random walk underlying the Normal distribution means that to scale up standard deviations, you multiply by the square root of time. I am grateful to Philippe Jorion for suggesting this calculation.

because it actually made predictions. As Modest would comment: 'Before the crisis we probably spent more time in risk management meetings talking about VAR than we did about stress loss'.

Perhaps it was the comfort blanket of VAR which added to the sense of confidence that led Meriwether and the other principals to hand back the $2.7 billion in December. After all, the following April, the Risk Aggregator said they could lose no more than $339 million – less than 10 per cent of capital – ninety-nine months out of a hundred. LTCM had only existed for 50 months. Surely there was no serious threat to the money machines.

If it was leverage that gave LTCM an advantage over Casanova, they had now pushed that advantage a long way. The effect of shrinking the capital base was to increase balance sheet leverage – the ratio of assets to capital – from 18.3 to 27.7. With its $1.25 trillion off-balance sheet positions, the fund's true leverage was even higher. No one questioned this leverage as excessive. According to Modest: 'We decided to go for leverage and we didn't think it would be much of a problem.'

But it was Merton and Scholes who had clinched the high leverage argument. I found this out after I paid LTCM a visit in April. Working for a finance trade magazine in London, I was putting together a special supplement to commemorate the 25th anniversary of the publication of Black, Scholes and Merton's groundbreaking options papers.

Merton and Scholes agreed to an interview, so I flew to the US to meet them. Arriving in Boston, I found Merton in his office at the Harvard Business School; putting on a brown tweed jacket, he walked me across the campus to the Business School Faculty Club where we had lunch overlooking the Charles River.

Merton was a charming host – he even apologised that some building work by the University was spoiling the view. With little prompting, he went into a lengthy exposition of the spiral of innovation, and the idea that economic functions were more important than the institutions that carried them out.

Merton was full of excitement about the brave new world of sophisticated financial products that he had helped bring about. The enthusiasm was sincere, but slightly disembodied, and he reminds me of Carl Sagan or Arthur C. Clarke – a believer that technology alone can make us into better and happier people.

LTCM hardly entered the conversation at all. The lunch continued for two hours, and as I listened to this amiable financial philosopher holding forth, I couldn't imagine anyone more different to the tense, high-strung derivatives traders I knew in London.

Perhaps this demeanour is responsible for Merton's image on Wall Street as a 'semi-detached' member of LTCM. All the bankers I know who have ever dealt with LTCM agree that Merton only had a peripheral role in the fund. 'He hasn't got a clue about trading', is a typical comment that they make. The truth is Merton was deeply involved in LTCM, but perhaps it suited both him and Meriwether that such perceptions were held.

Two days later, I found myself in the lobby of Osprey House in Greenwich, Connecticut – the headquarters of LTCM. I was there to meet Myron Scholes and I was an hour late. It didn't matter. No less charming than Merton, Scholes suggested we grab lunch in LTCM's cafeteria.

It was even more laid back and casual than the Business School Faculty Club. Scholes – wearing a V-neck golf club sweater – exchanged greetings with the young LTCM traders in the meal queue, then chatted to the cook behind the counter. Finally we returned to his office with our meal trays.

I didn't have much idea of what LTCM was in April 1998, and was more concerned with asking Scholes historical questions about his invention of the celebrated formula. But out of politeness, I asked about LTCM too. Was it an asset management company? Scholes responded, 'more like an asset and liability management company'. In other words, a hedge fund.

Scholes's style is very different from Merton. When Merton talks about financial innovation, people are mentioned only as cogs in the invisible mechanism. For Scholes, without the energy and drive of real people, none of it would ever have happened. Practical issues – such as liquidity – were constantly mentioned in our conversation.

Scholes seemed genuinely amazed at the impact of his formula on the world. Not only was he surprised at how existing options markets had grown in its wake but also he highlighted how the formula had led to the emergence of completely new markets such as interest rate options.

In retrospect, Scholes said some very revealing things during our conversation. He was particularly keen to point out the role played by the early Chicago options traders during the 1970s in the birth of risk management. But clearly he was also thinking about LTCM: 'How do you manage a leveraged book of business with people who don't have much capital? How do you finance their business efficiently?'

Even more pertinent was a comment about equity. He said, 'I like to think of equity as an all-purpose risk cushion. The more I have, the less risk I have, because I can't get hurt. On the other hand, if I have systematic hedging – a more targeted approach – that's interesting because there's a trade-off: it's costly to hedge, but it's also costly to use equity.'

For a long time, I didn't appreciate this statement. Then I found that Merton had said virtually the same thing in his December 1997 Nobel lecture: 'Non-financial firms currently use derivatives to hedge price risks. With improved lower-cost technology, this practice is likely to expand. Eventually, this alternative to equity capital as a cushion for risk could lead to a major change of corporate structures as more firms use hedging as a substitute for equity capital; thereby moving from publicly traded shares to closely-held private shares.'

These two statements say a lot about LTCM's fateful decision to hand back capital. In December, the principals had decided to reduce their 'risk cushion' by $2.7 billion. Why? Because the money machines towering above this capital, with their $120 billion of borrowed bonds and $1.25 trillion of derivatives, were themselves a substitute for it!

How? According to Scholes and Merton, the interlocking parts were now so perfectly engineered, that these devices were virtually capable of perpetual motion. As the technology of risk management continued to improve, the tiny sliver of equity underneath the inverted pyramid would vanish completely. There would be no need for excess cash to lubricate the money machines, and no need for irritating shareholders.

This last argument won over the former Salomon traders among the principals. According to one: 'I do believe that we viewed investors as a necessary evil. Ultimately, the fund was to become employee-owned. By that definition, you're setting up a situation where investors are going to lose out.'

Clearly, Scholes and Merton provided a philosophical basis for December's decision. At LTCM's zenith, they had a vision of zero capital and infinite leverage. It was Swift's flying island of Lapula all over again. Call it hubris or foresight, but this vision was soon to be tested to its limit.

Outliers

April 1998 was the last moment of innocence at LTCM; the last time all the models worked and the dream still appeared real. At this swansong, this final high point, what was LTCM doing? What were its biggest bets?

The latest LTCM annual accounts that are generally available are for the year end of 1997. Normally, such accounts were a closely guarded secret. A year later they were being touted around in an attempt to salvage LTCM's reputation, which is how they came into my hands.

The consolidated balance sheet shows $129 billion of assets and $124.5 billion of liabilities – like two paving stones propped apart by a $4.72 billion matchstick of equity. But the really astonishing numbers appear off-balance sheet. As we have already seen, LTCM's derivatives positions amount to a total of $1.25 trillion – most of this in fixed income derivatives such as swaps. The total equity derivatives notional is $35 billion.

How big is $1.25 trillion? It is roughly the size of Italy's national debt, or as one US congressman later pointed out, the same as the entire annual budget of the US government. Of course, LTCM didn't actually have this money, nor did it ever physically change hands.

In an interest rate swap, for example, the notional is used as an imaginary two-way loan which forms the basis of fixed and floating rate interest payments. It is these much smaller amounts that are exchanged between counterparties. The *net* amount changing hands is the difference between the fixed and floating payment, and that is even smaller again.

This kind of accounting prompts many derivatives advocates to criticise the fuss made over such huge numbers. They say that notional amounts are meaningless, and overstate the risk of derivatives. When talking about the original use of swaps, where investment banks do gentlemen's agreements with large corporations, this argument has weight. Every swap matches some existing form of borrowing, and probably does reduce risk rather than increase it.

However, with LTCM, that argument is wrong. We saw how LTCM used asset swaps to exert its muscle on the Italian bond market, without physically owning any securities. For LTCM, swaps were a means of leverage, giving it huge economic muscle power with virtually no capital. Merton and Scholes' giveaway statements above support this view. So in the case of LTCM, derivatives notionals are real numbers indicating the real economic effect of the fund. The actions of Alan Greenspan in October would bear this out.[4]

As for LTCM's bets themselves, they are buried somewhere in these numbers. We already know about the decision to sell long-dated index volatility. These trades started before Christmas 1997, and continued well into the New Year.

Another of Modest's trades involved stocks issued by the same company in different countries – for example Royal Dutch Shell (listed in New York) and Shell Transport (listed in London). Differences in investor appetite in each market made the stocks different in price. Called an equity pair trade,

---

4. The Counterparty Risk Management Policy Group discussed this issue in some detail as part of its June 1999 report.

the bet required owning the cheap stock and selling the expensive one short, to cash in when the stocks converged to the same price again.

There were several enormous trades in the US fixed income market. Meriwether's old favourite – the on-the-run/off-the-run Treasury trade – was there, along with another classic-type arbitrage trade between interest rate futures and the money markets. The biggest bet of all was that dollar swap rates were too big compared with equivalent Treasury bond yields.

In London, Victor Haghani had closed down the Italian money machine, and built a new one to take advantage of a subtle difference between the UK and German fixed income markets. His strategists had noticed the anomaly in what are called forward swap spreads. This is the difference between what the market expects swap rates to be in the future – say ten years' time – and what it expects government bond yields to be.

In the UK, this spread was 80 basis points (0.8 per cent) while in Germany it was only 20 basis points (0.2 per cent). But Britain was expected to join European Monetary Union within ten years, so the difference between the two forward spreads would have to decline to zero. So LTCM took a vast long position in UK forward spreads against a corresponding short position in Germany.

This was a complicated money machine *par excellence*. Part of it involved taking short positions in long-dated UK gilts. So big was LTCM's position that the usual way of shorting bonds wasn't enough.

With the help of Morgan Stanley, LTCM used an off-balance sheet solution called a 'total-return swap' which synthesised the effect of selling a long-dated gilt without a physical transaction taking place. As a result, say Morgan Stanley traders, LTCM's position was larger than the entire gilt market.

There were some other sizeable European trades, involving interest rate options, as well as Greg Hawkins's money machine built to exploit Danish mortgage bonds and some Soros-type bets on Scandinavian currencies. Meanwhile, Greg Hawkins's interest in Russia had led to some big positions in the Russian government bond market.

Far away in Tokyo, Arjun Krishnamachar had laid bets on the Japanese swap and government bond markets. Finally, Larry Hilibrand had found a new sideline betting on corporate takeovers and mergers, which was already bringing in significant profits. This last activity was slightly controversial among LTCM staff because there was no mathematical rule that said mergers had to take place.

Then, in May and June 1998, something strange happened. For the first time, LTCM lost serious amounts of money. For May, net returns were −6.42 per cent, corresponding to a loss of $312 million. June was even worse at −10.14 per cent, reducing LTCM's capital by $461 million. After staying within it for over four years, LTCM had breached its monthly VAR limit twice in a row.[5] It was a dangerous sign.

Why did it happen? It seems that the US mortgage market hit a rough patch, and one hedge fund went out of business at the time. But weren't the money machines supposed to be protected against such blips in the market? The explanation later given by Meriwether and his partners was to lay the blame at the door of the institution which had first allowed them to flourish: Salomon Brothers.

The firm had changed a lot since Meriwether cleared out his office back in August 1991. Buffett had gone, and in 1997, Salomon merged with the Travelers insurance group, whose CEO Sandy Weill took overall control. This was already a radical step, but then, in April 1998, Weill stunned Wall Street by announcing a further merger with Citibank. The stock of both companies jumped by $20 billion on the news.

Sandy Weill was a very different type of manager to John Gutfreund. Skilled at restructuring sluggish companies, Weill also knew what shareholders wanted: stable earnings and rising stock prices.

Meanwhile, Salomon's crowning glory, its bond arbitrage group, had lost its magic touch. By 1994, the group was losing hundreds of millions a year. Sometimes it would recoup, but the see-sawing earnings had made Salomon the butt of Wall Street analysts. The last straw for Weill came in 1997, when Salomon's London traders lost $200 million betting on the failed merger between British Telecom and MCI.

Some time around the Citibank merger announcement, Weill decided to get out of the arbitrage business. What the LTCM partners claim is that this decision immediately had an impact on the fund's positions. David Modest said: 'We had heard rumours that they were unwinding, and we thought that some of our poor performance was because of their unwinding.'

Modest's logic is that the Salomon arbitrage group had similar positions to LTCM's, particularly in US mortgage bonds and dollar interest rate swaps. If Salomon closed down these positions during May and June, and if they were large enough, the effect would be to move the market against LTCM.

---

5. Recall that the maximum monthly allowable loss is $244 million.

What we do know is that on 7 July 1998, Salomon Brothers announced that its legendary US bond arbitrage desk would be closed for good. So perhaps Weill had secretly shut down the positions to avoid tipping off the market, before making the announcement.

However, there is evidence which goes against LTCM's version of events. It comes from JP Morgan. According to a senior JP Morgan executive: 'We had specific conversations in May with Sandy Weill himself about taking over their arb book. He was committed to a tactical withdrawal from the US.'

Rather than simply shut down the operation, Weill was looking for buyers. Across Wall Street, traders were starting to wonder if arbitrage trading had had its day. Were the money machines being driven too hard in the quest for profit? Were those tightly interlocking parts starting to come loose?

Weill was warned about the danger, and urged to sell his money machines so that they could be carefully dismantled. The JP Morgan executive continues: 'We told him it was an accident waiting to happen. We were concerned that an exit by Salomon in a sloppy way would do real damage to the market, and we talked about taking it off them in one fell swoop.'

According to this source, when Weill finally did make the announcement in July, the positions were still in place. The ensuing wind-down, was 'botched' says the source, and cost Salomon $100 million.

Whatever actually happened, it seems that the LTCM principals genuinely believed that the source of their problems was Salomon. At first sight, things looked bad. The fund was now down 15 per cent on the year. It had never lost this much before. At a fateful risk management meeting during the last week of June, the principals debated what to do.

According to the Basle Committee rules followed by the big investment banks, a significant breach of VAR limits requires either an immediate increase in regulatory capital to cushion portfolios, or a corresponding reduction in positions.

As a hedge fund, LTCM wasn't bound by these rules, but the seasoned traders in the Greenwich conference room knew that they were based on sound principles. The sliver of capital underpinning the inverted pyramid had just got 15 per cent smaller. Would the edifice still stand up after another 15 per cent of these foundations went down the tube?

The principals agreed that the pyramid – LTCM's positions – should be cut back as a precaution. The daily dollar volatility of the fund would be reduced from $45 million to $35 million. But how? This figure for dollar volatility – the same as VAR – lumped together the combined effects of dozens of money machines, multiplying their volatility by the dollar size of each position.

Some of these money machines were fairly simple, like the on-the-run/ off-the-run Treasury trade. Others, such as sterling/deutschmark forward swap spreads or long-dated index volatility, were sophisticated and hard to dismantle. The question was, how significant were LTCM's May and June losses? Were they evidence that something was wrong with the models which had been used to design the machines?

This is an age-old issue in statistics. Suppose you are measuring the heights of a population of dogs with the help of some assistants. Most dogs are about a foot high, but just as you are about to calculate the mean and standard deviation, you notice that someone has measured a twenty-foot high dog. In statistical language, this is called an 'outlier', and the usual procedure is to throw out such nonsensical measurements.

Bill Krasker, the LTCM principal who had been Meriwether's chief quant at Salomon, had specialised in studying this problem while working in academia. In finance, a series of daily or monthly price returns takes the place of dog populations. Do you still ignore outlandish data? The danger is that this means ignoring the October 1987 crash like it was a twenty-foot dog.

Krasker believed that if you knew something about the system you were measuring, then this information could be used to decide whether outliers ought to be excluded. He called this 'qualitative robustness'. If you know you are measuring dogs, you exclude outliers, but if you are measuring an unknown animal, you leave them in.

Writing in an economics textbook, Krasker once said: 'The most reliable way to identify outliers in these contexts is to estimate robustly the model's underlying parameters, and check for observations that deviate greatly in an appropriate sense from the model's prediction.'

The returns on the S&P 500 index, which were subject to the whims of investors across the world, had no model behind them. In this case, freak events like October 1987 weren't outliers. They were part of the S&P's rich tapestry.

LTCM's returns were, on the other hand, the product of finely-tuned money machines. As one of the machines' chief designers, Krasker reasoned that he knew how they worked. In particular, they were designed to extract money as markets became efficient, and the spiral of innovation did its work.

Sandy Weill's decision to close the Salomon bond arbitrage desk didn't fit into that. It was nothing to do with the efficiency of markets – it wasn't 'fundamental'. The Salomon machines were similar to LTCM's; and eventually should make a profit. Pulling them to pieces was the senseless, clumsy act of an individual. For this reason, argued Krasker, LTCM's returns in May and June were outliers.

Krasker's reasoning was persuasive, as Modest would later recall: 'The fact that it wasn't for any fundamental reason probably made us over-confident. If you know why you're losing something, it's probably better than having no idea why you're losing it.'

The conclusion was that rather than dismantle the sophisticated money machines, LTCM should cut back the inverted pyramid by selling off things that could easily be bought back again in the market, when profits had risen again. In other words, LTCM should sell off its most liquid positions, like on-the-run Treasury bonds.

Then an objection was raised from the other side of the LTCM conference room. It came from Myron Scholes. A flavour of his views can be gleaned from what he had told me – with eerie foresight – two months earlier:

> Suppose you have a hedged book, and then you have to reduce the size of your balance sheet due to adverse hits on your capital. There's always a tendency to reduce or sell your more liquid securities first. If things continue to go against you, then you're left with the more illiquid securities, and a very unhedged book. So that's a very bad strategy. You should reduce your book proportionately – liquid and illiquid together.

Why did Scholes object so strongly? For him, there was a continuum between illiquid positions, such as long-dated volatility, through liquid positions like Treasury bonds all the way to the ultimate liquid security – cash itself. But cash was a major component of LTCM's equity capital, which was a last-ditch line of defence.

Liquid positions are so-called because they can be easily converted into cash. By getting rid of them, you are making it harder to raise cash if things really come to a pinch. In Scholes's view, liquid positions were like an option to raise capital – and that option was valuable.

This is what was worrying Scholes. When he had advocated replacing expensive equity cushions with carefully hedged money machines, he wanted this hidden option to be built in, like a parachute. Now his LTCM partners effectively wanted to throw the parachute out of the window to lighten the plane. Merton then spoke up in agreement with his fellow Nobel laureate.

Meriwether listened carefully. For him, however, it was his ex-Salomon protégés sitting at the table opposing Scholes and Merton who had what really counts on Wall Street – a track record. In particular, Eric Rosenfeld, Greg Hawkins, Larry Hilibrand and Victor Haghani had nearly fifty years of experience between them constructing these machines and earning billions of dollars with them.

Haghani's London lieutenant justifies his boss's views: 'People like Myron and Bob were not trading, and they were a little more distant from everything, so one of the reasons they might have been less convincing is that they were less informed.'

There was another reason why Meriwether came down on the side of his old colleagues. LTCM's illiquid positions – the elaborate money machines – were the most profitable. The liquid positions were the least profitable. The 15 per cent 'outlier' of May and June was an excuse to cut these positions out of the balance sheet.

Almost a year later, David Modest would recall this justification: 'If you're bringing the risk down 15 per cent, how are you going to do it? Are you going to cut everything across the board? We decided it was more rational to look at things trade by trade, close down the trades that were the least attractive, try and hold on to trades that were more attractive. That probably caused us . . .' Modest was unable to finish this sentence.

So at this crucial meeting in late June, Scholes and Merton were overruled. The giant money machines would be left intact. It was a fatal mistake. Now the carnage was about to begin in earnest.

Into the abyss

In July 1998, the boom in arbitrage trading – or 'relative value' to use the approved Wall Street marketing phrase – seemed unlikely to end. Hedge funds specialising in this strategy were being set up every week, following in LTCM's wake.

One such fund, Convergence Asset Management, founded in January by ex-Salomon trader Andy Fischer, raised $700 million in a single month purely from disgruntled investors denied a chance to buy into LTCM. Meanwhile, management consultancy Arthur Andersen offered advice for banks seeking some of the lucrative hedge fund business. As the bankers would later ruefully admit, the risks were largely ignored.

Hedge funds using relative value strategies were now a significant part of the swap market, accounting for 25 per cent of trading volume in London alone. Over in the proprietary trading departments of the investment banks, there was a similar frenzy. Goldman Sachs and Merrill Lynch were the biggest players, but others were fighting to catch up.

In March, for example, Goldman's top London proprietary options trader, David Seetapun, was headhunted by Credit Suisse First Boston. He had built up a huge position in the sterling options market at Goldman, and now did the same in deutschmarks and dollars at CSFB.

As July ran its course, some gossip circulated in London about LTCM's disappointing 15 per cent decline. But it was considered rather a symptom of a sluggish market than anything more ominous. LTCM would end July almost flat, with returns of 0.48 per cent. In retrospect, the fund probably lost money, but this was offset by the sale of liquid positions.

The mood lifted at LTCM that July, as Meriwether and the other principals joined Saman Majd and his Deutsche Bank colleagues for their, now, annual golf jaunt in the Scottish highlands. But it was the calm before the storm. When the first gusts of the impending hurricane started blowing in, they weren't a great threat. Perhaps because they came from a distant, unconnected source: Russia.

Over a year earlier, in April 1997, LTCM's Greg Hawkins had chaired a debate on Russia at MIT's World Economy Laboratory conference. The speaker was Maxim Boyko, one of the young reformists who was advising Russian president Yeltsin. In the audience was the usual mix of Federal Reserve governors, European foreign ministers and eminent economists.

Eighty years after Lenin's Red Guards stormed the Winter Palace in St Petersburg, a new breed of revolutionary was taking control of Russia. Instead of greatcoats, they wore suits. Instead of rifles, they wielded laptops and mobile phones. They were Russia's new capitalists.

The youthful reformers appointed to the government by President Yeltsin, such as Anatoly Chubais and Sergei Kiriyenko, painted the capitalists as a bulwark against the reactionary communist past. These dynamic entrepreneurs would have the energy to revitalise the country's decaying industrial base, which was state-owned. So in return for political support, the reformers began handing out shares, and a privatisation boom started. In 1997, the Russian stock market climbed by 149 per cent in dollar terms.

The reformers found eager supporters in the West. For 50 years since World War Two, the Soviet Empire had been a terrifying, well-armed monolith bent on global domination. Now, the collection of states which had emerged since the end of the Cold War had the potential to be the greatest free market the world had ever seen. Western money started pouring in, contributing to the stock market boom.

There were a few things that Russia hadn't sorted out yet – such as shareholder rights, bankruptcy law and tax collection – but these were mere 'inefficiencies' that would soon be ironed out in a warm bath of foreign investment. That is what brought Greg Hawkins and Maxim Boyko together in April 1997.

In the lecture theatres of MIT and Harvard, in the conference rooms of the International Monetary Fund and the State Department in Washington, the Russian reformers were saying the same thing. Just lend us enough money to build up our infrastructure, they said. If we can collect taxes, and keep the extremists at bay, the dream will come true.

So the IMF made loans to the Russian government, while Western banks and investors bought its debt. It seemed like a very good deal – the most popular Russian government bond, a short-term rouble-denominated Treasury bill called the GKO, paid annual interest of over 40 per cent. By lending to Russia, you might earn more than an investor in LTCM had made in 1995 and 1996.

Led by Credit Suisse First Boston, foreign investment banks set up large Moscow operations, to buy these bonds and package them for Western investors. Of course, Russian bonds were risky. If the government could collect taxes as promised, then like Italy, it could reduce its debt, and the bonds would go up in price. However, if the Russians failed to do this, the country would go bankrupt, and the bonds would default.

The hedge funds and proprietary desks now taking an interest in Russia were aware of this risk. Most developing countries issue two kinds of bonds – dollar bonds and local currency bonds. Back in the early 1980s, when Latin American countries defaulted on their debt, it was the dollar-denominated bonds they refused to pay.

Debt denominated in local currency was repaid by simply printing more money. This meant inflation, and then a sharp devaluation of the local currency against the dollar. The effect for foreign holders of local currency bonds is the same as if they had defaulted. So even though GKOs appeared unlikely to default, they were just as risky as Russia's dollar bonds.

But Greg Hawkins and the other hedge fund operators surveying Russia thought they had a way round the problem. With the help of a friendly investment bank, Hawkins constructed a money machine. The investment bank would buy the bonds, and in return for paying the bank a dollar floating rate, LTCM would receive the high GKO coupons, in roubles, which could be converted back into dollars again.

At the same time, LTCM entered into a forward contract (with a different investment bank) so that as soon as it received a rouble payment in a few months time, it could exchange the roubles for dollars at today's exchange rate. If Russia devalued the rouble in the meantime, LTCM would be protected.

This second bank would earn its fee on the transaction, which it would hedge by trading in the Russian domestic currency markets. To make life even simpler for hedge funds like LTCM, both halves of the money machine could be expressed as a value in dollars, to save the trouble of having to deal in actual roubles. In this case, the forward was called a 'non-deliverable forward'.

So in late 1997, on Hawkins's directions, Haghani's London traders entered into this trade. LTCM also did other Russian trades involving dollar bonds, which required going long on one security and selling another.

But by July 1998, Russia looked distinctly shaky. The stock market had plunged. Investors who travelled to Russia to claim share certificates or inspect the factories they supposedly owned found themselves threatened by thugs with baseball bats. What was going on?

The entrepreneurs who had been the great white hope of the reformists were nothing of the sort. Emerging as hated figures among ordinary Russians, these 'oligarchs' stripped the assets they had been given, and funnelled wealth out of the country. Organised crime was rampant. Chief prosecutor Yuri Skuratov estimated that half of Russia's gross national product was controlled by criminals.

The government wasn't much better. With the help of corrupt Russian bankers, IMF loans soon exited the country into offshore bank accounts, at the rate of $1 billion a month. In the beach resorts of south-east Asia, and the shopping malls of Dubai, Asian and Japanese tycoons were replaced by suddenly-wealthy Russians. According to Skuratov, half of Russian banks were mob-controlled.

Policymakers in Washington, perhaps fearing Russia's nuclear capability if the government lost control, pressed for the loans to continue, and so in July, the IMF delivered $17 billion into the waiting arms of the Russians. Immediately, $4.5 billion went into Swiss and Channel Islands bank accounts.

By early August, the yields paid on new GKO bonds rose to 70 per cent as investors grew nervous, and Russia was spending half its tax revenues on interest payments. It was obvious that soon Russia would either default on its bonds or devalue the rouble – or probably both.

But LTCM and the other hedge funds believed that their money machines protected them – whatever they lost on the GKO, they would make back on the forward contract. Feeling secure, most of the LTCM principals went on holiday at the beginning of the month, along with many other senior Wall Street traders.

However, when Russian Prime Minister Sergei Kiriyenko finally announced a combined rouble devaluation and GKO default on Monday, 17 August, there was a nasty surprise waiting.

The Russian government issued a decree forbidding domestic banks from honouring foreign exchange contracts for a month. That meant if you had sold roubles for dollars to a Russian bank at the pre-default rate, you weren't allowed to cash in what should have been a winning lottery ticket.

Up to that point, the Russian banks had been taking dollars from foreigners investing in GKOs (and other securities), while selling forward contracts to pay the dollars back again. Now, courtesy of their own government, these banks could hold on to the dollars.

Some Western banks would later try and sue these domestic firms, only to find that they were little more than marble facades with gangsters behind them. By this time the dollars were safely sitting in offshore accounts. Needless to say, many ordinary Russians had a similar experience, and lost their savings.

The Western banks suffered heavy losses as a result of this sneaky move. In particular, Credit Suisse lost over $2 billion. However, the hedge funds who had built GKO money machines were supposed to be protected, because they were insulated from direct trading in the Russian markets. Unfortunately, the investment banks which had so assiduously wooed these funds now showed their ugly side.

The High-Risk Opportunities fund (HRO) was a Cayman-registered hedge fund run from Miami. Part of a family of funds called III Offshore Advisors which had been founded during the 1980s by a bond trader called Warren Mosler, HRO had $850 million invested in the GKO money machine.

In time-honoured fashion, HRO had the two halves of the trade with several different banks. The GKO part was mostly with Lehman Brothers, Bankers Trust and Credit Suisse while the rouble forward was handled by French Banks Société Generale (SG), Credit Lyonnais and Dutch firm ING Barings.

After the combined GKO default and devaluation of 17 August, the first side of the trade was in the red, but the second side was supposedly profitable since it was a derivative contract based on published figures for the rouble/dollar exchange rate.

So while HRO now owed a large payment to Lehman, Bankers Trust and Credit Suisse, it should have received a similar payment from SG, Credit Lyonnais and ING. However, these latter three firms had hedged their exposure in the domestic Russian market, and were unable to trade because of the Russian government ban. They faced losses if they honoured their commitment to HRO.

Then canny lawyers at these three banks appear to have hit on a smart idea. With the money it owed to Lehman, Bankers Trust and Credit Suisse, HRO was theoretically bankrupt. According to an old legal principle called 'set-off', creditors can halt scheduled payments to a bankrupt counterparty, and wait until the liquidators move in. That is what the other three firms did on 18 August.

That immediately forced HRO to default on its payment on the GKO side of the trade, turning a theoretical bankruptcy into a real one. Mosler and his colleagues could only look on, impotent, as the fund was liquidated. It was now Wednesday.

LTCM experienced no such problems from its counterparties. Furthermore, the fund wasn't a dominant player in the Russian market and although it lost money, it didn't suffer a serious blow at this point. By late September, LTCM's total emerging market losses would total $400 million, but only part of this came from Russia. The damage was more subtle.

Like a spore of anthrax carried in the wind, the HRO incident caused the Russian disaster to spread. In New York and London, dealers began talking among themselves. The HRO trade was believed to be very large, and rumours began circulating that Lehman Brothers was in trouble (these rumours later proved baseless).

But it was not just rumour that spread the epidemic. What else was it? Not rogue traders or reckless risk takers. The agent chiefly responsible for transmitting the pathogen from trading floor to trading floor was the man in the white protective suit and the emergency vaccine. It was the risk manager himself.

We have seen how VAR became the near-universal means of controlling market risks after international regulators gave their final approval in 1996. The risk managers were powerful figures, and their radar systems were wired into the trading desks. Every minute that a position was marked-to-market, the VAR number on a risk manager's computer screen would pick up any changes.

And now, on the week of 17 August, the Russian losses began to filter through. All the biggest firms had been involved in this market to some extent, and all acknowledged that this was a volatile market.

But how is VAR calculated? Essentially, you multiply each position's volatility by its size in dollars and add them together, allowing for the fact that some risks cancel each other out by having negative correlation.

Now, with sudden mark-to-market losses, the Russian contribution to VAR rose rapidly. The effect was to cause many trading desks to breach their VAR limits. According to the Basle committee rules, once such a breach took place so many times, more capital would have to be allocated or positions had to be cut.

All the big investment banks are leveraged to some degree, and capital is a precious commodity. Cutting positions was the route taken. So risk managers would phone head traders and tell them to cut back – not just in Russia, but everywhere. Even when positions are profitable? asked the traders. Rules are rules, replied the risk managers.

A similar story was happening at dozens of hedge funds, many of which used VAR to manage their risks. Not having LTCM's luxury of choosing how to cut positions, many had to reduce exposure across the board, as capital was eaten away by the Russian débâcle. Many banks instructed their hedge fund clients to put up more capital against their trades – which had the same effect.

Where did the hedge funds and prop desks find the money to do this? They had to raid their other, still-profitable positions. The result was that capital began flowing out of those swap and government bond markets which LTCM, other hedge funds and the world's biggest proprietary desks had been specialising in.

Bob Litzenberger – a highly experienced quant at Goldman Sachs who would later become chief risk manager for the firm – describes what happened:

> Consider a situation when volatilities rise and there are some trading losses, VARs would be higher and tolerances for risk would likely be lower. For an individual firm, it would appear reasonable to reduce trading positions; however, if everybody were to act similarly it would put pressure on their common trading positions.

But why were VAR limits driving down prices? It was the same issue which had been overlooked all those years before, in October 1987: liquidity. Although VAR isn't the same as the option theory underlying portfolio insurance, both are built on the same assumption – that markets are liquid and continuous.

Cox, Ross and Rubinstein's garden of forking paths tells you how to replicate an option, each time the stock or other asset underlying it goes up or down in price. But on Black Monday, the build-up of orders from portfolio insurance programmes to sell index futures had overloaded the Chicago Mercantile Exchange, and replication no longer worked. The underlying market must be liquid in order to buy and sell at the correct price.

What about VAR? By telling you how much you can lose in a given day, most of the time, VAR is a warning system that can be used to control risks. If you breach that limit too often, you cut back in a controlled way until you return to the safety zone again. That is the theory.

But during August 1998, everyone tried to do this at once. As we saw with Black Monday, the result is inevitable. The opportunists who take advantage of short-term price drops disappear. Market makers widen the spread between buy prices and sell prices, and finally there are huge jumps downwards in price. Like the proverbial fire in a movie-theatre, everybody rushed for the exits.

However, the last two weeks of August were different to Black Monday. Instead of the old-fashioned stock market index, everyone was trying to shut down or at least reduce the speed of the complicated money machines which had been exploiting discrepancies between bond, swap and options markets around the world.

What hadn't been realised was that these discrepancies were only kept at bay by the machines themselves. The effect was horrific. The leveraged money machines at LTCM and all the other hedge funds and investment banks were so big in size, and were running so fast, that the sheer act of trying to shut them down made them blow up. According to Litzenberger:

> For relative trading value, the philosophy is, the more spreads widen from 'normal' levels – like a rubber band – the greater the tendency to pull back (i.e. mean revert). Of course, if you're putting a lot of force on a rubber band, there's a chance it could break!

In other words, massive positions like Haghani's recent sterling/deutschmark swap spread trade – which already had made a modest profit for LTCM – suddenly flipped into the red. That week, the gap between sterling and deutschmark ten-year forward swap spreads tripled from 25 to 75 basis points (0.75 per cent). This seems like a small move, but because of LTCM's leverage, it lost Haghani $200 million.

Nobody realised what was going on. In the fixed income markets, we have seen how many of the big money machines worked on a common principle. Something that seemed underpriced because of some irrationality among investors – such as a mortgage bond – is bought, while slightly more expensive securities such as Treasury bonds are sold against it.

The engine running the money machine often came from differences in liquidity. Investors value something they can quickly turn into cash, and undervalue something they can't. The granddaddy of all money machines, Meriwether's on-the-run/off-the-run Treasury trade, worked in this way.

And now, as the money machines started getting shut down, the effect was to drive the engine backwards – pushing prices of liquid securities up and everything else down. However, the traders couldn't see their own impact on the market. To them, it looked as if everyone was acting irrationally apart from them. The talk was of a 'flight to quality' or a 'flight to liquidity'.

This market virus was having an equally devastating effect on correlation. Under the VAR regime, the fact that different assets often moved in opposite directions suggested that you could take two risks for the price of one. Now, everything started moving in the same direction, except for on-the-run Treasuries, which moved the other way. Suddenly, risk seemed a lot higher, and this made the epidemic even worse.

Bob Litzenberger comments:

> If many arbitrage traders have similar trades and the aggregate position sizes are very large, it is like dry grass building up and just needs a match to ignite it. The very fact that the positions were held in common created the correlation.

At LTCM, it was not just the traditional money machines that were causing problems. Larry Hilibrand had made a large bet that telecommunications company Tellabs would successfully take over its rival Ciena. This was a 'risk arbitrage' trade, just like the one Merton had successfully done as a student all those years back.

But then, on Thursday, 20 August, Ciena revealed it had lost an important contract, and analysts speculated that the merger might be cancelled. The value of Hilibrand's trade declined by $100 million.

At LTCM, things were done differently to the banks. Rather than be forced to reduce positions according to a VAR computer program, the fund had contracts permitting it to maintain positions as long as it liked – so long as sufficient collateral was in place. But the mark-to-market losses moved positions 'off-market' triggering automatic calls for additional collateral. This began eating into LTCM's core capital balance.

By Friday, 21 August, the devastating effect was apparent. Shocked traders in Greenwich and London stared at their screens. By the end of the day, LTCM had lost a total of $551 million – over half a billion dollars.

That night, panicked phone calls were made to all the dispersed LTCM principals. Meriwether was called away from a formal dinner in Beijing. Hawkins had to abandon a house-hunting trip to California. Rosenfeld had to leave his wife and children on vacation in Colorado, and fly overnight back to Greenwich.

At 7 a.m. on Sunday, 23 August, the principals assembled in the glass-walled conference room overlooking Long Island Sound. Haghani and Hufschmid were connected by speaker from the London office, as were Krishnamachar and Chi-Fu Huang in Tokyo. The news was bad everywhere.

Just how bad was it? There was still nearly $4 billion left. According to one principal, a former Salomon trader, who attended the meeting that Sunday, it was already too late: 'Personally, I knew we were out of business on 20 August. We didn't have enough capital. My wife was in California at the time, and I told her "this thing is all done".' At the meeting, however, he said nothing. Instead he listened to Meriwether and Rosenfeld argue that the fund could survive – with the help of a big investor who could ride in and save them.

There was no time to lose. The equity foundation underlying the vast inverted pyramid was collapsing, and had to be shored up with new capital. LTCM had given $2.7 billion of capital back to investors in December. Now the principals would have to try and get some of it back.

No-one expected this to be easy, recalls Modest: 'August is probably not a good time to go out and raise money. A lot of people were on vacation in the Hamptons; Europe was on vacation. There was a lot of fear in the market.'

Rosenfeld started out by calling Warren Buffett in Omaha the same evening. He offered Buffett the entire Tellabs–Ciena trade as an outright purchase. The position had already lost $100 million, and stood to lose $200 million more if the merger was cancelled.

It must have been a humiliating experience for Rosenfeld. The problems with the Tellabs–Ciena merger were being widely discussed, even in the press, and analysts predicted it would fail. And now, here was a former member of Salomon Brothers' executive committee begging Buffett to take a lemon off his hands. Buffett said he wasn't interested.

On Monday, Meriwether phoned Merrill Lynch's chief financial officer Herb Allison, claiming that there were 'opportunities' in the market. He asked Allison to contribute $300 million, but the answer was no.

Then Meriwether tried calling his erstwhile friend Mathis Cabiallavetta in Zurich. This time he asked for $500 million. But since that champagne toast at the IMF meeting a year before, UBS had merged with its rival SBC, and Cabiallavetta had been elevated to chairman – with reduced day-to-day powers. He also said no.

Meanwhile, the disease was spreading around the world, transmitted electronically by VAR computer programs which triggered more cutting of positions. The markets in South-East Asia, still struggling since the crisis first broke the previous summer, dropped further. Latin America came next.

The hundreds of economic analysts paid by investment banks to produce daily reports for clients were lost for words, as the market appeared to go insane. Strange examples were everywhere. For example, according to the prices of emerging market bonds, Argentina, a healthy economy, was about to default on its debt within four weeks.

In Europe, Norway – which up to now was treated like member of Emu – suffered a sharp decline in its currency against the deutschmark. The difference between German and Norwegian bond yields was trying to say that Norway had broken free from the North Sea and drifted down to the south-eastern Mediterranean.

Usual economic relationships which seemed like fixed reference points for thousands of traders and analysts were suddenly meaningless. Yield curve models which linked government bond prices at different maturities together like segments of a string broke down as different parts of the string forgot that they were supposed to be joined together.

For the quants who had designed and tested money machines based on these models, it was a shattering experience. As one money machine exploded after the other, it was not only their intellectual world collapsing, but their personal wealth too.

Meriwether and the principals tried not to show their feelings to their 200-odd staff. The official line was that the markets were full of opportunities and that LTCM would weather the storm. Shustak went as far as borrowing $38 million from the Bear Stearn's cash account in order to pay all staff in advance up to Christmas.

But the strain was beginning to show. One of Haghani's lieutenants recalls: 'I asked him, "How bad is it?" He said, "Well, there's a 5 per cent chance that we are at risk here." That's stupid – we should never have been in that situation.'

On 27 August, Meriwether transferred some property he owned into his wife's name. LTCM sources insist that this was an ongoing part of Meriwether's state planning and not an attempt to hedge his own bankruptcy risk.

By the week ending 28 August, everyone in the firm could see that LTCM's mightiest bets were in deep trouble. For example, dollar swap spreads – one of LTCM's biggest single trades – were at levels which had not been seen since 1987. The giant inverted pyramid might even topple over unless capital was found to prop it up. The fear was that if news leaked out about how dire the situation really was, no-one would invest.

There was one alternative – cut positions. But everyone else was doing that already. LTCM had had its chance back in July, and had blown it. Against Scholes's advice, many of the relatively liquid positions which now could have given LTCM vital breathing space were gone. The last few of these – mostly Scandinavian currency bets and positions in the CME's Eurodollar futures contract – were unwound. Left behind were the big money machines – LTCM's so-called core positions.

To even attempt to unwind the illiquid positions at this stage would have revealed LTCM's predicament. According to the principal quoted above: 'You're like a rabbit sitting in the middle of a field being circled by dogs. You can't move. The notion that we could have unwound meaningful amounts of these positions is simply ludicrous.'

Modest recalls: 'We reduced our non-core positions; we were unable to liquidate most of our core positions because for some of the markets we were involved in trading had ceased. Nobody wanted to take positions. The people who would normally take positions off of us, namely the investment banks, were trying to step back at the same time.'

So a further desperate overture to Buffett was made on Thursday, this time in person by Larry Hilibrand. There was no question now of merely trying to off-load a failed risk arbitrage trade on the Sage of Omaha. Hilibrand went through LTCM's positions with Buffett, but again he said no.

It was now the end of the week, and soon LTCM would have to announce its August results. They would make grim reading. In a single month, the fund had lost $1.85 billion in capital, leaving it with $2,281,428,786. The net return was −44.78 per cent, which was a thirteen standard deviation event.

By then, the turmoil in the bond and derivatives markets was starting to infect the stock markets too. Over the first week after the Russian crisis broke, the S&P 500 had risen slightly. But now, between 26 August and 31 August, it fell by 12 per cent. European stock markets were similarly afflicted.

On 2 September, a remarkable letter was drafted and sent to LTCM's investors. It was signed 'John W. Meriwether'. He began: 'As you are all too aware, events surrounding the collapse in Russia caused large and dramatically increasing volatility in global markets throughout August.'

He continued: 'Investors everywhere have experienced large declines in their wealth. Unfortunately, Long-Term Capital Portfolio has also experienced a sharp decline in net asset value.' After revealing the month's returns, Meriwether's letter said, 'Losses of this magnitude are a shock to us as they surely are to you.'

He went on to attempt to explain why the losses had occurred, saying 'August saw an accelerating increase in the demand for liquidity in nearly every market around the world. Many of the fund's investment strategies involve providing liquidity to the market. Hence our losses across strategies were correlated after-the-fact from a sharp increase in the liquidity premium.'

In these words we see the self-delusion that blinded so many players during those weeks. Meriwether seems to be saying, 'everyone else out there is going crazy, but we're not. They're making our money machines run backwards, and we're the innocent victims.'

If that was delusion, the next part of the letter went to extremes in trying to sound upbeat. 'Risk and position reduction is occurring in some strategies', Meriwether continued. 'On the other hand, we see great opportunities in a number of our best strategies and these are being held by the fund. As it happens, the best strategies are the ones we have worked on over many years.'

There is a note of bravado here. Meriwether and the principals had no choice but to stick with their biggest positions, which were unsaleable. Even those which could be sold, LTCM could only sell at a substantial loss – which would further eat into precious capital. It was all wishful thinking.

In the letter, Meriwether went on to assure investors that 'our capital base is over $2.3 billion' – the glass was half full in other words – and that term financing arrangements ensured that LTCM would have all the time it needed to reduce positions. Just in case anyone thought of asking, the letter reminded investors that they couldn't withdraw any of their money until Christmas.

But the most poignant part of the letter came at the end. Meriwether said: 'Since it is prudent to raise additional capital, the fund is offering you the opportunity to invest on special terms related to LTCM fees.' It then gave Dick Leahy's phone number, in the vain hope that someone might take the bait.

The volatility trap

If during August, it was possible to imagine a kind of mass panic that spread out of Russia, in September, the penny finally dropped. The market looked, and saw itself in the mirror. As its monthly returns became public, and Meriwether's letter began to circulate, LTCM became the story.

David Modest recalls: 'While we view August as a kind of exogenous event, we feel that there was a fair bit of focus on LTCM in September. When we announced the net asset value, people started to worry "my God, what happens if they go under?" Obviously that didn't help matters much for us.'

'I don't think it was the August loss that was unanticipated, I think what we didn't fully appreciate was that once we lost that $2.5 billion, in some sense the game was over for us. The market's anticipation of the next $2.5 billion loss was more than we could withstand.'

What finally killed LTCM over the next three weeks was the supposedly foolproof mechanism which was designed to keep the money machines running for ever. It was the collateral management system, which piped Treasury bonds round the world, topping up counterparty accounts as needed.

LTCM's collateral agreements were the envy of other hedge funds. For the less esteemed funds, the investment banks offering prime brokerage services protected themselves using a built-in risk management device in all their contracts.

On top of the normal amount of collateral required from the fund, which equals the investment bank's current exposure on a given contract, an extra bit is required. This is called a 'haircut'. If the value of the contract declined sharply, and the hedge fund went bankrupt before it could transfer additional collateral, the haircut compensates the bank for any shortfall in collateral.

Consider what happens when buying a $100 million bond on repo. If you trade for an investment bank, you borrow the $100 million from a bank to pay for the bond, which you deposit with the bank as security. If the bond declines in price, the bank might ask for additional collateral to cover the loan.

But if you run a hedge fund, the bank will only lend you the $100 million if you deposit $102 million worth of bonds. The haircut is the extra $2 million which you must provide yourself.

Until the value of that $102 million in bonds declines below $100 million, the loan remains collateralised, cushioning the bank against losses. And where does that extra $2 million come from? It must be raised from hedge fund investors as equity, and will eat into the returns you earn on their capital.

However, LTCM and a few other select hedge funds were given VIP treatment and did not have to pay haircuts. This was highly significant for swaps. Since these are always entered into at zero value for both sides, LTCM didn't have to post any collateral at all. In other words, with no capital at stake, the fund had almost infinite leverage.

When the value of positions suddenly changed, counterparties would call for additional collateral, and LTCM would immediately open a tap on its Treasury bond pipeline, and top up the account.

But in September, as money machines around the world blew apart, the value of LTCM's positions was declining very rapidly indeed. During the first three weeks of the month, the fund lost over half a billion dollars every week. Now everyone knew it was in trouble, where was that collateral going to come from?

The problem was especially acute for those who had bought long-dated index options from LTCM. In its role as the Central Bank of Volatility, during early 1998, LTCM sold huge quantities of options, mostly on the French CAC-40 and German DAX indexes.

The historical long-term average volatility for these indexes was about 15 per cent per year. The options were priced as if volatility would be around 22 per cent for the same length of time in the future. LTCM wasn't interested in holding the positions until maturity in five years' time. But by periodically buying back the options it had sold, and selling new ones, the fund would capture most of the profit as implied volatility declined back to normal levels.

The way the system worked for the counterparties was for each to set up a special trading account in LTCM's name. This account, managed by the bank, actually sold the option to the bank itself. The bank then sold on the volatility to the structured product market, or to another bank seeking reinsurance.

With its money machine sitting safely inside an investment bank, LTCM would run it by remote control from Greenwich or Conduit Street. All LTCM had to do was top up the machine – or account – with collateral when needed from its pipeline of Treasury bonds.

Like LTCM's other positions, the amount of collateral was set to equal the mark-to-market value of the options sold. If this value went down, LTCM would receive collateral back. If it went up, LTCM would have to pour in some more. And of course, there was no haircut. Bernard Oppetit at Paribas comments: 'They didn't want to give haircuts to anybody, because they were on top of the world, and why should they? Like everybody else, we said fine.'

But during August, the implied volatility of CAC and DAX long-dated index options had gone up, not down. There were factors at work even before the Russian crisis broke. For example, the top heavy bull market was driving down the relative value of stock dividends, making it more expensive to delta-hedge option positions.

However, Russia triggered a repeat of the previous October's crisis, as a rise in short-dated options – needed for gamma-hedging – pushed up the price of long-dated options. The VAR virus then made its presence felt as risk managers ordered traders to cut positions. But how? They needed to buy reinsurance – in other words, buy the options on the market.

Since October 1997, the number of players in the market had gone down by half. The fate of Ramy Goldstein had demonstrated how dangerous the market was, and only a few firms were willing to develop the expensive trading and risk management infrastructure needed to safely sell long-dated options.

Jeremy Isaacs, a senior executive at Lehman Brothers and a veteran of this market, uses a colourful analogy: 'There was no fresh supply. And that's unlike anything else in life that I can think of. With anything else, there's a natural limit in price because you can create more supply. This is like fine art. Why would anyone pay X million for a Picasso? It's because there's not going to be another one.'

So in early September, implied five-year volatility on the CAC and DAX – as well as other indexes – climbed to astronomic levels, crossing 30 per cent for the first time. Like Casanova's Martingale, LTCM was expecting a sure profit when volatility went down in the long run, but this increase had the effect of a series of black cards while the bet was on red. The fund had to put more and more cash on the table to stay in the game.

As a result, LTCM's collateral pump was working overtime to supply its many index volatility money machines. Every time that CAC or DAX implied volatility went up by one percentage point, another $100 million worth of precious Treasury bonds would be handed over.

But after Meriwether's now famous letter to investors appeared, the counterparties started worrying. What if LTCM ran out of money and went bankrupt, while the machines still needed to be fed collateral? Yet they had one crucial edge on LTCM at this point.

According to their collateral agreements with LTCM, these counterparties were responsible for marking the money machines to market. While there was some scope for LTCM to use independent price quotations from brokers, long-dated index options were so illiquid that third-party quotes were unreliable.

This minor detail cost LTCM over a billion dollars. Because LTCM had received red carpet treatment and was exempt from haircuts, counterparties had no cushion as implied volatility jumped upwards. But if they used the opportunity to mark-to-market at as high-a-rate as possible, then they could force LTCM to hand over extra collateral which would serve effectively as a haircut.

So by trying to protect themselves, counterparties forced prices against LTCM all the more. According to Oppetit: 'They wouldn't have had this problem if they'd given a haircut in the first place, because people wouldn't have pushed volatility against them.'

During those final weeks, implied volatility rose beyond 30 per cent and started heading for 40 per cent – purely as a result of LTCM. But some banks had more sinister motives. If LTCM did go bankrupt, what would happen to a bank to whom it had sold long-dated volatility?

Physically speaking, the option had been sold to the bank by a special account which was controlled and funded by LTCM. If LTCM could no longer fund the account, it would become property of the bank's own equity derivatives traders. But because it had been continuously marked-to-market and rolled over, the option now would have an implied volatility of 40 per cent instead of the 22 per cent it had at the outset.

At this price, some traders had an incentive to sell on the option and realise an instant profit. David Modest, who conceived LTCM's index option strategy, may have thought 22 per cent was an over-estimate when compared with 15 per cent historical volatility. He was wrong, and paid dearly for his mistake. But 40 per cent was unheard of – in the words of Isaacs, a 'once in a lifetime event'. Any trader selling index options at this level would have to make a profit because volatility would *have* to go down.

According to Oppetit: 'When it became apparent they were having difficulties, we thought that if they are going to default, we're going to be short a hell of a lot of volatility. So we'd rather be short at 40 than 30, right? So it was clearly in our interest to mark at as high a volatility as possible. That's why everybody pushed the volatility against them, which contributed to their demise in the end.'

Back at LTCM, Haghani, Modest and all the traders working for them were horrified, as they felt their counterparties easing them into a death spiral. The brokers who were supposed to provide independent third-party price quotes joined in the feeding frenzy, setting up trades on one phone line while quoting against LTCM on the other. There was scant sympathy. Many felt that LTCM was finally getting a taste of its own medicine. Commenting almost six months later, Modest was restrained: 'I think there were a lot of people who were potentially hedging our bankruptcy risk. All that was doing was pushing our trades further away from us, causing us to need to raise more capital; the more you needed to raise, the harder it was to raise it.'

What also was killing LTCM at this point was its notorious secrecy. Some of its mightiest money machines – such as the sterling/deutschmark forward swap spread trade – were split up between different banks. For example, Morgan Stanley was only given bond transactions, while JP Morgan was assigned the swaps.

Taken as a whole, much of the risk in this money machine cancelled out – although the bit that remained was still grievously damaging. But the counterparties with different parts of the trade could only see what was in front of them, and naturally they assumed the worst. So marking-to-market was used to raise extra collateral here too.

Now working 15-hour days, seven days a week, Rosenblum and Chatfield struggled to squeeze the last drop of collateral out of the system. The now discredited Risk Aggregator was re-programmed to give an up-to-the-minute detailed breakdown of counterparty exposure.

By the second week of September, unwelcome visitors began appearing. At Bear Stearns, the senior executive responsible for handling the relationship with LTCM was Warren Spector. As LTCM's cash balance declined, Spector was concerned that the balance might be unable to cover the margin calls on LTCM's huge futures position. Also, with up to $10 billion a day in cash passing through the account, there was the nagging fear that LTCM could go bust before one of the large payments had been settled. To reassure Spector, Rosenfeld invited Bear Stearns to send a team to sit next to Rosenblum on the financing desk and listen in on phone calls with counterparties.

Meanwhile, UBS had finally realised the full implications of the covered call option deal it had sold on LTCM's performance the year before. It was also a very significant swaps counterparty with the fund. Exercising a right built into the bank's contracts with LTCM, UBS's chief risk manager Andy Siciliano sent a team to Greenwich to perform 'due diligence' on the fund, to discover what UBS's credit exposure was.

The giant option deal was more of a problem. Back in the halcyon days of early 1997, Cabiallavetta had touted the deal as a clever way of allowing UBS to own a $800 million stake in the fund. Strictly speaking, the stake was only a temporary hedge for the option it had sold to LTCM.

In desperation, Siciliano engaged a top Wall Street law firm to prove that this made UBS a counterparty, rather than an equity investor with a stake now approaching zero in value. If this were true, then the $800 million could be treated like a loan rather than equity, and UBS would have a much stronger claim on LTCM's assets. The bad news from the lawyers was that they were unable to justify this argument, and Siciliano lost his job as a result.

By the third week of September, Meriwether could see the end coming, as capital fell below $1.5 billion for the first time. Although no margin call was unpaid, and no contracts yet in default, the tower of leverage was unsustainable and about to topple like a mountain hitting Wall Street. No-one had answered Meriwether's plaintive plea on the investor's letter of 2 September. His priority was now sheer survival.

The last seven days of LTCM's independent existence have a strange feel of their own. Thirty years of finance theory has proven itself useless. Billion dollar track records and Nobel Prizes are now meaningless. 'Strategic relationships' are as transient as the bubbles in the champagne used to celebrate them.

All that is left is a poker game. At the centre is John Meriwether, the soft-spoken Irish kid from the South Side. He was always there, of course, but before he was hidden behind his dazzling, outspoken acolytes. Now they cluster behind him in silence.

Facing Meriwether across the green baize table-top are about two dozen investment banks. At first sight they hold all the cards. They have deeper pockets than him. They also have the keys to his money machines, and very soon will have the legal right to turn them off or claim them as their own property.

Some of these banks, especially those who bought index volatility from the fund, want LTCM to die. For them, it is a zero-sum game – if Meriwether loses, they win. These players are out for themselves only. However, other players see things differently. If LTCM were liquidated, and they took over some positions, they would have to sell them immediately with no hope of realising their full value.

Many of these players have also copied LTCM's bond and swap strategies. They are no less ruthless, but to some degree, they are chained to Meriwether inside the cockpit of his stricken plane. They want to land the plane first and then finish LTCM off. The last thing they want to see is Meriwether filing for bankruptcy protection in the Cayman Islands.

For Meriwether, these players are vital. Their fear makes him stronger, because it forces them to keep the game going. They can give him time. And when you are bleeding to death to the tune of $500 million a week, time is money.

The obvious play for time was to find that elusive sugar daddy who could offer LTCM a quick blood transfusion of capital. Meriwether had already tried that and failed miserably. But what if one of these fearful investment banks did it on his behalf? He was free to choose who.

So on Thursday, 17 September, Meriwether played his first card. He drove down to Manhattan, to see the man who had been his classmate 25 years earlier at the Chicago Business School. A man who had become his fierce competitor in the game of arbitrage. That day, Meriwether – accompanied by Merton and Rosenfeld – entered Goldman Sachs to meet Jon Corzine.

Game theory

Ten years before, Corzine had struggled to imitate Meriwether's magic touch at Salomon. Now, he was in on the secret, and Goldman was Wall Street's top trading firm. In the first half of 1998, 43 per cent of Goldman's $5.5 billion earnings came from trading – a considerably higher proportion that its rivals.

The arbitrage group headed by Lloyd Blankfine behaved like a Long-Term Capital Management embedded inside Goldman, and the firm's balance sheet leverage, which stood at 36 in May, was largely due to this group's activity. Like LTCM, it was both aggressive and secretive – somewhat different in style to Goldman's traditional investment banking business.

And like LTCM, the arbitrage group was being savaged by the turmoil. Between July and September, the firm would eventually report record trading losses of $1 billion – nearly half of that occurring in September alone.

Unlike LTCM, Goldman was about to go public in what was supposed to be Wall Street's most eagerly awaited Initial Public Offering (IPO). The idea was that by giving up its hallowed private partnership status, the firm could use its shares as a currency to take over other companies. However, with global stock markets in decline, it was the worst possible time to float the company.

Corzine had pushed hard for the IPO, while his co-chairman Henry Paulson – who came from the investment banking side – was less enthusiastic. Corzine had also nurtured the trading business which was now doing so badly. So as he sat with Paulson facing the LTCM principals, Corzine's career was on the line.

Corzine didn't quite realise it at the time. He had been shadowing Meriwether from afar for so long, and now here he was in the flesh. Corzine wanted to increase, not reduce, Goldman's risk taking, and was intoxicated at the thought of absorbing LTCM's innermost secrets. He later said: 'We wanted access to their intellectual capital, their programs, their judgement. An alliance would broaden and deepen our understanding of the markets.'

Meriwether then outlined what LTCM needed to stay alive: at least $2 billion in fresh capital from Goldman investors. This would give them nearly a two-thirds stake in the Long-Term Capital Portfolio. So desperate was Meriwether at this point that he offered more – the investors could also take a 50 per cent stake in LTCM itself, and enjoy both a share of the 25 per cent fees and the UBS option payoff.

But this wasn't enough for Corzine – he wanted control over LTCM's risk management, which had clearly failed dismally. He also insisted on oversight of LTCM's investment strategies. No problem, replied Meriwether. Satisfied, Corzine pledged to find LTCM the investors it needed.

As the two men shook hands, they appeared friendly. But the billion-dollar poker game had begun in earnest. It was Corzine's turn to make the next move. What other cards, however, did Meriwether have up his sleeve? Events were now moving quickly.

As it turned out, Meriwether got his move in first. The opportunity came from an unexpected direction. A US government official came to the poker game thinking he was an umpire, not realising that in this game, everyone is a player.

Bill McDonough, the President of the New York Fed, was getting worried. As the giant money machines at LTCM and elsewhere started to topple over one-by-one, the bond and swap markets which they had exploited were seizing up in turn.

The reason was simple. Anything which LTCM might conceivably own, would be immediately worth a lot less if LTCM went bankrupt and was forced to liquidate its positions. And in the climate of fear, rumour was widespread. Who would be dragged into oblivion with LTCM? Lehman Brothers fought furiously to quash speculation that it was about to file for bankruptcy protection from creditors.

Because of this panic, the normal work the markets were supposed to perform stopped being done. For example, in the US, high-yield bonds have replaced commercial loans as a means of financing growing companies. Open competition in this market usually makes borrowing cheaper than one-to-one lending relationships. But now there was no market, as all the high-yield investors stayed at home. It was the same in the mortgage bond market.

Interest rate swaps were invented to manage risk by turning one kind of loan or bond interest payment into another. But now, because of LTCM's giant swap spread money machines, this market too was frozen. That in turn discouraged even the largest companies from issuing bonds.

Not just in the US, but all over the world was the pattern repeated, as markets ceased to function. For all their aggression and greed, the big investment banks that made these markets played an important role. And if LTCM went under, things would surely get worse.

After taking over from Gerry Corrigan as New York Fed President in 1993, McDonough had presided over a great expansion in the bond and derivatives markets. Since June 1998 he had also been chairman of the Basle Committee, the conclave of central bankers which set international rules on capital standards, and was pushing the Committee to go further in allowing banks to use their own models for managing risks.

On Friday, 18 September, McDonough phoned Wall Street's leading investment bankers to find out the latest news on LTCM. All were gravely concerned – about their own fortunes, and for the markets as a whole. However, McDonough's mood lifted after he spoke to Corzine and learned that an attempt was being made to find investors.

By now, Goldman had some detailed information about LTCM, and Corzine wanted to share it with McDonough, but needed Meriwether's permission first. On hearing that the Fed was taking an interest, Meriwether might be expected to have mixed feelings. Back in 1991, the New York Fed, under Corrigan, had been pivotal in ending his career at Salomon.

But Meriwether also remembered how Corrigan had relented on his punishment of Salomon when Buffett raised the spectre of 'systemic risk', and the dangers of allowing a major bankruptcy on Wall Street. Perhaps McDonough – who had no personal dealings with Meriwether – could be played in the same way.

So Meriwether refused Corzine permission to brief McDonough, and asked to be allowed to do so himself. When McDonough phoned Greenwich, Rosenfeld invited him to visit on Sunday, 20 September. What McDonough didn't realise was that he was now a player.

However, McDonough was due to fly to London that day in preparation for an announcement that the Basle Committee was planning to make further concessions to banks on credit risk models. After McDonough had conferred with Fed chairman Alan Greenspan, his deputy, Peter Fisher, agreed to visit LTCM instead.

Meanwhile, Corzine's men were making some discoveries. Goldman partner Peter Kraus called Buffett that Friday, and learned that Buffett had already turned down the chance to invest in LTCM. Phone calls to George Soros and top hedge fund manager Julian Robertson yielded similar information – they had been approached by Meriwether, but had turned him down.

This was not the virgin territory Corzine had hoped for, as he later commented: 'It took me personally by surprise. It makes you feel a little like Secondhand Rose.' So that weekend Kraus went back to Buffett, who was by now beginning a three-week vacation in the Alaskan wilderness with Microsoft CEO Bill Gates.

It was just as well that Meriwether was meeting the Fed on Sunday, because the offer that Corzine and Buffett put together by satellite telephone was crystal clear about the ideal status of Meriwether and the other LTCM principals: unemployed. There was no other way that Buffett would provide the billions needed to prop up LTCM's teetering money machines.

At 10.00 a.m. that Sunday, two cars with government plates drove north out of Manhattan to Greenwich. In one was Fisher; the other car contained Treasury Assistant Secretary Gary Gensler. As they entered the lobby of Osprey House, it was an important moment – the US government was paying a visit to an unregulated entity which had been conducting most of its business offshore.

They were greeted by an old colleague – David Mullins. Once upon a time, Mullins had worked with Fisher, trying to make the global financial system safer. Now, Mullins and his partners at LTCM were part of the greatest threat that system had ever seen. Mullins was also in the process of losing his entire personal fortune. But he showed no emotion.

As they crossed LTCM's trading floor to the glass-walled conference room, Fisher and Gensler noticed more than just haggard LTCM employees. There were teams from Goldman and JP Morgan intently studying spreadsheets of the firm's positions, trying to understand where they fitted into the stricken money machines.

In the conference room, Meriwether painted a terrifying picture for Fisher and Gensler. It must have made an impression on McDonough, because he later gave a vivid description to Congress:

> During this meeting, we learned the broad outlines of Long-Term Capital's major positions in credit and equity markets, the difficulties they were having in trying to reduce these positions in thin market conditions, their deteriorating funding positions and an estimate of their largest counterparty exposures. The team also came to understand the impact which Long-Term Capital's positions were already having on markets around the world and that the size of these positions was much greater than market participants imagined.

By now there was another wave of fear travelling up the spines of LTCM counterparties. The Long-Term Capital Portfolio was based in the Cayman Islands. If Meriwether filed for bankruptcy, Cayman law would apply. While US law allows creditors to immediately liquidate positions and sell collateral in the event of bankruptcy, Cayman law does not.

US counterparties would have to wait for several months while a Cayman-appointed trustee went through LTCM's books and worked out who owed what. By that time, the markets would have plunged further, and collateral would no longer cover losses. When McDonough suggested to Congress that the counterparties stood to lose $3-5 billion apiece if LTCM were liquidated, this is what he meant.

The next day, Monday, 21 September, was yet another disaster for LTCM. The previous Friday, the Tellabs–Ciena merger had finally been called off for good, and now Hilibrand's doomed trade lost another $200 million. Rising implied index volatility, dollar swap spreads and a squeeze in the British gilt market accounted for a further $350 million.

At $552 million, the loss was only slightly more than that of a month earlier, but as a fraction of LTCM's dwindling capital, it was a mortal wound. By the day's end, the capital balance fell to $800 million. It was a reminder to Meriwether and the other principals that for all their poker skills, much of the portfolio was beyond their control.

The prison-like building that houses the US Federal Reserve Bank of New York is an architectural misfit. All around it, at the southern tip of Manhattan, are the cream of Wall Street banks. All their buildings are glass and steel skyscrapers, which disappear into the mist on overcast days. By contrast, the New York Fed building on Liberty Street is a defensive cube of granite blocks and barred windows.

At 8 a.m. on Tuesday, 22 September, three groups of men descended from their glass and steel eyries, and passed through the Fed's modest pair of wooden doors. Inside, surly cops with handguns passed their briefcases through an X-ray machine. High on the lobby wall, like a Trojan's shield, a circular bas-relief celebrated the Fed's founding in 1913.

The men were shown into a dining room on the eleventh floor, where Fisher shook their hands. Each group had a leader. One was David Komansky, chairman of Merrill Lynch. Another was Sandy Warner, CEO of JP Morgan. Finally there was Jon Corzine.

Questioned by Fisher over breakfast, all three agreed that a forced liquidation of LTCM would be a catastrophe. Almost as unpalatable was the prospect of injecting the required capital and taking over LTCM themselves. However, they decided to explore the possibility of this 'consortium approach' should it become necessary.

The ideal solution would be for that elusive big investor to take the entire problem off their hands. But neither Komansky nor Warner knew of such an investor, while Corzine kept quiet about his negotiations with Buffett.

It was then that a new idea took shape. What if the enormous positions at LTCM were taken over by the three firms? In other words, the still-whirring money machines could be eased off their crumbling foundations and delicately moved onto new, secure ones. The three decided to send two teams to Greenwich to investigate this possibility, while a third working group would assemble at JP Morgan's Wall Street offices to explore the consortium approach.

Meanwhile, McDonough was at London's Barbican Centre giving a press conference on behalf of the Basle Committee. Invited as the star turn of a conference organised by Britain's regulator, the Financial Services Agency, McDonough was supposed to be announcing a more liberal regime in which banks could use their own credit risk management methods.

While only a few of those present were fully aware of the breaking crisis, it was the worst possible timing for such an announcement, and McDonough looked miserable as he answered questions. How could international banking regulations be liberalised when clearly, bank risk management techniques had failed appallingly?

On his way to the airport afterwards, McDonough joined a conference call with Fisher. Although UBS had now joined JP Morgan, Merrill Lynch and Goldman Sachs in attempting to solve the crisis, the working groups had reported back from Greenwich with bad news.

It had emerged that LTCM's positions were so complicated, and the components of money machines so dispersed among the fund's counter-parties, that transferring the positions in a simple way was impossible.

Meanwhile, Bear Stearns had warned that if LTCM's capital fell below $500 million, it would stop clearing the fund's trades. In response, Meriwether now called on the Chase Manhattan syndicated loan for $500 million. Because the facility was in the process of being re-negotiated, Meriwether had promised not to touch it. In protest, two members of the loan syndicate refused to pay their share, so only $470 million was handed over.

That evening, the four firms met at the New York Fed to reconsider the consortium plan. By 8.30 that night, a total of 13 firms had become involved – all counterparties with large exposures to LTCM. They included Morgan

Stanley, Credit Suisse, Bankers Trust and Salomon, and all sent their CEOs
to the fortress on Liberty Street.

While most of the firms present were now committed to making the
consortium approach work, some of the aggressive poker players now made
their presence felt. For those with large index volatility positions, there was
no question about what should happen. In the words of one participant:

> When it came to bailing them out, we were completely opposed to that.
> We wanted them to bite the dust. We would have been short volatility at
> 40 per cent and would have had one hell of a ride. We would have made a
> ton of money.

At 9.30 the next morning, on Wednesday, 23 September, everyone began
gathering again in the Fed boardroom. Then at 10 a.m., McDonough was taken
aside by Corzine who told him of the deal he had put together with Buffett.

For the original investors in the Long-Term Capital Portfolio, Buffett's
offer rammed home how their dream was no more. All of their stake would
be bought out for the sum of $250 million. Owning the lion's share at 40 per
cent, Meriwether and the LTCM principals would not only lose their stake,
but their jobs too.

In return, Buffett would put $3 billion into the fund. He had persuaded
Hank Greenberg, chairman of the American International Group (AIG) to
put up $700 million. Corzine had delivered the final $300 million, bringing
the total offer to $4 billion. Goldman's traders would take over admini-
stration of the fund.

McDonough was delighted. After calling Buffett to confirm the good
news, he asked the assembled bankers in the conference room to wait while
the offer was considered. At 11.40 a.m., the Buffett/AIG/Goldman offer was
faxed to Meriwether. He was given 50 minutes to respond.

Corzine thought he had played a winning hand in the poker game. Here
was the big investor everyone had been begging for. Now, instead of
grappling with the coronary-inducing terror of LTCM's collapsing
portfolio, everyone in that Fed conference room could return to their glass
and steel eyries and get on with being investment bankers again.

However, Corzine had lost the game as soon as he had played the hand.
And it would be him, not Meriwether who would lose his job. Why?
Corzine's mistake was to give Meriwether a choice.

What Meriwether knew was that now the Fed had become publicly
involved, there would have to be a deal, which would leave him and the

LTCM principals with at least something. McDonough saw himself as guardian of the financial system, and LTCM's bankruptcy was even less acceptable to him than it would be to Meriwether. So Meriwether guessed rightly that he could reject the Buffett offer out of hand.

Calling McDonough back, Meriwether – joined on the phone by David Mullins – used the excuse that he didn't have the legal authority to accept the offer because it required the unanimous consent of all of LTCM's limited partners. Because this could not be done by 12.30 p.m., the offer would have to lapse.

Although LTCM's original prospectus clearly states that the 'general partner' – that is, LTCM itself – has far more rights over the running of the fund than ordinary investors, McDonough lost his nerve at this point. He was now a player in the poker game, not an umpire, and he didn't like the sensation. Rather than out-bluff Meriwether, McDonough caved in. He was only a regulator after all, and he didn't want to 'force a solution'.

So at 1 p.m., the CEOs of 16 banks and securities firms reconvened in the Fed conference room, and the ensuing meeting continued for the next five hours. The main sticking point was how much each firm should contribute to the bailout.

By now, LTCM's capital had fallen to $400 million, and Bear Stearns refused to contribute anything, insisting that its risk was high enough already. Banque Nationale de Paris also declined to join, although BNP officials deny that this was due to any large index volatility positions being held by the Bank.

To pull other recalcitrant banks into line, Merrill Lynch chief financial officer Herb Allison is said to have phoned a *Wall Street Journal* editor from the conference room and given a tip-off that the meeting was taking place. Pointing out that reporters would be waiting downstairs, Allison warned everyone that they had better emerge from the Fed with a deal agreed. Merrill Lynch spokesmen deny that Allison did this.

That evening, the deal finally came together. The consortium members Goldman Sachs, JP Morgan, Merrill Lynch, Morgan Stanley, Credit Suisse, UBS, Salomon Smith Barney, Bankers Trust, Deutsche Bank, Chase Manhattan and Barclays Capital contributed $300 million, while Société Generale, Lehman Brothers and Paribas contributed $100 million.

Totalling $3.625 billion, the consortium investment would leave the original investors' remaining capital of $400 million intact, but it would now only be a 10 per cent stake in the fund. Meriwether and his principals would keep their jobs, but they would be watched over by a team of six seasoned traders appointed by the consortium.

It was just after 6 p.m. A round of applause was heard in the conference room by people waiting in the corridor outside. The ordeal was over at last.

Back in Greenwich the news filtered through to stunned LTCM staff over the next two days. One of the traders who had invested his own life savings in the fund broke down in tears in Eric Rosenfeld's office. Now he was wiped out, he would have to cancel his wedding.

Meanwhile, a hundred-strong due diligence team from Goldman was pouring over LTCM's positions – all 60,000 of them. And the losses were stupendous. Emerging markets trades – such as Russia – accounted for $430 million. Directional bets took care of $371 million, while equity pair trades lost $306 million. But the two killer blows came from Modest's equity index volatility trades at $1.314 billion and the fund's core fixed income arbitrage trades which lost $1.628 billion. Total losses were $4.6 billion.

In New York, now that the broad outline of a deal had been agreed, negotiations shifted from the Fed to the law firm Skadden, Arps, Meagher and Flom where lawyers from all the consortium members hammered out the details. Meriwether and other LTCM principals were told to wait outside the conference room during discussions.

It was agreed that the 'oversight committee' would have powers over strategy and risk management, as well as hiring and firing. The six men would take sabbaticals from their firms, and would be forbidden from sharing information about LTCM with their colleagues. Meriwether and the other principals would keep their jobs, and be paid a salary of $250,000 per year – modest by Wall Street standards. Their own position in the fund now stood at $27.74 million – a decline of $1.8 billion since January.

Larry Hilibrand protested. With his $24 million loan, not only had he lost all his money, but was now in the red to Credit Lyonnais. Having recently built a $4 million house in Greenwich, Hilibrand pushed desperately for the bailout to cover his debts. His request was refused.

In London, the Consortium members walked into LTCM's Conduit Street offices to take control. At first, Victor Haghani was his old, pushy self, firing probing questions at his visitors. He was soon brought to heel. According to one of those present: 'We told Victor to shut up and start answering questions for once. After that, he was very accommodating.'

And what about LTCM's spiritual founding fathers, Scholes and Merton? How did they feel now that their wealth had declined virtually to zero? How did they feel as the world's press fed on this story of the mighty laid low?

All the assumptions buried in the small print of the Black–Scholes formula – liquid and continuous markets, Normal distributions – had broken down that summer, as well as older shibboleths such as diversification.

For Scholes, Merton and the tight-knit group of quants they had nurtured over the years, the world they invented had fallen apart. The Nobel Prizes now must have felt like an albatross hung round their necks.

When the young Fischer Black had crossed the Charles river bridge to work with Scholes, 29 years earlier, the film *2001: A Space Odyssey* was in the movie theatres. In that film, a computer, HAL runs amok and tries to kill the hero. And now, during August and September 1998, LTCM's computerised money machines had also gone berserk, and had destroyed their creators.

9

Aftermath

My chief care
Is to come fairly off from the great debts
Wherein my time, something too prodigal
Hath left me gag'd.
William Shakespeare, *The Merchant of Venice*

In Morgan Stanley's global fixed income division, Brian Leach was the numbers man. As head risk manager, he was responsible for determining the market value – or marking-to-market – the division's huge trading portfolio of bonds, swaps and options, every day. The numbers, or 'marks' Leach and his team produced were vital to the career of every Morgan Stanley fixed income trader: Were their positions profitable? Were they too volatile? Should they be cut back or expanded?

Brian Leach had a lot of power and he didn't wear it lightly. In appearance, he resembles Willem Dafoe in the role of an FBI agent – square glasses, brown hair combed sideways. Neat and serious. He loved his job, because it fitted his moral code: Traders are only human, but the numbers don't lie.

Arriving early at Morgan Stanley's fixed income trading floor near Times Square on Monday, 28 September, Leach didn't expect an easy day. LTCM was one of his firm's biggest counterparties, and for over a month now, the stricken fund had been hanging over his traders, ready to swamp them with disgorged positions in the event of a forced liquidation.

Not only did the Morgan Stanley traders need to anticipate what LTCM might do; there were their rival Wall Street firms to think about too. And behind the traders was Leach, marking everything to market. A former trader himself, he was acutely aware of the dilemma they faced. Normal 'flow' business had disappeared as corporations, pension funds and insurance companies backed away from the turbulent markets. It was too risky for them.

But for a firm like Morgan Stanley, not trading was not an option. Why? Without the evidence of real live deals from the traders, the risk manager would have to guess the value of their positions. In a volatile market, these guesses might be wildly wrong. The firm would be like a battleship without radar, blind during the heat of battle. Yet with the markets paralysed, the mere act of trading created volatility, as Morgan Stanley and its rivals thought and acted alike, creating even greater shifts in the market. That was the dilemma.

Leach explains: 'You have 25 Wall Street houses, all of them with a large position in bonds and each of them trying to find out where to mark the bonds. The way that most people do that is to buy and sell. They're bumping into each other, all slightly tilted to the bid or the offer, and as a consequence the price keeps moving.'

And now there was the Fed-mediated bailout to contend with. Sitting at his desk that morning, Leach knew that Morgan Stanley was involved. When the firm's senior management invited him upstairs for a meeting, the last thing Leach expected was to be asked to take an immediate, indefinite leave of absence and travel to Greenwich to join the six-man LTCM Oversight Committee.

At this point, Leach hesitated for a second. He was being asked to represent his firm and help save the entire market from meltdown. Part of him itched to get back to the safety of his desk, and continue guiding his firm through the turmoil. He was a loyal company man, and had worked continuously at Morgan Stanley for his entire 17-year career. Leach recalls: 'You're being asked to leave a firm you have a great deal of emotional commitment to, to try and help another institution without the same emotional ties.'

Finally, Leach accepted the assignment. From that moment, everything moved at lightning speed. There was only a very brief moment for goodbyes with his team, and he headed off to the offices of law firm Skadden, Arps, Meagher and Flom to meet the Consortium – and his new colleagues.

Of the six men who turned up that morning, to try and save LTCM and, more importantly, the banks who were so heavily entrenched in the fate of LTCM, only two had ever met before. There was Leach and five others. Who were they? Some were well-known names in the derivatives industry. Connie Voldstad for example. Back in the 1980s, he had helped found the swaps business at JP Morgan; now he was co-head of global debt markets at Merrill Lynch.

Mike Allen had been one of the first advocates of VAR in the early 1990s
– now he was a senior risk manager at UBS. As the committee's sole firm-
wide risk manager, Allen's job would be to replace the discredited Risk
Aggregator with something that actually worked. Then there was John
Fullerton, who held a troubleshooting role at JP Morgan, as special advisor
to chairman Sandy Warner.

Next came Rick Stuckey, soft-spoken and bespectacled. Now head of
fixed income derivatives at Salomon Brothers, he had once reported to John
Meriwether himself. Finally there was David Rogers from Goldman Sachs.
Head risk manager for the firm's equities division, his experience was
required to handle LTCM's giant equity positions. Indeed, he had already
visited LTCM's offices twice as part of Goldman's due diligence team.
Imbued with a Goldmanesque sense of irony, Rogers struck a wry
counterpoint to Leach's seriousness.

Greeting each other in the Skadden, Arps boardroom, the six men sat
down to be briefed by the Consortium's board of management, headed by
Duncan Hennes. In charge of global trading and sales at Bankers Trust,
Hennes was a big personality who peppered his conversation with expletives.

For Leach and the others, an invisible 'Chinese Wall' now suddenly
surrounded them. What Hennes told them about LTCM couldn't be shared
with any colleagues at their own firms, let alone the public at large. They
were truly alone – and would remain like that for over a year. According to
Rogers: 'We thought it might be a month or a couple of months. If we'd
known it was going to be a 14–15 month thing, we would have thought
about it differently.' That same afternoon they arrived at LTCM's
headquarters in Greenwich.

Emerging from the lift in Osprey House, the six could immediately
sense the invisible carnage around them. In the words of Rogers: 'It was a
pretty shook up place from the top to the bottom. There were a lot of
principals who had been wiped out, and a lot of the employees who'd gone
way back to where they were.'

For Meriwether and the principals, this was a tense moment. Rogers
comments: 'According to the deal that was struck that weekend, we legally
could have fired all the principals if we wanted to. We could have fired
Meriwether if we wanted to.' So when Meriwether shook hands with the
six it was with the plaintive voice of a man greeting his executioners that he
said: 'I'm so glad they sent the A-Team.'

In moral terms, this is the moment where many feel that the Committee
and the Consortium made a mistake. Meriwether and the 15 principals were

perceived by the world as a greedy bunch of incompetents. Not only had they destroyed the wealth of themselves and their investors, but they had also imperilled the global financial system. They should have been fired on the spot.

In reality, Leach and the other five's hands were tied. The firing clause had only been included at the behest of Jon Corzine. The failure of Buffett's buyout, and the very existence of the consortium, suggested that the principals still had a role to play. And so they were spared the humiliation of dismissal. Rogers comments: 'Within two weeks, we realised that would be the wrong thing to do.'

In carefully chosen words, Leach justifies the Committee's decision: 'We wanted to provide stability. It was not going to be helpful to destabilise the management structure or how people acted internally if we were trying to get at the primary risk, which was the portfolio. So what we tried to do was adapt to the structures they had in place and work within those.'

These words have a sound of weakness to them. Adapt to the structures? Work within them? Surely this sounds a little too over-respectful in the circumstances. The structures built by LTCM – in risk management terms at least – had brought them to disaster. If Larry Hilibrand or Victor Haghani – the two biggest risk takers – had been Morgan Stanley traders, Leach surely would have dismissed them for losing his firm so much money.

However, as LTCM's figureheads, there was a danger in the Committee's eyes that these principals' sudden departure might trigger an exodus of loyal junior staff from Greenwich. Reliant upon this backup, the Committee had no choice but to work with the principals as colleagues. Morality took a back seat behind practicality.

So instead of being fired, Meriwether and the principals were given an act of penance on a salary of $250,000 a year – to help Leach and the committee unwind the portfolio. They seized at the chance like drowning men. According to Rogers: 'They were all pretty responsive and co-operative. They tried their best to understand that while they didn't have the same goals we had, it was in their best interest to try and help us.'

For Leach the relationship was no more than a means to an end – reducing the risk: 'The way things worked was that we had the ultimate say, and if we wanted to do something, it got done. We asked them a lot of questions and they helped us understand what the best route was, and then we would make the hard decisions.'

As it turned out, the committee needed all the help they could get. In the world outside the fish tank of LTCM, things looked worse, not better, in that critical week following the bailout. The world's bond markets and swap markets remained paralysed in the wake of LTCM's collapse. A modern-day Atlantis had just disappeared beneath the ocean and no-one could believe what had happened.

The Committee maintained a news blackout, only pausing to issue the odd press release giving the most basic scraps of information. LTCM's own PR man, a sphinx-like character named Peter Rosenthal, was no more forthcoming. 'The boys are having a hard time right now', was all he would say, when asked for comments from Meriwether and other principals.

On Wall Street, the leading securities firms and banks behind the bailout were getting pummelled in the stock market. By early October, Merrill Lynch shares fell to 75 per cent of their value at the beginning of the year, while Lehman Brothers – still fighting off bankruptcy rumours – declined by 60 per cent. Goldman Sachs, meanwhile, had cancelled its IPO.

On 29 September, Alan Greenspan and other Federal Reserve officials met for their regular Open Markets Committee meeting. While the US economy was in rude health, the malaise in the markets crept into the discussion, and then Bill McDonough reported on the LTCM bailout. Greenspan decided to cut interest rates by 0.25 per cent.

By allowing banks to borrow money at slightly cheaper rates, Greenspan hoped to jolt the markets back to their senses. It didn't work. The hidden land of collapsing money machines was too big.

In Greenwich, the Committee was now working frantically to prevent these very machines collapsing before the Consortium's $3.6 billion ran out. 'Obviously you have to maintain the funding capability or you can't open the next day', says Leach. Rogers concedes that it was touch and go: 'We had extreme swings in P&L during the entire month of October. We spent time thinking about whether we were properly capitalised. That issue was a strong incentive for us.'

At the root of the Committee's troubles was not lack of cash, but market psychology, recalls Leach: 'The concern in the marketplace was that LTCM was going under. We had to change that perception.' Ever since it crystallised around the time of Meriwether's letter to investors in early September, this perception had been lethal.

At one extreme was the hostile marking-to-market conducted by Paribas and other counterparties that bought long-dated index options from LTCM – a conscious attempt to suck collateral out of the fund. Then there were firms (some of them counterparties) that took speculative positions against the fund in anticipation of a LTCM fire sale. Finally, there were traders with similar positions to LTCM who were trying to liquidate what they had before LTCM went bankrupt and drove prices through the floor. All three of these had the effect of draining LTCM's capital.

With Meriwether, Rosenfeld and the others now acting like helpful retainers, the committee drew up a plan of action. There was no time to lose, Leach recalls: 'We had to make a reasonable dent in the most vulnerable positions in a brief window of time. We did not think the markets would function efficiently over the Xmas period given what had happened. So we really only had an opportunity in October and the first half of November to realistically make the dent.'

Of course, the existence of this time window was kept a closely guarded secret. Then there was another problem facing the committee members – the fact that they were on secondment from six firms all active in proprietary trading. Even if LTCM was no longer trying to 'pick off' weaklings in the market, what if information leaked across the Chinese Wall back to traders at these firms? The solution was to always have two committee members present during phone calls with counterparties.

Now it was time to get their hands dirty. With 60,000 swaps positions alone, unwinding LTCM's portfolio would be a Sisyphean task, but two positions in particular were causing the most damage – long-dated index option trades and sterling swap spreads.

Why? Both positions were large and illiquid, and since LTCM was known to have outsized positions in both trades, marking them to market amounted to guessing what LTCM would do. As Leach puts it: 'The positions were large, but the rumour mill had it going that they were probably even larger.' This feedback effect made trading impossible between LTCM and its counterparties. Leach comments: 'Those two the market already knew an infinite amount about, and there was a lot of volatility based on us.'

As a numbers man, Leach realised that he had to do more than stabilise the mark-to-market value of LTCM's portfolio in sterling swaps and index options in order to effect a sale; first he had to stabilise the entire market. He had to broadcast the price to everybody like a TV station. But in such illiquid markets, only actual sale prices count. The answer? Take a leaf from the US or UK Treasury's book and conduct regular auctions, providing full disclosure of positions that were sold.

Leach comments: 'We wanted to show a very orderly process, and hopefully the market could re-evaluate and re-price based on that information.' Conducted in London, the auctions began in October, and would continue until January.

Meriwether and his principals looked on in wonder as the Committee achieved what they hadn't been able to do. In the words of one principal: 'People had to say, hey, we can't bet against LTCM any more. They had pre-bought on the assumption that LTCM would have to liquidate, and now they had to sell again.'

If the tide was starting to turn inside LTCM itself, out in the market at large things were very different. Although the S&P 500 index had stopped declining by the second week of October, financial stocks didn't, and the banks were forced into an uncomfortable reckoning with shareholders.

In an attempt to claw back credibility, Merrill Lynch and its cohorts started releasing figures for their exposure to LTCM and other hedge funds. These reassuring statements all followed a similar line: exposures were 'fully collateralised' with US Treasuries.

And the reporters who covered the story were easily hoodwinked – how were the exposures marked-to-market? Was the collateral really sufficient to cover illiquid positions? These questions were never asked.

Perhaps there were just too many juicy disaster stories to write about which diverted their attention. On 23 September, UBS had marked down its $766 million LTCM investment to $64 million – a humiliating loss of $694 million on a deal which had been Cabiallavetta's pride and joy. In a letter to shareholders, UBS CEO Marcel Ospel admitted 'At no time was this structure justifiable from a risk/return perspective.'

Credit Suisse followed suit by writing off its own option deal with LTCM to the tune of $55 million. Meanwhile, Bank of America revealed a $1.4 billion loss on its investment in hedge fund DE Shaw, which under the guidance of founder David Shaw, had built up a similar menagerie of money machines to LTCM. The hedge fund Convergence Asset Management declined by 70 per cent, losing $500 million. Other leveraged hedge funds complained bitterly as they were brusquely forced to cut positions by banks.

But some of the worst losses had been experienced by the investment banks' own proprietary traders. Goldman would report a loss of almost $1 billion, and Salomon lost over $1.3 billion. Merrill Lynch would top all these figures when it later revealed a hit of over $1.8 billion.

For Merrill's portly chairman David Komansky, there came an embarrassing revelation. Back in the glory days of 1994, after Merrill Lynch salesmen had raised $1.1 billion for LTCM from investors, the firm's $10 million fee was reinvested in the fund, where it grew to $25 million. In 1997, Merrill had decided to fold this proprietary stake into a deferred compensation plan for senior executives. Staff awarded a deferred annual bonus filled in a form giving a list of investment choices; well over a hundred ticked the box for LTCM, including Komansky himself.

And now Komansky was forced to splutter his way through press conferences, defending his decision to take a personal stake in the fund. Merrill Lynch employees and shareholders alike were appalled that while Merrill's stock had plunged in value, their chairman had pledged $300 million of the firm's precious money apparently bailing out his own private nest egg.

In fact, the allegation was somewhat unfair to Komansky. Worth over $100 million, most of his personal wealth was tied up in Merrill stock and options, while the LTCM stake accounted for less than 1 per cent. Under the terms of the bailout, Komansky's LTCM investment had now declined by 90 per cent. His firm's $300 million contribution was intended to shore up LTCM and prevent it from causing even more trading losses to Merrill than it had already. But he was visibly stung by the criticism.

In the wake of the losses, there next came a prolonged night of the long knives on Wall Street and beyond. UBS led the way. On 6 October, Cabiallavetta, Siciliano and two other top executives were forced out by Ospel. Bank of America soon followed suit, dismissing its own raft of senior executives. At Salomon, global head of arbitrage, Costas Kaplanis, 'retired' in November.

Merrill Lynch joined in when its head of risk management, Daniel Napoli, abruptly left the firm. This was followed by a swathe of sackings among fixed income and emerging market traders, in which Merrill fired almost 5 per cent of its workforce.

The style was brutal. A head trader or quant would turn up for work and try to log on to his computer. Finding his password was invalid, he would call the IT department for assistance. Instead of an IT manager, however, security guards would then arrive and frog-march the hapless trader out of the building, in full view of his colleagues.

Far away in Rome, the governor of the Bank of Italy was forced to explain to the Italian parliament the circumstances of its Foreign Exchange arm's investment in LTCM.

Meanwhile, on 1 October, Greenspan and McDonough testified on the LTCM bailout before the Banking and Financial Services Committee in the US House of Representatives. Bewildered Congressmen struggled to make sense of it all. LTCM was invisible. It didn't have any voters or factories or armed forces. How could it threaten the global financial system so badly?

Greenspan and McDonough struggled to explain. Greenspan put LTCM in a wider context, saying, 'What is remarkable is not this episode, but the relative absence of such examples over the past five years.' McDonough focused on the details of the bailout itself, inevitably highlighting his own role.

It was this that bothered the Congressmen. While Greenspan was treated with respect, McDonough endured a grilling. Why, they asked, had the US government got involved in rescuing a group of high-rolling gamblers while lone mothers were being forced off welfare into low-paid jobs?

On the defensive, McDonough pointed out that no government money had been used to save LTCM. The Congressmen responded by accusing McDonough of patronising them. According to former colleagues of McDonough, his credibility in Washington suffered a permanent blow as a result of the LTCM bailout. In the words of one, 'McDonough messed up. He left the Fed's fingerprints all over it'.

Greenspan had been around Washington for too long to be bothered by hostile Congressmen, and his status as an icon was secure. But he was increasingly worried by the paralysed state of the fixed income and credit markets. So on 14 October, he spoke to his fellow Fed officials by conference call, and decided to cut short-term rates by an additional 0.25 per cent.

The quarterly cycle of Fed committee meetings, with the resulting interest rate decisions, is one of the rhythms that drives Wall Street. It was something close to heart failure in the market that drove Greenspan to deliver an additional jolt that October day. And it worked. Not only did stock markets rebound with a vengeance, but the hidden credit markets slowly began to unfreeze. Greenspan administered a further 0.25 per cent jolt for good measure at the next scheduled committee meeting on 17 November. After that, the crisis was officially over.

Somehow, amid all the hurly-burly of the bailout, Myron Scholes went through with his wedding to Jan Blaustein early that October. It was a much-needed, albeit brief, opportunity to escape. At the reception, held in Manhattan's Pierre Hotel, Meriwether was seen dancing with his wife Mimi, apparently enjoying the occasion. It was a tribute to the power of positive thinking. Worth over $150 million a few months earlier, he now had less than 10 per cent left.

As for Scholes, he became the first partner to leave LTCM, along with Bill Krasker, in late January. Moving permanently back to California,

Scholes worked on building his new house near Stanford, which was a therapeutic experience for him. Krasker, by contrast, appeared traumatised by his experiences at LTCM, say those who have met him since he resigned.

At this point, Meriwether made one of his rare forays to the press, when he and the other ex-Salomon principals at LTCM invited *Liar's Poker* author Michael Lewis to interview them at Greenwich. It was Meriwether's chance to let off a head of steam that had built up over the previous months, as he watched his old rivals pick through the bones of LTCM.

Unable to directly attack the firms which had bailed him out, Meriwether hurled invective at financial conglomerate AIG, blaming this firm's traders for driving index volatility positions against LTCM. There were also some unattributed pot-shots at Goldman Sachs, highlighting this firm's contradictory role as both architect of the Buffett bid and Consortium member.

By the time the article appeared, however, Meriwether's main target, Jon Corzine had been forced to step aside as co-chairman of Goldman, and would shortly leave the firm completely. While the long-awaited Goldman IPO would finally go ahead that spring, Corzine had already paid the price for his misjudgments the previous year.

The appearance of Lewis' article irked the Consortium, who forbade any more press contact. But Meriwether was now on phase two of his rehabilitation scheme. Armed with a computer presentation, he, Rosenfeld and the other core LTCM principals began visiting investors, 'explaining' the previous summer's disaster as a once-in-a-lifetime event that was unlikely to be repeated.

Astonishingly, they also claimed that LTCM's leverage was not excessive. One chart misleadingly compared LTCM's balance sheet leverage with that of large Wall Street securities firms and commercial banks, without pointing out that these other firms have genuinely diversified businesses, in contrast with LTCM. What many found hard to take was the principals' refusal to accept any blame.

Back in Greenwich, the real work was being done by Leach, Rogers and the other four committee members. Along with the remaining 12 principals, most of the LTCM staff were still there, although about 20 per cent who had been involved in researching new trading strategies were dismissed because their roles were now redundant.

That January, the six committee members could afford a sigh of relief. The auctions of sterling swap spread and index option positions had been a success, in that at least they had sidestepped the perils of the cat-and-mouse game of dealing directly with counterparties. More important, they had defused the two most explosive parts of the portfolio.

But auctions were not a panacea. For LTCM's more liquid positions, the Committee could do much better on the interdealer market. But that meant re-entering the fray, together with the risks that entailed.

In particular, there was the risk of falling prey to the constant rumour mongering that dogged the fund. One of the loudest of such rumours concerned the gold market. For some time, the price of gold had been falling, and gold industry lobbying groups started blaming LTCM.

In fact, LTCM had never touched the gold market, since none of the principals had any expertise in commodity trading. When the Committee pointed this out, it didn't make any difference. Rogers chuckles; 'We actually had somebody who said they knew we were lying. We know you have gold.' Finally, Eric Rosenfeld was ordered to take legal action against websites that carried the rumour.

Against such a climate, attempting to distinguish genuine buyers was a fraught process, says Leach: 'People fished for negative answers. They would name ten items, hoping to have you throw out one, then another, so they could back into what you actually owned.'

Eventually, the serious buyers started to show up, says Leach: 'There were times where people came in expressing interest in a specific security in the portfolio, and we were able to agree on a trade that was very discreet.'

David Modest's pairs trades are one example of how this worked. The biggest involved the US and Dutch-listed shares of multinational oil company Shell, but there were many others. Goldman Sachs' London equity derivatives team prepared a prospectus and after getting Rogers' agreement, sold much of this part of LTCM's portfolio to its European pension fund clients.

This was small beer compared to LTCM's vast network of interest rate swaps contracts. Swaps were the sinews of the portfolio. They were the engines of LTCM's biggest fixed income trades – dollar and sterling swap spreads, Japanese, German and French yield curve trades, Italian government bond bets. They also were a tool that made other trades possible – the US mortgage bond money machine, for example, depended on dynamic swaps trading to extract hidden option value. So Leach and his colleagues would have to trade swaps whether they wanted to or not.

Sterling aside, there were two types of swaps in the portfolio. First was dollar swaps, which had remained relatively liquid even at the height of the crisis. Here, the committee could sell LTCM positions directly into the market. With the help of LTCM's dollar swaps trader Buddy Robinson, they began as soon as they arrived. The second type included swaps linked to Japanese and major European interest rates, where liquidity was more precarious. As they tried to trade this second category, the committee encountered a new obstacle.

It was through swaps that LTCM really insinuated itself into the global financial system. In terms of notional values – the imaginary two-way loan that determined the size of interest payments in the swap – the fund's portfolio accounted for almost 5 per cent of the global swap market. But this remarkable figure alone can't explain how LTCM's tangled cats cradle of contracts snagged every firm on Wall Street so badly.

The problem arose from the profligate way in which LTCM built the portfolio. When Larry Hilibrand or Victor Haghani entered into a swap spread trade, they signed ten- or twenty-year contracts, but they had no intention of staying with them that long. Typically, after a few months or a year, the trade would have 'converged'. If they were long dollar swap spreads for example (paying fixed interest payments on the swap) a widening in spreads meant that the trade was now profitable in mark-to-market terms. By dismantling the money machine they could turn that value into cash.

However, that isn't what Hilibrand and Haghani did in practice. The reason is that swap contracts are designed to stay in place for their full term. As a result, banks charge a lot more to dismantle (or 'unwind') swap contracts early, than they do to enter them in the first place. So to save money, LTCM did something else. If it wanted to get out of a 20-year swap after one year, it entered into a brand-new, opposing 19-year contract that cancelled it out exactly – except for the profit that LTCM had earned on the trade.[1]

Because of this, LTCM's swaps portfolio resembled a coral reef. There was the 'living' part near the surface – contracts that hadn't yet made a profit. Then there was the much bigger 'dead' part underneath – contracts that were no longer economically active and had been cancelled out with opposing contracts. At this point one might ask, so what? Shouldn't a pair of opposing contracts be equivalent to no contract?

---

1. If the trade diverged and went into the red (in mark-to-market terms), LTCM's philosophy was to simply hang on and wait until it converged back again. It saw this as a 'free' option made possible by the fund's long-term financing arrangements with counterparties. As it turned out, there was no such option.

It wasn't, because of the way LTCM traded. Suppose Hilibrand had done the 20-year swap trade above with Goldman Sachs, and wanted to take a profit after 12 months. Would he phone the Goldman swaps desk to do the opposing 19-year trade? Probably not. Goldman knew he had the original trade on. Goldman's proprietary desk might have the same trade. There was the fear – justified or not – that the prop desk might hear that Hilibrand was exiting the trade, and then get out first, pushing prices against him. So Hilibrand would do the opposing trade with a different firm – perhaps UBS.

During 'normal' times this was fine. LTCM's trades were so large that dealers competed for its business, in order to earn fat commissions. Once signed, the contract would be shunted off to the back office and forgotten about. Then came the crisis. Suddenly the top 30 global firms realised that they had hundreds of billions of dollars worth of outstanding contracts with LTCM, of up to 30-year's maturity. They had no way of knowing which were live and which were 'dead coral'.

Credit officers at these firms naturally assumed the worst: that they stood to lose the full economic value of all these contracts if LTCM went bankrupt. So they reacted by increasing calls for margin payments, collateral haircuts and also by marking-to-market in as hostile a way as possible. For LTCM, this was disastrous because its leverage now depended on the gross rather than the net value of all its swap contracts. Effectively, the defunct trades had become dead weight, pulling it below the surface.

It was through this tangle of swap trades that LTCM became a ticking bomb at the heart of the global financial system. The staggering economic losses projected by each LTCM counterparty brought Wall Street to a shuddering halt. These projected losses, along with the effect of proprietary trading losses, cut into the leading firms' core equity capital so badly that Alan Greenspan was forced to act, and cut interest rates.

But how could anyone defuse the bomb? Inheriting this dire situation, the Committee knew it had to reduce the mountain of swap contracts in order to cut LTCM's enormous leverage. According to Leach: 'Each counterparty thinks that there's effectively a unique position. The longs see only long exposure between them, the shorts see only short exposure between them. Everybody wants a haircut because they think its gross exposure, where we internally see it as a net exposure.'

It was the Japanese and European swaps that were a priority, because LTCM had historically made massive bets in these markets (such as the Italian trade in Chapter 7) that now accounted for most of the deadweight. However, unwinding or selling the swap contracts – all 10,000 of them –

was unfeasible: 'It would have incurred a huge transaction cost and would have been very onerous to the fund', says Leach. The ultimate solution, which was devised by Rick Stuckey and John Fullerton, became known as the swap project.

What Stuckey and Fullerton did was turn the cats' cradle to their advantage. LTCM's counterparties had big outstanding swap exposures with each other, as well as LTCM. What if this exposure was cancelled out by a swap trade that went through LTCM?

Leach offers an example which just hints at the complexity involved: 'Let's say that Goldman is long a swap from Morgan Stanley. And we now have the LTCM portfolio which is short a swap from Morgan Stanley and long a swap from Goldman, and these are perfectly offsetting. What happens is, by handing Goldman the Morgan Stanley swap on LTCM's book, we neutralise the original Morgan Stanley one on their portfolio. That's a massive change for Goldman. That reduces counterparty exposure to LTCM, and it reduces counterparty exposure to Morgan Stanley. If you can find the right collection of swaps, it obviously is extremely attractive to everybody.'

In practice, the fit wasn't perfect. Either the maturity of the swaps didn't quite match, or the counterparty wasn't the same. But just like dismantling a fiendishly complicated bomb detonator, Stuckey and Fullerton gradually removed the tangle of swaps from LTCM's portfolio, and by the end of the year they had reduced it to nothing. It was a remarkable achievement.

In April 1999, the assets controlled by the fund had already shrunk by 50 per cent, while the capital increased by 20 per cent – representing a significant reduction in leverage. So Meriwether widened his rehabilitation campaign. Chosen perhaps because he was the least well-known of all the principals, David Modest went on a speaking tour of top US business schools and university finance departments, delivering the investor presentation to the academic community.

But Meriwether's decline was slowly becoming apparent as some of his closest cohorts began to desert him. Hans Hufschmid left in May to start a company providing back office services for hedge funds. He was followed by Merton in June. In July a further six partners announced their departure: David Mullins, Greg Hawkins, James McEntee, Robert Shustak, Chi-Fu Huang and David Modest.

For Merton, it was quite a contrast to the 'delicious excitement' he had spoken of on winning the Nobel Prize. He was no longer a multimillionaire. However, Merton chose not to look back, and avoided any mention of how his theories had been tested to destruction in 1998.

Instead, returning to the public gaze at conferences, Merton took refuge in the cosy, ideal world of the financial innovation spiral, where progress is endless, and markets behave predictably.

Out in the real world, however, the markets were still refusing to behave themselves. While equities enjoyed unprecedented growth as the New Economy boom held sway, the summer of 1999 saw another wave of turmoil pass through the sterling swaps market. Around this time, Goldman's new chairman Hank Paulson finally decided to shut down Corzine's proprietary trading group for good.

Across the industry, a strict regime of risk management now took hold. An inter-bank working party set up to explore the lessons of LTCM's collapse recommended a much more cautious approach to hedge funds, incorporating liquidity and leverage considerations to risk management.

As a result, stringent demands for collateral and limits on leverage squeezed many hedge funds out of business, at the same time as proprietary desks were being shut down as being too risky. One trader estimates that the total liquidity provided to the market by these players has declined by over 90 per cent. At the same time, an ongoing buyback of outstanding debt by the US and other leading governments has further added to the shortage of liquidity.

The fate of one Credit Suisse arbitrage trader, David Seetapun, is symbolic. In 1995 Seetapun had just completed a PhD in mathematical logic at the University of California, Berkeley, and was believed to be one of the most promising young mathematicians of his generation. Then he was lured to Wall Street.

Seetapun became an options arbitrage trader first for Corzine's group at Goldman and then for Credit Suisse, until he lost nearly $100 million in September 1998 and was dismissed. After that, he spent several months as a professional gambler in Las Vegas. Today, he works on a deep-sea fishing boat in Florida.

By October 1999, LTCM had repaid $2.6 billion of capital to the Consortium. The Long-Term Capital Portfolio had been reduced in size by 90 per cent, and was now leveraged about ten times on its capital base. In January 2000 a final payment of $925 million was made, and LTCM closed its doors for ever.

One man could barely hide his joy at the news – Bill McDonough. Speaking at a Chicago Fed conference in October, McDonough said: 'I'm happy to tell you that LTCM is very close to being out of business. I can assure you that is a result that pleases me considerably.'

Meriwether was now surrounded by a hardcore band of followers: Eric Rosenfeld, Victor Haghani, Larry Hilibrand, Dick Leahy and Arjun Krishnamachar. Creating new partners from loyal LTCM staff (two of them former Merton PhD students), Meriwether began raising money for a new hedge fund, the Relative Value Opportunity fund. The management company for the fund he called JWM Associates after his own initials.

Planning to raise a billion dollars, Meriwether turned to his old golf partners Edson Mitchell and Saman Majd at Deutsche Bank, but investors coughed up only $400 million. The fund began trading in February 2000. By the time of writing, it had grown by 7 per cent – reasonably good compared with the S&P 500 but only slightly better than the Lehman Brothers bond index.

Meriwether and Rosenfeld now talk a very different game. After the bravado of 1999, the duo now openly admit that LTCM's risk management was hopelessly flawed. They also admit treating their investors with contempt when they forcibly returned capital in late 1997.

Preaching this new-found penitence, in August 2000 they gave extensive press interviews to the *Wall Street Journal, Financial Times* and the *New York Times*. In them, Meriwether reveals how he has taken up yoga to help relax, while Rosenfeld recalls selling his wine collection after being wiped out in 1998. Apologising for the first time, Meriwether says: 'I feel enormous remorse. Our employees and investors entrusted us and I feel terrible about that'. According to Rosenfeld: 'The fundamental foundation of what we built the fund on was wrong.'

As for JWM, its leverage is restricted to ten times the fund's asset value, according to Rosenfeld. The revamped risk management system is completely governed by stress testing rather than a historical statistics-based system such as VAR, he adds. Trades now revolve around the swap and bond markets, and LTCM's ill-judged foray into equities is now consigned to history.

What about the Oversight Committee? Their job done, Leach, Rogers and Stuckey returned to the relative anonymity of their old posts. Fullerton now runs JP Morgan's private equity division. Voldstad and Allen have both left the industry.

Scholes, meanwhile, has completed his house and now runs a venture capital fund on behalf of Texan billionaires the Bass brothers. In contrast to Merton, Scholes central concern is liquidity and its pitfalls. Like Merton, he maintains a dignified silence on the fall of LTCM. But building a house is different:

Building a house is seeing the future and trying to hold a tremendous number of interrelated decisions together. You start off with an infinite number of decision nodes. Over time the nodes get reduced as decisions are made. (Once the wall board is in, it is difficult and expensive to change the wiring). I like puzzles, infinite nodes and their efficient reduction in a reduced form way. (You can't enumerate all possibilities. You have to decide on what is first order and what is second order.) Isn't finance like this as well?

Sources and Further Reading

Some of the bibliographical details in this list are incomplete, and I apologise for any omissions.

Introduction

This is the paper Merton wrote during his sophomore year at Columbia University:

'The "Motionless" Motion of Swift's Flying Island' by Robert C. Merton (*Journal of the History of Ideas*, 27, April–June 1966)

Chapter 1

For more on the connection between primate evolution and economics, see:

'The Two Faces of Adam Smith', by Vernon L. Smith (Southern Economic Association distinguished guest lecture, 1997)

A good source on the South Sea Bubble is:

The South Sea Bubble by John Carswell (Sutton 1993)

An excellent introduction to the history of statistics (and much more), along with comprehensive references, can be found in:

Against the Gods by Peter L. Bernstein (Wiley 1996)

The impact of statistics on nineteenth century physics, and the story behind Einstein's work on Brownian motion is discussed in:

Subtle is the Lord: A Scientific Biography of Albert Einstein (Clarendon Press 1982)

Bachelier's career is outlined in:

Capital Ideas by Peter Bernstein (The Free Press 1992)

An alternative view of Bachelier by a fellow Frenchman is given in:

Fractals and Scaling in Finance by Benoit B. Mandelbrot (Springer 1997)

An English transaction of Bachelier's 1900 paper is to be found in the following volume, now out of print:

The Random Character of Stock Prices edited by Paul Cootner (MIT 1964)

Myron Scholes and Robert C. Merton both provided extensive autobiographical material to the Nobel Foundation which can be found on its website:

http://www.nobel.se/laureates/economy-1997.html

A good account of Markowitz's, Samuelson's, Fama's and Sharpe's discoveries is given in Bernstein (1992)

Chapter 2

The Code of Hammurabi exists in numerous translations, and has been posted on the Internet. The following translation by L.W. King is on the Yale Law School website:

http://www.yale.edu/lawweb/avalon/hamframe.htm

For material on the early years of the Chicago Board of Trade I have drawn extensively on this well-researched book produced to celebrate the CBOT's 150th anniversary:

Market Maker by William D. Falloon (Chicago Board of Trade 1997)

The discovery of the Black–Scholes formula is covered by Bernstein (1992) and by Black himself in:

'How we came up with the option formula' by Fischer Black (*Journal of Portfolio Management*, Winter, 1989)

The two crucial papers that eventually won Scholes and Merton a Nobel Prize:

'The Pricing of Options and Corporate Liabilities' by Fischer Black and Myron Scholes (*Journal of Political Economy*, May–June, pp. 637–54, 1973)

'The Rational Theory of Option Pricing' by Robert C. Merton (*The Bell Journal*, Spring, pp. 141–83, 1973)

Chapter 3

Economist William N. Goetzmann is writing a book on the origins of finance and has posted a fascinating chapter about ancient Mesopotamia, 'Financing Civilisation', on the following website:

http://viking.som.yale.edu/will/finciv/chapter1.htm

A comprehensive historical reference for the material in this chapter is:

A History of Interest Rates by Sidney Homer and Richard Sylla (Rutgers University Press 1991)

The only substantial biographical material on John Meriwether's early life can be found in:

'Dream Team' by Leah Nathans Spiro (*Business Week*, 29 August 1994)

A short biography of Richard Sandor and details of the CBOT's invention of interest rate futures can be found in Falloon (1997)

The impact of Robert Lucas's rational expectations theory on US Federal Reserve policy can be traced back to this influential paper:

'Rational Expectations – Fresh Ideas that Challenge Some Established Views of Policy Making' by Clarence W. Nelson (Federal Reserve Bank of Minneapolis Annual report essay, 1977)

Chapter 4

There is a vast amount of literature by and about Richard Feynman. His own non-technical explanation of Quantum Electrodynamics is a good place to start.

Qed: The Strange Theory of Light and Matter by Richard P. Feynman (Princeton Science Library 1988)

For mathematically-inclined readers, this graduate textbook contains an accessible introduction to Feynman's sum–over–paths technique in quantum mechanics:

Quantum Field Theory by Lewis Ryder (Cambridge University Press 1985)

The two papers that brought Feynman's insight into finance:

'The Valuation of Options for Alternative Stochastic Processes' by John Cox and Stephen Ross (*Journal of Financial Economics*, 3, pp. 145–66, 1976)
'Option Pricing: A Simplified Approach' by John Cox, Stephen Ross and Mark Rubinstein (*Journal of Financial Economics*, 7, pp. 229–63, 1979)

An entertaining history of the capital markets over the last 30 years:

'Heroes and Villains' by David Shirreff (*Euromoney*, June 1999)

This is the paper that introduced no-arbitrage arguments to the theory of yield curves:

'An Equilibrium Characterisation of the Term Structure' by Oldrich A Vasicek (*Journal of Financial Economics*, 5, pp. 177–88, 1977)

The early relationship of Mitch Kapor and Eric Rosenfeld is described in:
   The Hacker Crackdown by Bruce Sterling (Mass Market 1993)

For many, this best-selling book by an ex-Salomon bond salesman is the
definitive account of Wall Street during the 1980s. It is also the source of the
most famous, but almost certainly apocryphal anecdote about John
Meriwether. Every former Salomon executive I have spoken to complains
about the factual inaccuracies in the book and nearly everyone of them wishes
he had written it
   Liar's Poker by Michael Lewis (Coronet 1990)

Chapter 5

A detailed history of portfolio insurance, from birth to eventual death, can be
found in Bernstein (1992)

Benoit Mandelbrot's unsuccessful one-man campaign against finance theory
orthodoxy is commemorated in Mandelbrot (1997). This collection of
papers includes a contribution by Eugene Fama

Merton's jump model ('the ant and the flea') was first outlined in this paper:
   'Option Pricing when Underlying Returns are Discontinuous' by
   Robert C. Merton (*Journal of Finance*, 31, pp. 125–44, 1976)

The Brady Commission report is more accurately known as:
   'Report of the Presidential Task Force on Market Mechanisms' (Brady
   Commission, January 1988)

The experience of Meriwether's Salomon arbitrage group during the
October 1987 crash and afterwards is recounted in a subjective way in Spiro
(1994) and:
   'How the Eggheads Cracked' by Michael Lewis (*New York Times*, 24
   January 1999)

This textbook describes the kind of sophisticated interest rate models used by
the Salomon arbitrage group:
   Financial Calculus by Martin Baxter and Andrew Rennie (Cambridge
   University Press 1996)

A popularly accepted account of the Salomon Brothers Treasury auction
scandal and its aftermath is given in:
   'Warren Buffett's Wild Ride at Salomon' by Carol J. Loomis (*Fortune*,
   27 October 1997)

Chapter 6

When reading Merton's magnum opus, the trick is to spot the LTCM members in the bibliography. Also note the absence of 'liquidity' in the index:

 Continuous Time Finance by Robert C. Merton (Blackwell 1990)

Scholes explains how derivatives can reduce your tax bill in:

 Taxes and Business Strategies: A Planning Approach by Myron S. Scholes and Mark A. Wolfson (Prentice Hall 1991)

The US law relating to hedge funds is outlined in:

 'Hedge Funds, Leverage and the Lessons of Long-Term Capital Management: Report of the President's Working Group on Financial Markets' (April 1999)

The history of the European Exchange Rate Mechanism leading up the 1992 crisis is told from an economics perspective in:

 Financial Markets and European Monetary Co-operation by Willem Buiter, Giancarlo Corselli and Paolo Pesenti (Cambridge University Press 1994)

LTCM's search for investors and the relationship with Merrill Lynch is discussed in this news feature, which repays careful reading:

 'How Salesmanship, Brainpower Failed at a Giant Hedge Fund' by Michael Siconolfi, Anita Raghavan and Mitchell Pacelle (*Wall Street Journal*, 16 November 1998)

David Mullins talks about his early life in this interview:

 'David W. Mullins Jr' (*The Region magazine*, US Federal Reserve Bank of Minneapolis, 1991)

This highly influential think-tank paper pushed senior bankers and regulators decisively in the direction of using Value at Risk models for risk management:

 'Special Report on Global Derivatives' edited by Charles Taylor (Group of Thirty 1993)

Chapter 7

An account of Fischer Black's last years is given here by his close collaborator Emanuel Derman:

 'Reflections on Fischer' by Emanuel Derman (*Journal of Portfolio Management*, December 1996)

Alberto Giovannini discusses the role of financial markets in adjusting public
debt imbalances in this paper presented at a 1995 conference. David Mullins
was also invited to the conference.

    'Solutions for Developed Economies' by Alberto Giovannini (*Proceed-
ings of the Federal Reserve Bank of Kansas City Annual Symposium*, August
1995)

Emanuel Derman and his co-workers at Goldman Sachs have written
extensively on the trading of volatility. Here is an accessible example:

    'Investing in volatility' by Emanuel Derman, Michael Kamal, Iraj Kani
and Joe Zou (Goldman Sachs Quantitative Strategies research paper,
1996)

The story of LTCM's option deal with UBS is covered in Siconolfi *et al.*
(1998) and also in:

    'Another fine mess at UBS' by David Shirreff (*Euromoney*, November
1998)

The background to the 1997 Asian crisis is discussed in this series of news
features:

    'Global Contagion: A Narrative' by Nicholas D. Kristof, Edward Wyatt
and David Sanger (*New York Times*, 15–18 February 1999)

In 1999, after the bailout, LTCM agreed to co-operate with Harvard Business
School professor André Perold (who has co-authored papers with Merton) in
the preparation of two case studies for MBA students. The first of these
analyses the fund's decision to return capital in late 1997. This analysis also
contains LTCM's own (erroneous) justification of the philosophy behind its
swap spread trades.

    'Long-Term Capital Management, LP (A)' by André Perold (Harvard
Business School case study N9-200-007)

Chapter 8

Casanova's engrossing life story is told in this readable twelve volume
translation:

    History of my Life by Giacomo Casanova, trans. Willard R. Trask (Johns
Hopkins University Press 1997)

Here are the two papers that brought the Martingale into finance theory:

    'Martingales and Arbitrage in Multiperiod Securities Markets' by
Michael Harrison and David Kreps (*Journal of Economic Theory*, 20, pp.

381–408, 1979)
'Martingales and Stochastic Integrals in the Theory of Continuous Trading' by Michael Harrison and Stanley Pliska (*Stochastic Processes and their Applications*, 11, pp. 215–60, 1981)

All comments by David Modest on LTCM in this chapter were made at this conference. I am grateful to Til Schuermann of Oliver, Wyman & Company and Anthony Santomero of the Wharton School for making it possible for me to attend.
'Measurement and Management of Global Financial Risk: A Financial Engineering Roundtable' (Wharton Financial Institutions Centre Conference, 29–30 April 1999)

My visit to see Scholes and Merton would not have been possible without the help of Jean-Michel Lasry, head of quantitative research at Paribas.

Scholes speaks about the role of equity and liquidity as part of his interview given three months before LTCM's meltdown, published in
'The Risk Tamers: 25 years of Black–Scholes–Merton' edited by Nicholas Dunbar (*Futures & OTC World* magazine, 1998)

Merton discusses the role of equity in:
'Applications of Option Pricing Theory: Twenty Five Years Later' by Robert C. Merton (Nobel Lecture, December 1997)

The second of Perold's case studies focuses on the situation facing LTCM's principals on 21 August 1998. While little tactical detail is provided, the study does list the biggest trades in LTCM's portfolio at this time.
'Long-Term Capital Management, LP (C)' by André Perold (Harvard Business School case study N9-200-009)

An attempt to quantify the leverage of an entity like LTCM is made in Appendix A of this industry response to the crisis which can be found on the website:
http://www.crmpolicygroup.org
'Improving Counterparty Risk Management Practices' by Stephen Thieke and Gerald Corrigan (Counterparty Risk Management Policy Group, June 1999)

The background to the Russian crisis is discussed in Kristof *et al.* (1999) and in:
'A Superpower Falls Apart' by Ronan Lyons (*Euromoney*, September 1999)

Krasker discusses outliers in an econometric context in his contributions to the reference text:

The New Palgrave: A Dictionary of Economics edited by John Eatwell (Grove 1988)

The events of August and September 1998 and their impact on LTCM are discussed in Siconolfi *et al.* (1998) and in great detail by Modest at the Wharton School conference as well as in:

'The Failed Wizards of Wall Street' by Peter Coy and Suzanne Woolley (*Business Week*, 21 September 1998)

'The Gamble that Shook the World' by David Thomas (*Saturday Telegraph Magazine*, 12 December 1998)

Chapter 9

All quotes by Brian Leach and David Rogers in this chapter form part of an extensive interview I conducted for *Risk* magazine in December 1999. I am grateful to Peter Field and the Risk Waters Group for granting permission to use these quotes. Some of the quotes appeared in the following article:

'The *Risk* Awards 2000: Risk Managers of the Year – the LTCM Oversight Committee' (*Risk*, January 2000, p. 32)

Meriwether and the other principals revealed their feelings (without naming the key names) about LTCM's index volatility counterparties in Lewis (1999) The story of John Corzine's relationship with Meriwether, and his role in the Warren Buffett bid is told in:

'Corzine, Meriwether Rivalry Climaxes in Long-Term Capital Deal' by Katherine Burton and Monique Wise (*Bloomberg*, 29 December 1998)

The story of Buffett's involvement is told from his perspective in:

'A House Built of Sand' by Carol J. Loomis (*Fortune*, 26 October 1998)

The Federal Reserve Bank of New York has released McDonough and Greenspan's accounts of the LTCM bailout in separate form. However, they are best read as part of a six-hour marathon session of the US House of Representatives Committee on Banking and Financial Services, together with a question and answer session involving hostile Congressmen. The full transcript of the session, which took place on 1 October 1998, is available on this website.

http://commdocs.house.gov/committees/bank/hba51526.000/hba51526_0.htm

Index